*Pālkhī* at Diva Ghat, 1979.
*(Photo courtesy of Anne Feldhaus.)*

Dnyaneshwar's *pādukās* in the *pālkhī* at Diva Ghat, 1979.
*(Photo courtesy of Anne Feldhaus.)*

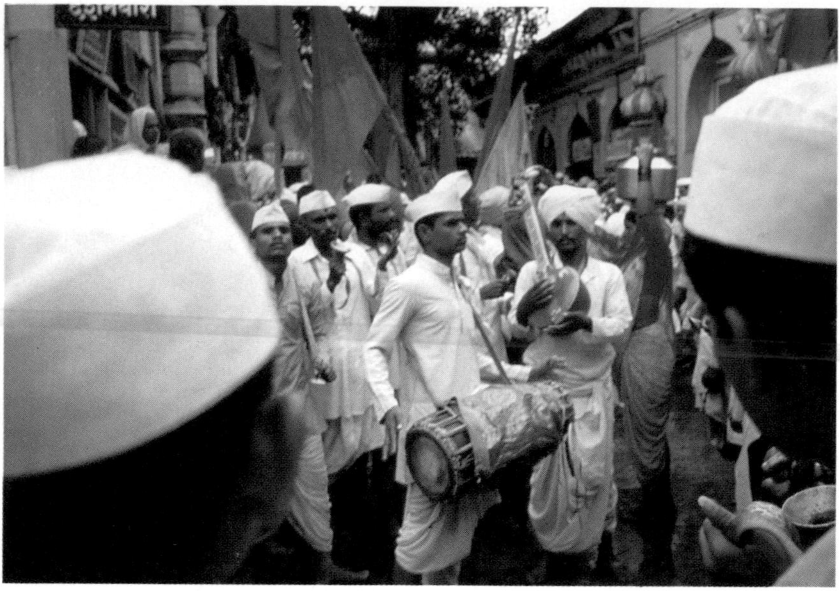

The *pālkhī*'s departure from Alandi, 1986.
*(Photo courtesy of Anne Feldhaus.)*

The *pālkhī* with *pādukās* in Alandi, 1986.
*(Photo courtesy of Anne Feldhaus.)*

# PALKHI

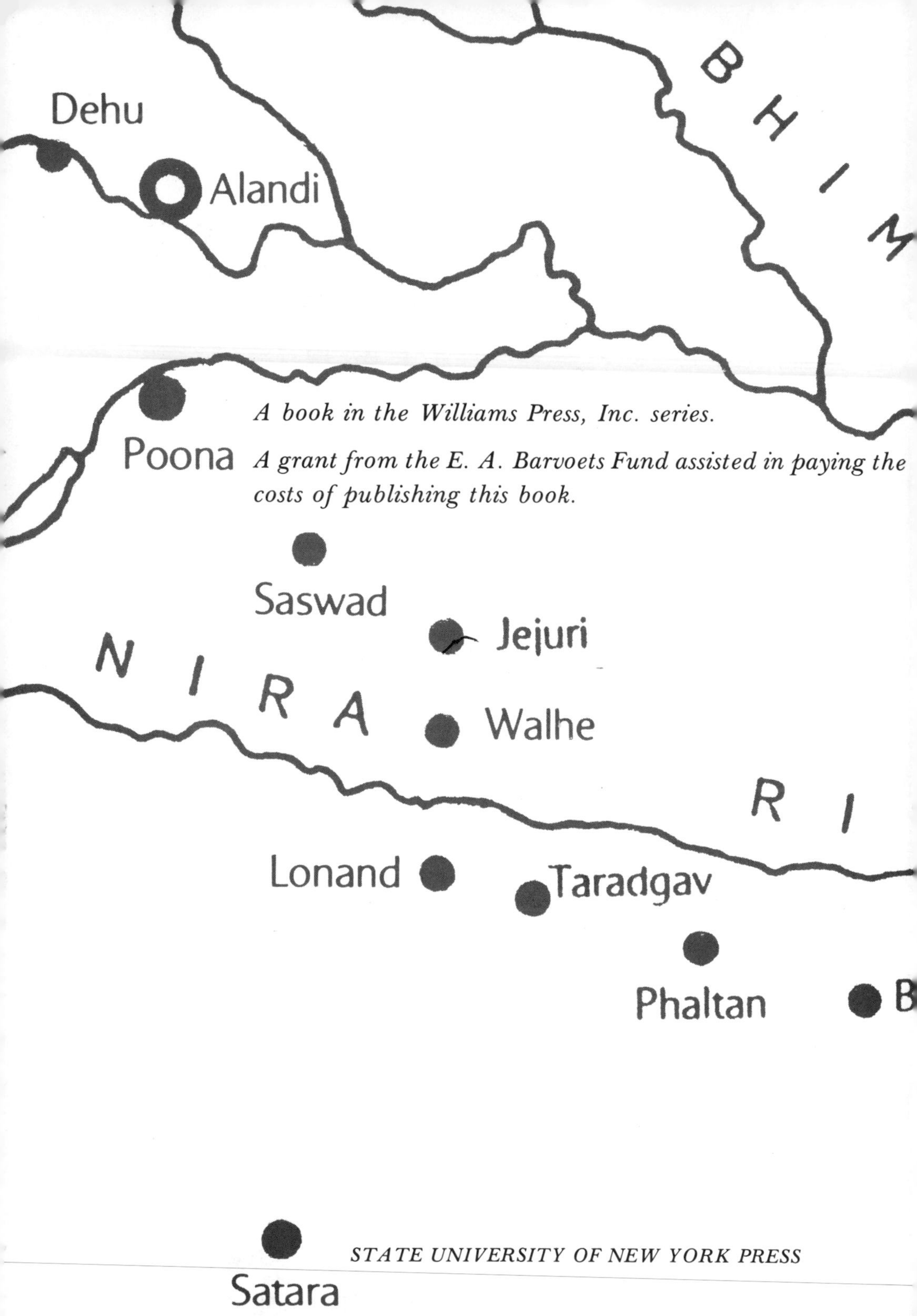


*A book in the Williams Press, Inc. series.*

*A grant from the E. A. Barvoets Fund assisted in paying the costs of publishing this book.*

*STATE UNIVERSITY OF NEW YORK PRESS*

# PALKHI

## *An Indian Pilgrimage*

*BY D.B. MOKASHI*

*Translated from the Marathi*
*by Philip C. Engblom*

*With Introductory Essays*
*by Philip C. Engblom*
*and Eleanor Zelliot*

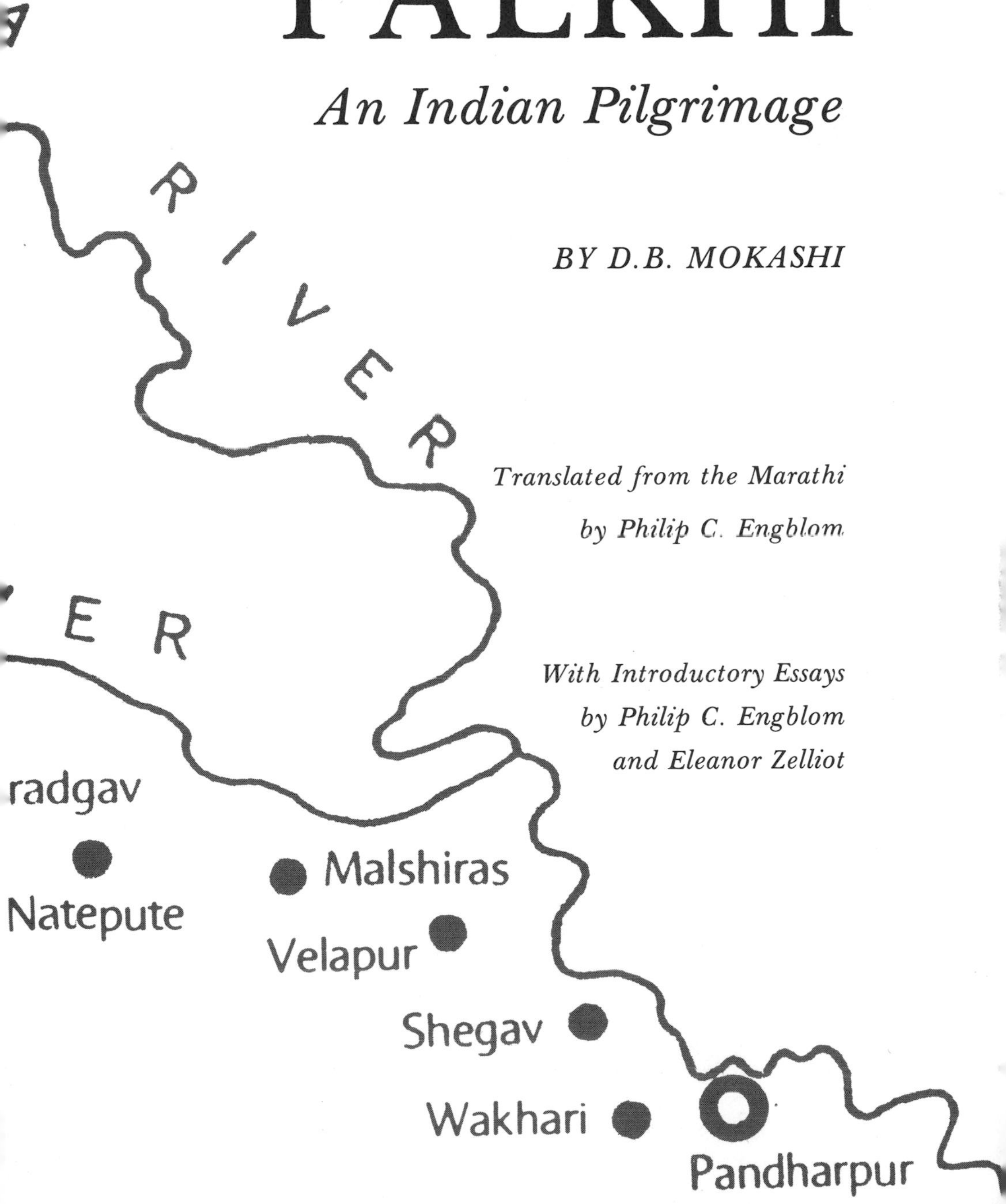

*Cover photo by Anne Feldhaus.*
*Cover and text design by Sushila Blackman.*

Published by
State University of New York Press, Albany

Printed in the United States of America

For information, address State University of New York Press, State University Plaza, Albany, N.Y., 12246

**Library of Congress Cataloging in Publication Data**

Mokashi, Digambar Balkrishna, 1915-
Palkhi, an Indian pilgrimage.
Translation of: Pālakhī.
1. Mokashi, Digambar Balkrishna 1915- —Journeys—India. 2. India—Description travel— 1947-1980. 3. Authors, Marathi—20th century—Biography. 4. Hindu pilgrims and pilgrimages. 5. Varkari sect. I. Engblom, Philip C., 1951- . II. Title.
PK 2418.M6Z47513 1987 891'.468703 [B] 86-30001
ISBN 0-88706-461-2
ISBN 0-88706-462-0 (pbk.)

10 9 8 7 6 5 4 3 2

*CONTENTS*

*When a man wakes from a sleep, will he*
*try to rescue himself from the river in*
*which he dreamt he was drowning? Then*
*the dream in which he thought he would*
*find knowledge disappears and he himself becomes*
*that heaven in the form of knowledge in*
*which there is neither knower nor*
*object of knowledge.*

*Dnyaneshwar*

# *ACKNOWLEDGMENTS*

This translation has involved the generous help of many people off and on over the years during which it was in preparation. It would never have begun without the instigation and steadfast encouragement of Pramod Kale, a previous translator of Mokashi, who sat down with the author and myself on the occasion when the translation was first being planned. Subsequently he carefully went over the manuscript with me at various stages.

I am equally indebted to D. B. Mokashi himself for the way in which he always made himself so freely available to me and my many questions. I marvel most especially at his unquenchable cheerfulness. Seriously ill as he was, just months before he died, he painstakingly went through the entire first draft of the translation and made many suggestions that improved it. His wife, Malini Mokashi, often sat with us and helped. I remember with deep gratefulness the warm welcome I always received in their home.

Several other friends read and commented on the manuscript at various stages. I am indebted in this respect especially to Vidyut Bhagwat, who spent many hours and much energy in going over the manuscript with me. Eleanor Zelliot, Anne Feldhaus, and Lee Schlesinger also all read the manuscript and contributed the most helpful suggestions. For assistance and advice generously rendered me specifically for the preparation of the introduction, I wish to thank S. G. Tulpule and P. V. Patankar. Judy Carra volunteered her timely help for proofreading and for preparation of the Index.

The passages from the *Jnāneshvari*, tr. V.G. Pradham (Albany: State University of New York Press, 1987) that precede each chapter were selected by the staff of SUNY Press.

Without the help of all these friends the translation would have remained a mere shadow of what it is. What deficiencies remain in it are of course entirely my responsibility.

Finally, I wish to dedicate this translation to my father.

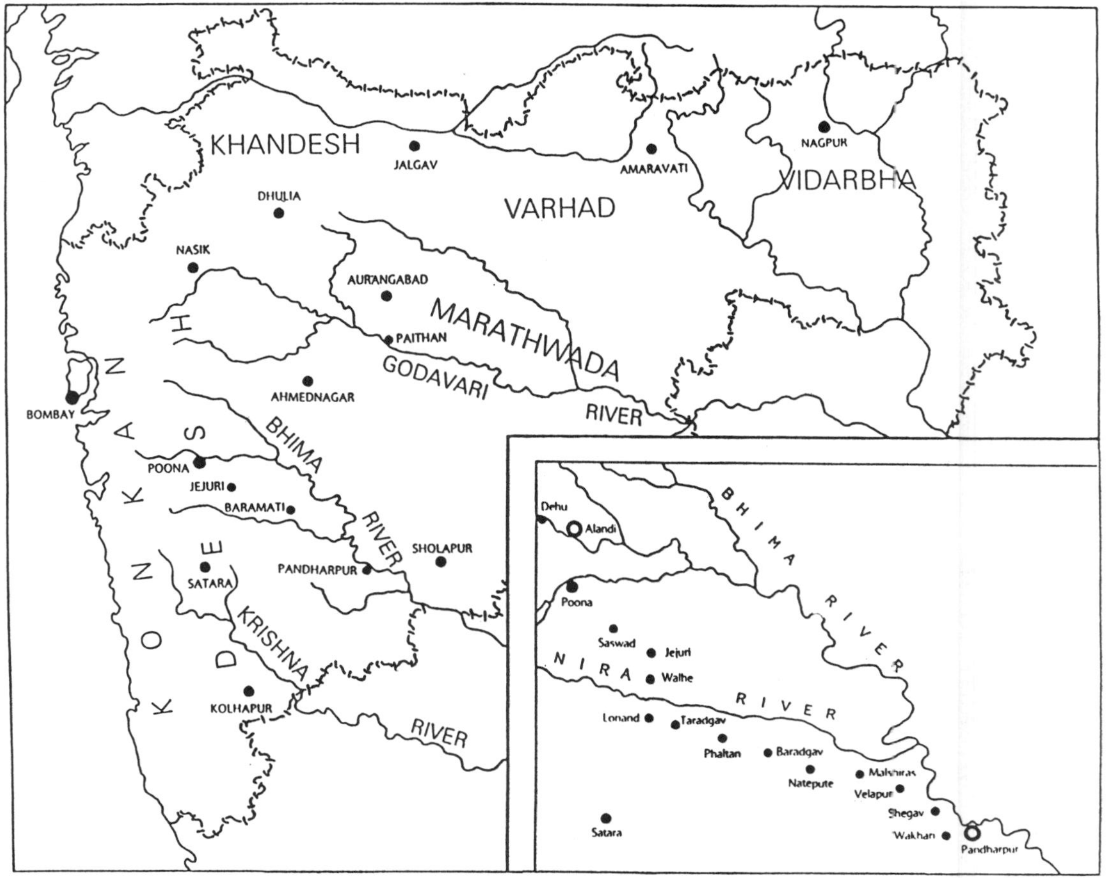


Map by S.Y. Waghmare

## *INTRODUCTION*
## *by Philip C. Engblom*

Pilgrimage is one of the most visible and pervasive features of Hinduism. Even today, in the modern secular state of India, pilgrims continue to go by the millions each year to sacred sites scattered all across the country. The diversity of these pilgrimages is as great as their number: they are all, in major or minor ways, different. Each pilgrimage site has its own very particular history, lore, and functions within the religious life of the communities that attend it. Every pilgrim in turn has his own specific motivations, ranging from the most mundane to the soteriologically most lofty. Pilgrimage in India reflects, in short, the complexity and diversity of India itself. It remains, however, a characteristic religious act that, whatever the nature of the motivations or whatever the status of the sacred site in the hierarchies of sanctity (from local shrine to pan-Indian *tīrtha*), virtually every Hindu performs at some point in his life.

Pandharpur is a pilgrimage site of great importance in the present-day Indian state of Maharashtra. It is situated about 200 miles southeast of Bombay on the Deccan Plateau and has a resident population of about 55,000. Its recorded history has been traced back as far as a

Rashtrakuta-dynasty copperplate inscription dated AD 516 (Vaudeville, "Pandharpur" 138), but it has certainly been a settled community much longer than that.

The origins of Pandharpur specifically as a sacred site remain a matter of speculation. But what has given the town its particular religious significance during the last seven or eight centuries is the temple of *Viṭṭhal*—the Maharashtrian *svarūpa* or original form of Vishnu—which forms the focal point not just of the town itself but also of the preeminent Maharashtrian Vaishnava devotional sect, the *Wārkarī Panth.* Every year, four times a year, large pilgrimages take place, which draw people from every corner of the Marathi-speaking region of India to Pandharpur. During the most important of these pilgrimages, in the lunar month of Ashadh (roughly speaking, the end of June and the beginning of July), the number of pilgrims reaches five or six hundred thousand. It is without a question the largest yearly *yātrā* (pilgrim gathering) anywhere in Maharashtra.

Given the size and importance of this pilgrimage, it is rather surprising that until fairly recently it was not very well known outside of Maharashtra. This may have been simply because it is so uniquely a Maharashtrian pilgrimage—that is, a pilgrimage restricted almost solely to the Marathi-speaking people of Western India—so it has not had the renown of the more pan-Indian pilgrimage sites such as Hardwar, Prayag, or Varanasi. Recently, however, quite a number of observers and scholars who have either written in English or been translated into English have made serious attempts to study and understand Pandharpur and the *Wārkarī* pilgrimage that centers there. Still missing from the literature is a detailed day-by-day account of the progress of the *Wārkarī* processional groups (*pālkhīs*) on their way by foot to Pandharpur each year. The present book, *Pālkhī*, which is a translation of one prominent Marathi writer's account of going with a *pālkhī* procession on the *Wārkarī* pilgrimage, will help fill this lacuna as well as add a vivid new facet to our understanding of what Victor Turner called the "great Maharashtrian pilgrimage."

## *D.B. Mokashi and the Dnyaneshwar* Pālkhī

In 1961 one of the preeminent Marathi novelists and short story writers of the immediate post-Independence generation, D.B. Mokashi, joined the *pālkhī* of one of the great Maharashtrian *Wārkarī* saints, Shri Dnyaneshwar, on its pilgrimage to Pandharpur. He subsequently wrote an account of his experience, based on the diary and notes he kept at the time, which he published in Marathi in 1964. The book begins straightforwardly with his departure from his home in Poona and ends with his arrival in Pandharpur. In between these points it describes the sequence of events as the *pālkhī* progressed along its way day by day. It is a travelogue, in short, of the author's personal experiences and observations.

Mokashi was not himself a *Wārkarī*, it is important to keep in mind. He came from a Brahman family out of the Konkan, the coastal district of Maharashtra, which because of its isolation by the Western Ghats has traditionally had only the most tenuous connection with the *Wārkarī* pilgrimage. His family deity was Narsimha, the man-lion avatar of Vishnu, based upon whom he wrote in the late 50s a beautiful semi-autobiographical novel, *Farewell to the Gods*, about one family's ties with its family gods. Like many others of his class who grew up in the middle of the Nationalist Movement, however, he himself espoused secular, humanist values, and he did not observe any overt religious practices. During most of his adult life he lived in the largely Brahman neighborhood of Poona called Sadashiv Peth. He made his living by running a radio repair shop in the same locality. But clearly his great interest and love throughout his life was his writing. And as a writer he was highly regarded in Maharashtra for his realistic, perspicacious prose fiction. Indeed he is recognized as being one of the group of formative "Realists" who transformed Marathi prose fiction in the post-Independence period.

But like all Maharashtrians, Mokashi also knew and respected the *Wārkarī* tradition. It is, after all, the single richest treasury of traditional Marathi literature and culture, and its great poetry especially pervades Maharashtrian society at all levels. But beyond merely this natural cherishing of tradition there is something deeper and more intangible in the feeling Maharashtrians have for the *Wārkarī* tradition. Another prominent, present-day Marathi writer, Durga Bhagwat, has written revealingly, "Somewhere there exists some inner link between Paṇḍharī [i.e., Pandharpur] and every Maharashtrian. . . . The kind of inner attachment one has for one's family and ancestors one feels also for Paṇḍharpūr" (112). Many contemporary Marathi writers have given evidence of this "inner link" to Pandharpur in their writing. In Mokashi's case one finds a strong, life-long sympathy for the *Wārkarīs*. It is apparent from his occasional use of *Wārkarī* subjects and characters in his writing, as for example in his poignant study of *Wārkarī* mentality in the short story, "An Experience of Immortality" (*Journal of South Asian Literature* 17 [1982]: 6–18). But he also felt a strong personal religious identification with the great poems of Dnyaneshwar and Tukaram in particular, which became especially important during his final illness. He went a step farther than most other writers, moreover, in that he decided to test his own "inner link" with Pandharpur through actual experience of the pilgrimage there.

This was not so simple a matter as it might appear to the casual observer. It should be borne in mind that social differentiation is a basic feature of life in India. As Deleury puts it, "Now, as before, the *Vārkarīs* come mostly from the countryside, being farmers, Brahmin landlords or petty officers, craftsmen, and traders. Few of them are from towns. . . . Fewer still are drawn from the ranks of the middle class or small businessmen or from the ranks of professional men such as teachers, professors, doctors, and lawyers" (5). Middle class literary society, especially in the major cities like Poona, has been particularly alienated, at least intellectually, because of the modern values in which it has been educated. For many it has become nothing less than a battle between the values of the mind and of the heart. As Mokashi addresses this very question at several points throughout *Pālkhī*, it is evident that he himself felt this conflict very acutely. He was, first and foremost, a highly regarded, modern, middle class writer with a considerable acquaintance with world literature, and he was cognizant especially of the style and technique of modern fiction in English. At the same time he retained strong feelings for the Marathi religious and cultural tradition; and though he was well-read and conversant in English, he was intellectually more at home in Marathi. To go along on the pilgrimage (and thereby to participate in one of the most venerable Marathi traditions) meant that he had to confront this conflict of values directly. It also meant that he had to set aside for a time his established position and role within middle class literary society.

Mokashi is not the only person who has left a written record of his experience with the *pālkhī*. G.A. Deleury accompanied the Dnyaneshwar *pālkhī* to Pandharpur in 1950 as a part of his research for *The Cult of Viṭhobā*, and much of his chapter on the actual pilgrimage is based on his personal observation. Likewise, Irawati Karve, one of the preeminent modern Marathi intellectuals, went on the pilgrimage in the early 1950s and left a much-admired account of her experience, as seen from her sociologist's perspective, in the form of the article, "On the Road: A Maharashtrian Pilgrimage." Other accounts, of greater or lesser extent, are also available in Marathi. Mokashi's record of the pilgrimage in *Pālkhī* remains, nevertheless, unique. It is, first of all, the only account in Marathi or English of the day-by-day experience of the pilgrimage over the two weeks of its progress toward Pandharpur. In addition, Mokashi had his own particular perspective on the pilgrimage. He was not an academic, and his account in no way has pretensions of that sort. Nor was he, on the other hand, an uncritical devotee of the *pālkhī*. Consequently, *Pālkhī* is neither a systematic study of the *pālkhī* pilgrimage nor a devotional guide to it. It is instead a vivid, realistic picture of the pilgrimage and especially of the pilgrims themselves as seen through the eyes of a practiced novelist. Incidentally (and for the most part indirectly) it also gives considerable insight into the frame of mind of modern Marathi literary culture and the manner in which it is trying to come to terms with its own traditions.

*Pālkhī's* special value lies in its complete authenticity. This is indeed Mokashi's hallmark as a writer. It arises out of the close attention he always paid to people's characters, to their social circumstances, and to physical settings. And to that is added the total sincerity with which he recounted what he observed. Twenty years have passed since the publication of *Pālkhī* in Marathi, and yet it still gives, in almost every respect, an authentic picture of the pilgrimage as it exists today. The individual *Wārkarīs* have changed, but the tradition carries on with remarkable fidelity. There are more pilgrims now than twenty years ago, but that reflects the increased population of Maharashtra itself.

Where changes have occurred is in the socio-political and economic context in which the *pālkhī* pilgrimage and the *Wārkarī Panth* exist. Economic development has advanced massively in certain areas of Maharashtra during the last two decades, and it has, as one consequence, exacerbated existing social inequities in Maharashtrian society. The communities of former untouchables have especially suffered from the increasing disparity between affluence and poverty in the society, and they have reacted by mobilizing increasingly vocal and concerted efforts to improve their position. This wider social and political mobilization of the former untouchables has also been reflected in the *Wārkarī Panth* to some extent in efforts made by *Wārkarīs* of untouchable background to gain a more equitable position within the *Panth* and to increase their participation in its affairs. In the late 70s this led to a series of incidents and satyagrahas that produced at least one significant change in the *pālkhī* pilgrimage: whereas the *diṇḍīs* (the traveling *bhajan* groups) of the former untouchables had always walked ahead of the actual *pālkhī* procession they were now given a new position within it, among all the other established *diṇḍīs* of the higher castes.

Nevertheless, the *Wārkarī Panth* and especially the *pālkhī* pilgrimage remain virtually a symbol in modern-day Maharashtra of unwavering continuity in a period that everywhere else is marked by rapid and stressful change. It is a continuity not only of the customs and rituals of a particular devotional sect but of a supremely important part of the history, character, and spirit of the larger Maharashtrian society. Mokashi's *Pālkhī*, through its depiction of the pilgrimage, allows us a glimpse of that perennial spirit of Maharashtra.

## *Vitthal, His Temple, and His Pilgrimage*

In order to put the *Wārkarī*'s *pālkhī* pilgrimage in context, it is important to establish its religious, socio-cultural, and historical foundations. Because the god Vitthal (known also as Vithoba and Panduranga) constitutes the primary focus of the *Wārkarī* religion, attention will first be given to the cult of this god and to his temple and the related sacred complex in the town of Pandharpur. Secondly, the *Wārkarī Panth* itself needs a careful look, especially the history and organization of its most public manifestion, the great *pālkhī* pilgrimage. How the individual *Wārkarī* differs from but also relates to the larger subcontinental Hindu pilgrimage tradition can then be addressed. In a related essay Eleanor Zelliot reviews the history of the *Wārkarīs* both as a strong religious tradition in its own right and also as an integrating Maharashtrian "national" symbol.

Several observers of the sacred complex at Pandharpur have been struck to find there two coexistent traditions surrounding the principal deity, Vitthal: the ritual temple worship of Vitthal on the one hand and the *Wārkarī* pilgrimage on the other hand. At a certain level they are of course related and mutually dependent. At least at certain periodic climactic occasions they share the same sacred space and the same sacred symbols. But in many other important ways they are also clearly distinguishable. Ian Raeside most sharply delineates the differences:

> There are two traditions of Pandharpur. For the pilgrims, who today are predominantly Vārkarīs, the concept of Pandharpur includes the road, the fortnight of singing and prayer as the diṇḍīs [traveling *bhajan* groups] make their way from Alandi and Dehu. . . . As *bhaktas* they experience the god directly all along the way. . . . [T]hey show their devotion to him by visiting his sanctuary in the great temple at Pandharpur, but they can worship him just as well in their hearts by repeating his names and the hundreds of *abhangas* devoted to him by the 'poet saints.' . . . But for the locals, for the badvas or hereditary priests

> and all the other Hindus who live in the narrow streets around the great temple, Viṭhobā is neither Viṣṇu nor Śiva. Viṭhobā is Viṭhobā, and the main temple is only the central point of a complex of shrines and temples and *tīrthas*, each with its own ministrants and rituals. (82)

Deleury also comments at some length on the evident incongruity of the fact that although the *Wārkarī Panth* has been largely responsible over the centuries for developing the importance and renown of Vitthal and of Pandharpur, the *Wārkarīs* themselves have had essentially no connection with the temple or with any of the other administrative or ritual aspects of the whole sacred complex that surrounds the temple. As he puts it, "There are therefore two distinct elements in the cult of Viṭhobā. The ritualistic worship carried on by the baḍvās, and the spiritual worship patronized by the Vārkarīs" (64).

These two "traditions" or "elements" of Vitthal-worship certainly do intersect, most especially on the occasion of the large *Wārkarī* pilgrimages four times a year that bring many thousands of *Wārkarī* pilgrims to the temple of Vitthal in Pandharpur. But these are clearly climactic occasions. In between times the pilgrims disperse to their own villages all over Maharashtra to continue at home the devotional practices expounded by their own tradition; and the temple and town for their part simply carry on with their day-by-day round of ritual activities, which includes attending to the needs of many non-*Wārkarī* pilgrims. The periodic *Wārkarī* visitation is clearly an irruption into (and to a great extent a disruption of) the normal ritual life of the temple and of the town.

The *Wārkarīs* themselves are conscious of their distinctiveness within the larger community of those who worship Vitthal. S.V. Dandekar, for many years the spiritual head of the Dnyaneshwar *pālkhī* (see pp. 258–60), was emphatic on this point: "Every *Wārkarī* is a Vitthal devotee, it is true, but every Vitthal devotee is *not* a *Wārkarī*" (*Wārkarī* 10). The *Wārkarī Panth* is a devotional (*bhakti*) sect, first and foremost, and it is therefore primarily interested in the traditional disciplines (*sādhanas*) of the *bhakti* way—and of these chiefly the singing of *kīrtans* and *bhajans*. When the *Wārkarīs* go to Pandharpur on pilgrimage they are in fact admonished *not* to engage in the varied and elaborate rituals that Pandharpur offers by right of its being a *tīrtha* of some note. On the occasion of the two largest *Wārkarī* pilgrimages in Ashadh and Kartik, when hundreds of thousands descend on the temple of Vitthal, the whole elaborate daily ritual of worship (*pūjā*) that normally surrounds the god is severely curtailed for five days in order to allow the *Wārkarīs* access, day and night, to the simplest ritual of all, *darśan*, standing in the presence of the god, seeing and being seen.

This is one illustration of how the orthodox temple worship of Vitthal clearly accommodates itself to the needs of the *Wārkarīs*—in the same way that, conversely, the *Wārkarīs*, by their active patronage of the temple over the centuries, have been the largest factor in enhancing its prestige and fortunes. It is a relationship of mutual benefit, in which both nonetheless preserve their distinctiveness. The temple—along with the whole sacred complex that surrounds it—has an identity outside of the *Wārkarī* patronage. Pandharpur offers the entire array of ritual services that are commonly expected of any major *tīrtha* in India, i.e., *snāna* (ritual bathing) and life-cycle rites such as *muṇḍana* (tonsure), *upanayana* (investiture of the sacred thread), and *śrāddha* (consignment of funerary ashes to the holy waters). Families of Brahman ritual guides (*tīrthopādhyāyas*), of many generations' standing, attend to these ritual services. The keepers of the temple rituals in the

Vitthal temple are similarly Brahman families having long hereditary rights to those duties. They also provide worship services (*pūjā*) for specific patrons. As we have seen, though, it is not the *Wārkarīs* who for the most part patronize these various rituals. Other pilgrims besides the *Wārkarīs*, in other words, also come to Pandharpur. They come not only from Maharashtra but from at least as far afield as Andhra Pradesh and Karnatak (Deleury 77).

The evidence strongly suggests that Pandharpur was a sacred pilgrimage complex, a *tīrtha*, long before the *Wārkarī Panth* existed and even, in all likelihood, before the worship of Vitthal came into being there—at least in its Vaishnava manifestation. What the origins of Vitthal-worship were—and when—remains the subject of serious scholarly debate. Given the prevalence of a Vitthal cult in Karnatak and the fact that Pandharpur remained under the dominion of Kannada dynasties until the thirteenth century (by which time the earliest part of the present-day Vitthal temple had been built in Pandharpur), it seems probable that the cult originated in Karnatak. Specifically with regard to the Pandharpur *kṣetra*, Charlotte Vaudeville argues persuasively that, given the overwhelming predominance even today of Shaivaite shrines there, "Viṭṭhal, as a form of Viṣṇu or Kṛṣṇa-Gopāl, was not the original deity worshipped there . . . his cult had displaced older cults, most probably that of Pāṇḍurang (alias Śiva), which was associated with some primitive Devī cult and with the cult of the monkey god Mārutī" ("Pandharpur" 149). This seems to be further corroborated by the fact that Vitthal's arrival in Pandharpur on a certain very specific occasion is part and parcel of all the traditional accounts of the god. In other words, he had not always been there.

What (or rather who) brought Vitthal to Pandharpur and caused him to stay constitutes in fact the charter myth of Vitthal-worship, both in its temple and in its pilgrimage

(*Wārkarī*) manifestations. The story revolves around the mysterious figure of a *muni* (sage) named Pundalik, whose *samādhi* or commemorative shrine, a small temple containing a Shiva *liṅga*, remains the second most revered shrine in Pandharpur after the Vitthal temple. Pundalik was in essence the first and archetypal Vitthal *bhakta* in Pandharpur. The story goes that Pundalik, after a self-indulgent youth during which he horribly mistreated his parents, repented and became thereafter a model of filial respect and loving-kindness. One day, as Pundalik was massaging his father's feet, Vitthal came to visit him and required hospitality from him as any guest would. Pundalik paused only long enough, out of the fervor of his devotion for his father, to throw a brick over his shoulder for Vitthal to stand on. This act of such absorbing filial devotion so pleased Vitthal that he decided to stay in that spot forever; and there he still remains, standing upright on his brick in the main temple at Pandharpur.

The earliest account of this story is given in a Sanskrit text, the "Pāṇḍuraṅgamāhātmya," which claims for itself a place in that great medieval compendium of myths, the *Skanda Purāṇa.* R.C. Dhere argues at some length for the relative antiquity of this text, placing it before the time of the great Yadava-dynasty minister, Hemadri, that is at the very least, before the middle of the thirteenth century (*Śrī Viṭṭhal* 26-40). This means that the advent of Vitthal-worship in Pandharpur long antedated the first acknowledged *Wārkarī* Saint, Dnyaneshwar, and by extension, the *Wārkarī Panth.* The account as given in the *Skanda Purāṇa* "Pāṇḍuraṅgamāhātmya" has been recognized by the entire subsequent tradition. Dhere credits it with being the foundation upon which the Vitthal-dominated sacred complex in Pandharpur arose (*Śri Viṭṭhal* 26). The *Wārkarī Panth* also made much of this account: "Puṇḍalīk is hailed by the whole Maharashtrian tradition, especially by the

[*Wārkarī*] poet-saints of Maharashtra, as their benefactor since it is he who brought Viṭṭhal to the spot . . ." (Vaudeville, "Pandharpur" 144).

Pundalik provides the traditional link, then, between the temple and the pilgrimage. He not only brought Vitthal to stay at the temple and thereby established the sacred complex surrounding him; he also provided, by his example, the archetype of devotion for all the subsequent long lineage of *Wārkarī* saints (see Eleanor Zelliot's following essay) and established the basis for the tradition of *Wārkarī* devotion to the saints.

The *Wārkarī* saints, most especially Dnyaneshwar and Tukaram, constitute in fact one of the most significant and distinguishing features of the *Wārkarī Panth*. S.G. Tulpule points out that the *Panth* has never been a "church" in any strict doctrinal or organizational sense: "It is a spiritual movement, or rather a body of spiritual groups gathered around saints belonging to Paṇḍharpūr" (*Classical Marathi Literature* 328). The importance of the saints is manifested in many ways. For one thing, the "literature composed by them constitutes the real 'scriptures' for all Mahārāṣṭrian Vaiṣṇavas" (Vaudeville, "Pandharpur" 156). But what is more, they are themselves the object of cultic worship among the *Wārkarīs*, almost as important as Vitthal himself, and as such they are fundamental to the meaning of the *Wārkarī* pilgrimage. Deleury most clearly expresses the nature of the *Wārkarī* regard for their saints:

> In many other Hindu sects the 'gurus', the 'swāmis' . . . are highly honoured and respected by their followers and disciples: indeed one could say that it is a common feature of Hinduism. But in the Vārkarī Panth, this veneration takes a peculiar aspect. Not only are the 'santas' [saints] venerated as avatāras of god at the place of their Samādhī by the group of their disciples and their descendants, not only are

> temples erected in their honor, but they are considered as still present in a spiritual way, as still living for the good of the community. This fact is at the root of the very existence of the pilgrimage.
>
> When he lived, the 'santa' used to go on pilgrimage to Pandharpur with the group of his disciples. While on the way, he assumed a very special holiness in the eyes of the ordinary Vārkarī, he was God himself walking across the country, giving to everybody the possibility to come near him and receive his blessing. To have a darśana of a 'santa' on his way to Pandharpur was to have a darśana of Viṭhobā himself. (73)

The saints went to Pandharpur on regular pilgrimage, as much to recognize and honor Pundalik, their archetype of sainthood, as to worship Vitthal. Even today the rule is for *Wārkarīs* to visit the shrine of Pundalik first upon arrival in Pandharpur, before they go take *darśan* of Vitthal (Vaudeville, "Pandharpur" 145).

What began as a recognition of Pundalik extended in time to the *Wārkarī* saints as well. And Pandharpur came to be known as the great meeting place of the saints:

> Paṇḍharpūr is the City of the Saints, the place where all the saints and all those who endeavor to follow them have always converged. The famous . . . pilgrimage to Paṇḍharpūr . . . is for [the *Wārkarīs* ] a way of joining all the saint-poets of Maharashtra in Paṇḍharpūr. The strenuous efforts of the pilgrims is motivated not only by the longing to contemplate the joined feet of their beloved Viṭhobā on the 'brick' but also to congregate with all the saints in their holy city. (Vaudeville, "Pandharpur" 157)

It can be said, indeed, that the entire *Wārkarī Panth* is organized around the saints. Certainly on the occasion of the climactic yearly ritual of the *Panth*, the *pālkhī* pilgrimage in Ashadh to Pandharpur, the organization of the *Panth* around the various saints as represented by their *pālkhīs* is explicit. But in many other less obvious ways, too, the *Panth* illustrates its coalescence about the saints. Each one of the saints, for example, has his own *samādhi* (like Pundalik's in Pandharpur), typically in the form of a commemorative temple, in the particular Maharashtrian town with which tradition has most closely identified him. There are many of these *samādhis*, and they are distributed over virtually every section of Maharashtra except the Konkan or coastal area. Each of these *samādhis* inspires its own customary yearly pilgrimage gathering and festival (*yātrā*). The most prominent ones (e.g., Dnyaneshwar's in Alandi, Tukaram's in Dehu, and Eknath's in Paithan) draw as many as one or two hundred thousand *Wārkarī* pilgrims every year and are themselves therefore among the more noteworthy *yātrās* in Maharashtra. The *samādhis* of the saints have become, in effect, the *Wārkarī Panth's* nodal organizing centers. So although the *Wārkarīs* worship the Vitthal of Pandharpur as the primary focus of their devotion, they have also kept their independence and distinctiveness by holding fast to the equally important tradition of their own saints, by honoring their *samādhis*, and by following the particular path of devotion they advocated.

## *The* Pālkhī *Pilgrimage*

Each year, from every corner of Maharashtra, the *Wārkarīs* converge on Pandharpur on the eleventh day (*ekādaśī*) of the fortnight of the waxing moon in the months of Ashadh and Kartik (and to a lesser extent in Magh and Chaitra) in order to honor Pundalik and to worship at the feet of Vitthal. This tradition dates back at least as far as the thirteenth century, to the time of the first great *Wārkarī* saint-poets, Dnyaneshwar and Namdev. Since then all the subsequent *Wārkarī* saints have, by their continuing example, established this pilgrimage as the preeminent ritual of the *Panth.*

To be a *Wārkarī* is first and foremost to make this pilgrimage faithfully, at least once and preferably twice, every year, in the company of all the other *Wārkarī* saints. As Deleury points out, the word *santa* (saint) in *Wārkarī* terminology is applied "to any pilgrim on his way to Paṇḍharpūr" (75). So the company of the saints on the pilgrimage includes all the ordinary *Wārkarī* men and women as well as their present gurus— that is, the entire living *Wārkarī* community of today. But it also includes all the great saints of the past. Because these saints are also taken along faithfully each year on the most climactic of all the *Wārkarī* pilgrimages and festivals, the one in the month of Ashadh. They are taken along carried in palanquins—*pālkhīs*—under the representation of their *pādukās.* These latter are a traditional type of clogs with wooden pegs as toeholds (but in this case rendered in silver) that represent the pilgrim saint's feet; and they are, hence, a powerful emblem of the pilgrim path he trod when he was living.

Around each one of these saints' *pālkhīs* there has coalesced over time a traditional procession of hundreds or thousands or even, in the most important instances, tens of thousands of *Wārkarī* pilgrims who accompany the saint from his *samādhi* or commemorative temple, wherever it happens to be in Maharashtra, to Pandharpur. The oldest, most traditional, and most revered of all these *pālkhīs* is that of Dnyaneshwar, which starts from his temple in Alandi (some fourteen miles north of the city of Poona) and journeys then for fifteen days over a distance of about 150 miles to Pandharpur on the occasion of the Ashadh pilgrimage. At the same time, between twenty and thirty other *pālkhī* processions from virtually every corner of

Maharashtra also travel to Pandharpur. On the eve of the great *Wārkarī* holy day of the eleventh day of the bright fortnight of Ashadh, they all enter Pandharpur together in their combined forces of hundreds of thousands.

A *pālkhī* is, in the strictly literal sense of the word, a palanquin. The *pālkhī* from which Mokashi's book gets its title is, physically speaking, also a palanquin: ". . . the pole is covered with silver plating, the seat is inlaid with precious metals and the framework is finely carved. Its weight is considerable and eight or ten men are required to carry it on their shoulders" (Deleury 82). But this is only the plainest denotative sense that the word *pālkhī* conveys in Marathi.

For Marathi-speakers "*pālkhī*" has certain connotations that are both more specific and more general than the literal meaning of "palanquin." That is why the word has been left as it is in the title and throughout the text of this translation. Palanquins have long since disappeared as a mode of transportation in Maharastra except in one special context: the religious procession. There is one particular palanquin, moreover, that every Maharashtrian knows and to some degree identifies with, and that is the *pālkhī* that bears the silver *pādukās* of Saint Dnyaneshwar from Alandi to Pandharpur each year. It is so central and integrating an emblem of the pilgrimage that it in fact represents to Maharashtrians not only Saint Dnyaneshwar but also the pilgrimage and, by extension, the entire *Wārkarī* movement, hence, one of the richest parts of Maharashtrian society's heritage as a whole.

The Dnyaneshwar *pālkhī* holds pride of place among all the *Wārkarī pālkhīs*. In the sense both of the physical palanquin and of the organized procession that accompanies it, it is the oldest and most traditional, so it has provided the legitimation and the model for all the others—including some begun as recently as the last couple of decades. In this way the Dnyaneshwar *pālkhī* has become the focus around which the *Wārkarī* pilgrimage has coalesced.

In terms of the continuous seven-century tradition of *Wārkarī* pilgrimage to Pandharpur, however, even the Dnyaneshwar *pālkhī* is relatively new. It was begun only at the very end of the eighteenth century. Before that time, the regular *Wārkarī* pilgrimages each year in Ashadh, Kartik, Magh, and Chaitra were certainly taking place but in a much less organized way. Even then the Ashadh pilgrimage was the largest and most significant, and the *pādukās* of Dnyaneshwar were taken to Pandharpur for that yearly occasion carried around the neck of some leading *Wārkarī* saint or guru—a tradition to which Mokashi refers in *Pālkhī* respecting Tukaram (see page 104). The use of a *pālkhī* to carry the Dnyaneshwar *pādukās* was an innovation that is credited to a rich nobleman from Satara District by the name of Haibatravbaba Arphalkar. This great devotee of Dnyaneshwar not only provided for the *pālkhī* and the paraphernalia of tents, carts, horses, and—at one time—elephants that surrounded it, but he also more fully organized the *Wārkarīs* themselves around it on the occasion of the yearly Ashadh pilgrimage (Dandekar, *Wārkarī* 62). He established the first official *diṇḍīs* (*bhajan* or singing groups) and brought them together in a set order within the *pālkhī* procession. Likewise, he arranged the daily order in the singing of the *bhajans*, which is still in use today. As Dandekar puts it, "The Ashadh *pālkhī* festival is entirely his fruit" (*Wārkarī* 62). As recognition of his sterling devotion to Dnyaneshwar and to the *Wārkarī Panth*, Haibatrav lies buried now under the first step of the Dnyaneshwar temple in Alandi (Neurgavkar 16).

All the other *Wārkarī pālkhīs* were established later, clearly on the model of the Dnyaneshwar *pālkhī*. The Tukaram *pālkhī*, which carries the *pādukās* of Tukaram from Dehu to Pandharpur in Ashadh, was begun in the nineteenth century not long after the Dnyaneshwar *pālkhī,* and it is regarded as second only to the Dnyaneshwar *pālkhī* in sanctity. The other *pālkhīs* have all been organized in the twentieth century.

The custom is for all the *pālkhīs* to arrive together in-Wakhari—the small town four miles northwest of Pandharpur—in time to participate in the great combined processional into Pandharpur on the eve of the bright *ekādaśī* (eleventh) of Ashadh. This means that some of the *pālkhīs* from farthest away must leave a month or more in advance (Neurgavkar 10). The combined processional from the last camp in Wakhari to Pandharpur begins each year at noon on the bright *daśamī* (tenth day) of Ashadh. Several hundred thousand pilgrims participate in it. Not all of them have come with the various *pālkhīs* the whole way. Even for the Ashadh pilgrimage, the majority of *Wārkarīs* come to Pandharpur independently, mostly by bus or train; but they do participate at least in the final four-mile processional. In the mid-50s Dandekar estimated that fifty to sixty thousand *Wārkarīs* actually accompanied the various *pālkhīs* on their way to Pandharpur (*Wārkarī* 78). The number is by now probably more likely to be in the vicinity of 100,000. As Mokashi clearly shows, however, the *pālkhīs*, like rivers with many tributaries, keep growing in numbers all along their separate ways the nearer they get to Pandharpur. To go on foot with the *pālkhīs* is clearly recognized as a special honor and distinction, the most public token of a *Wārkarī*'s serious commitment to the *Wārkarī Panth* (Neurgavkar 2-3). Even to go a short ways, if only the last four miles, with the *pālkhīs* is to share in what has become the core ritual of the *Wārkarī Panth*.

Every year the order, the route, and the schedule the Dnyaneshwar *pālkhī* follows remain virtually unchanged. Deleury observes, "The Jñāneśvara *pālkhī* is not an indiscriminate mass of pilgrims gathered around the palanquin. It has a very definite organization" (83). In accordance with the system of lunar months, some years there may be one or two extra days and some years one or two days fewer. These are accommodated for by spending more or fewer days respectively in stopovers at two or three of the larger towns along the way. Otherwise, the stopovers themselves are the same from year to year, except when really exceptional circumstances intervene as in Phaltan the year Mokashi went along (see pp. 234–35). The order of the procession, of the *diṇḍīs* within the procession, of the singing of the *bhajans*, and of all the other devotional and ritual performances (as described by Mokashi) is the same every year.

The *diṇḍīs* are the principal organizational units of the *pālkhī* procession. These are normally local groups of *Wārkarīs* who have gathered together voluntarily. They may have from twenty or thirty to several hundred members, and they are typically formed along caste lines. Some of the oldest *diṇḍīs* are as old as the *pālkhī* itself. New *diṇḍīs* are added from time to time (following an established petition process), and they are given a place in the order of the procession on the basis of seniority: the oldest *diṇḍīs* are nearest the *pālkhī*, the newest ones the farthest away. The *diṇḍīs* function of course to provide for the physical needs of their members all along the way. But just as importantly they also provide a disciplined daily regimen of *bhajan* singing, dancing, *kīrtans*, and religious discourses (*pravacanas*) that keep the members constantly engaged in the devotional purpose of the pilgrimage.

As is clear from Mokashi's observations in *Pālkhī*, however, many *Wārkarīs* do accompany the *pālkhī* independently—that is, unaffiliated with any *diṇḍī*. Most are poor *Wārkarīs* who cannot afford the *diṇḍīs*' fees. They either bring their own provisions along with them or accept the charity of pious townspeople along the way. As they must also arrange for their own lodging, many hundreds go on ahead of the procession to reach the designated stopover early; while, conversely, similar numbers of the weak and old come trailing along behind the procession (Neurgavkar 32). Mokashi himself gives several memorable vignettes of these people who come along however they can behind the procession. But the most interesting of the independent *Wārkarīs* are those who have committed themselves to making the pilgrimage from Alandi to Pandharpur and back to Alandi every month. In the mid-60s Neurgavkar estimated their numbers as between two and three hundred (57). The *pālkhī* procession in Ashadh corresponds with their own more stringent pilgrimage program, so they accompany it both coming and going on that one occasion during the year. Although unaffiliated with the recognized, official *diṇḍīs*, these various independent *Wārkarīs* do participate in the broader organization of the *pālkhī*, at least in the minimal sense of staying tied with it stage by stage along the way and of participating in the more public of the many devotional and ritual performances that attend the *pālkhī*'s progress.

The *pālkhī* procession's organization holds only for the duration of the out-going journey from Alandi to Pandharpur. As soon as it reaches its destination, the Dnyaneshwar *pādukās* are ensconced in their designated place in Pandharpur, and the pilgrims themselves are left to their own devices. Typically, after arriving with the *pālkhī* in Pandharpur on the evening of the bright *daśamī* (tenth) of Ashadh and having *darśan* of Pundalik, "on the *ekādaśī* (eleventh) they fast, take *darśan* of Shri Panduranga, and spend the whole day in doing *bhajans*" (Neurgavkar 6). They remain in Pandharpur, ideally, for five days until the full moon day, when they all disperse to their own towns by whatever means they can.

The full moon day marks the departure of the Dnyaneshwar *pālkhī*, too, on its way home to Alandi. The return trip could hardly be more different than the journey to Pandharpur. Only some three hundred chosen *Wārkarīs*, including those who make the journey each month, accompany the *pālkhī*, and the daily walk is doubled, since they must arrive in Alandi on the dark *daśamī* (tenth) of Ashadh to reinstall the *pādukās* at the right time in the Dnyaneshwar temple there. All the festival aspects of the *pālkhī* procession during the pilgrimage going to Pandharpur are dispensed with on the return. And thus, thirty-two days after setting out, the great pilgrimage returns full circle and comes to an end each year.

## *The* Wārkarī

The importance to the *Wārkarī Panth* of the great historical saints in its tradition should not obscure the fact that the living *Panth* is made up of many hundreds of thousands of ordinary people who live and work in the everyday world. It is one of the great attractions of the *Wārkarī Panth* that it is not an esoteric cult limited to religious specialists but that it is so open to all. The great saints were themselves for the most part householders, not *sannyāsīs*. They advocated the practice of the path of devotion (*bhaktimārga*) even while living within the entanglements and responsibilities of life in the family and in society (*samsāra*).

Being a *Wārkarī* (except for those who take the vow of monthly pilgrimage) does not exempt one from fulfilling familial, social, and religious obligations (*dharma*) as defined by one's own particular station in life. In this respect the *Panth* is orthodox and in accord with the overarching Hindu system. As Dandekar explains the *Wārkarī* ethic:

"Each one should act according to his own caste (*varṇa*) and stage of life (*āśrama*). But in the Kali Yuga more is needed. So the Way of Devotion (*bhaktimārga*) and the remembrance of the names of God (*nāmasmaraṇ*) have been given in addition. But the most important aspect of personal conduct [for a *Wārkarī*] is the rule of going twice a year on pilgrimage" (*Wārkarī* 75). It is clear that pilgrimage for the *Wārkarī* is not subsidiary or supererogatory but essential to his particular path of devotion.

To be a *Wārkarī* is, as we have seen, first and foremost to make the commitment to go on pilgrimage to Pandharpur regularly each year. This is the most characteristic and, indeed, self-defining religious act of the *Wārkarīs*. The word *Wārkarī* itself means in essence "pilgrim":

> *Wārkarī* means one who makes a *wārī*. He who makes a *wārī* is a *Wārkarī*. *Wārī* means "coming and going." So one who comes and goes is a *Wārkarī*. This "coming and going" takes place from one's own town to the town of the worshiped deity and back, and it takes place regularly. Chosen deities—Khandoba, Vithoba, Devi—are many. But the word *Wārkarī* is applied only to the devotee who worships the Vitthal of Pandharpur. Each year he must regularly and without fail go on the bright *ekādaśī* of one of the four [specified] months. . . . The majority of *Wārkarīs* accept especially the *ekādaśīs* of Ashadh and Kartik. (Neurgavkar 6)

It is clear from this that "*Wārkarī*" is a special word with a clearly defined and limited meaning and that the *Wārkarī* man or woman is therefore a special type too.

The standard Marathi word for "pilgrim" is *yātrekarū*, i.e., one who performs *yātrā*—the Sanskrit term for "pilgrimage" that occurs commonly in Marathi and all across India. The word *yātrā* (and more specifically *tīrtha yātrā*) applies to and typifies pilgrimage in a "Great Tradition" sense. When Maharashtrian Hindus go on pilgrimage to Banaras, Hardwar, Rameshwaram, or, closer to home, to Nasik and other Maharashtrian *tīrthas* of established sanctity, they speak of themselves as doing *yātrā*. Invariably, Mokashi himself in *Pālkhī* uses the term *yātrā* for every other pilgrimage to which he or other characters in the book refer.

Yet for a *Wārkarī* there is a clear difference between making his *wārī* to Pandharpur and doing a *yātrā*. The one he does regularly and punctually every year; while the other he *may* also occasionally do as an additional, supererogatory merit-earning action. (See, for example, the story Mokashi narrates of two *Wārkarīs*, uncle and nephew, who one year do a *yātrā* to Banaras, pp. 167-68.) "Supererogatory" is the term Agehananda Bharati uses to characterize the typical Hindu view of and regard for pilgrimage (*tīrtha yātrā*): it is an action that is "highly meritorious, though not essential to spiritual welfare" (136). Herein lies the crux of the difference between *wārī* and *yātrā*. Both are voluntary actions, which are thought to benefit the performer spiritually. But the one—*wārī*—is, above and beyond that, essential also to the definition of the performer of the action. As Deleury so aptly puts it:

> To go every year on pilgrimage is indeed for the Vārkarī an obligation: but this obligation should not be considered as an external rule. . . . The Vārkarī is obliged to go on pilgrimage because if he did not he would not be a Vārkarī. He became a member of the panth in order to go on pilgrimage, since it is the pilgrimage that makes the Vārkarī. (103)

The *wārī* is, paradoxically then, an obligation voluntarily undertaken. One chooses to do it because it is the only true way to define oneself as a *Wārkarī*. The *wārī* is, indeed, regarded by the *Wārkarīs* as the one most essential *sādhana* (spiritual discipline or means) of the particular devotional path they have chosen.

Like all *bhakti* sects in India, the *Wārkarī Panth* also, however, attaches tremendous importance to *bhajan* and *kīrtan*. These assume special significance in the context of the *wārī* to Pandharpur. *Bhajan* is the singing as a group of the devotional songs composed by the saints of the tradition. *Kīrtan* is a religious performance in which the leader expounds the devotional literature to the assembled devotees by means of song, dance, and narrative. The differences between these two devotional forms, at least in the *Wārkarī* tradition, can be rather ill-defined. A *kīrtan* may assume the character of a *bhajan* and vicc versa, a good example of which can be seen in Mokashi's description of the Kaikadibuva's *kīrtan* in *Pālkhī* (pp. 126–27). Worshiping together in a group, as a community of *bhaktas*, is the significant common factor.

*Bhajan* is, for the *Wārkarī*, his principal act of worship. As Mokashi points out: "For a *Wārkarī, bhajan* takes the place of *pūjā*" (p. 183). Dandekar, too, claims unequivocally that "*kīrtan* and *bhajan* are the major means of making the *Wārkarīs* one with Bhagawanta (God)" (*Wārkarī* 79). What makes *bhajan* so attractive a *sādhana* (spiritual means) is that it is comparatively accessible to the common man or woman and does not require esoteric disciplines:

> According to Tukaram the unblemished state that is attained by the *sādhanas* of yoga can also be attained by an easy way through the *sādhana* of *bhajan*. Instead of killing the passions—lust, anger, etc.—[as is the aim of *yoga*] one simply turns them over to Hari. (Dandekar, *Wārkarī* 86)

This implies that *bhajan* is an act (at least ideally) of the most complete self-abnegation and total self-surrender to Vitthal. It comes from a recognition of the insufficiency of the individual to realize his spiritual goals. This attitude underlies not only the *sādhana* of *bhajan* but also the *sādhana* of the *wārī* to Pandharpur; it is the common ground that vitally connects the two. The *wārī* represents in reality an apotheosis of the *bhajan sādhana:*

> The singing of the hymns [*bhajans*] is one of the most important functions of the pilgrimage. As most of the pilgrims are illiterate . . . the singing of the religious hymns is for them what the reading of spiritual books is for other communities. It is through the medium of these hymns that the Vārkarī traditions and teachings are transmitted from generation to generation. This makes, as long as the pilgrimage lasts, a true school of spirituality . . . a long retreat. (Deleury 88)

The supreme importance of the *bhajan* singing to the meaning of the *wārī* pilgrimage also impressed itself very forcefully on Irawati Karve. She perceived the singing to be the principal factor in creating the sense of community, of spiritual interdependence that she found to be characteristic of the pilgrimage in spite of residual caste and class differentiations:

> All were Marathi-speaking people—coming from different castes, but singing the same songs, the same verses of the Varkari cult, speaking to each other, helping each other, singing songs to each other. ("On the Road" 22)

As noted earlier, the sense of the community of *bhaktas* is fundamental to the *bhajan.* It is also, as we can see, basic to the *wārī* (as an extension of the *bhajan sādhana*) and indeed basic to the entire *bhaktimārga.*

*Bhajan* and *wārī*, then, are not separate phenomena; they are in fact all of a piece, joint parts of the overall *Wārkarī* path, of the *Wārkarī* practice of the *bhaktimārga.*

The *wārī* is the yearly culmination of the year-long practice of *bhajan* in the life of the *Wārkarī* community. As the "going and coming"—that is, the actual journeying to and from Pandharpur—the *wārī* has great significance therefore, in terms of the *Wārkarī* devotional path, as a spiritual *sādhana* in its own right. As Deleury puts it: "The pilgrimage must be considered as a real 'tapa'. A special line of mortification [that] will give to the Vārkarī the opportunity to exercise the virtues required for getting at the perfect 'bhakti' " (108). It is clear then that the journey with the *pālkhī* to Pandharpur is more than just a means to attain the goal of *darśan* of Vitthal in Pandharpur. It has great importance itself as a spiritual discipline.

The relative emphasis the *Wārkarīs* place on the actual journeying portion of their pilgrimage is one of its principal distinguishing features within the overarching system of pilgrimage in India. Journeying to and from a sacred center is common to all pilgrimage, it is true. E. Alan Morinis, in *Pilgrimage in the Hindu Tradition*, uses as his principal defining criterion of pilgrimage that special kind of journey that transfers "an individual from a profane and familiar environment to a sacred place which is spatially separated from surrounding everyday life" (259). But the emphasis in most instances of pilgrimage in India, it seems clear from the literature, falls relatively less on the journey itself (and the merit accrued from it) and more on the sacred center as the goal and the overriding *raison d'etre* of the journey. Morinis himself, in his study of pilgrimage in West Bengal, comes to the conclusion that pilgrimages there "seldom involve journeys which are themselves structured as ritual behaviour" (219). The typical pattern of pilgrimage in Bengal as he describes it (even at Vaishnava pilgrimage sites such as Navadvip, which have a strong *bhakti* orientation) is for pilgrims to come in occasional, small family groups (164). Their interest is focused entirely on the sacred center itself and the spiritual or mundane benefits to be obtained there because of its special holiness and its characteristic concentration of "orthodox ritual symbolism" (213). Bhardwaj presents a similar picture, in his geographically more dispersed study of pilgrimage sites in North India, with respect to most of the instances he studied. He uses the relative distance the pilgrims travel to particular sites as one of his principal criteria for determining the pilgrimage fields of these sites—and their consequent status in a theoretical hierarchy of sanctity. But once again this is seen to be not so much a factor of the spiritual efficacy of the journey as it is a valuation of the sacred center to which the journey is made. There certainly are exceptions, such as the pilgrimages to Kedarnath and Badrinath high in the Himalayas, the rigors of the journey to which are a distinct factor in the merit accruing from them. But here too there is a difference between the clearly supererogatory action of an individual pilgrim's accrual of merit on dangerous and difficult pilgrimage routes, perhaps once in a lifetime, and the *Wārkarī* pilgrim's cherishing of the devotional path he walks, in the company of his fellow saints—the community of *bhaktas*—year after year, as a voluntarily assumed obligation.

The *pālkhī* pilgrimage, it is clear therefore, is not a typical example of pilgrimage in India. The *Wārkarī* himself does not view it as such, and its very evident differences from the common pattern of Hindu pilgrimage in India seem to support his view. The *Wārkarī*'s *wārī* relates to the broader (pan-Indian) pattern of pilgrimage (*tīrtha-yātrā*) only at a relatively abstract level of analysis: the *wārī* *is* a journey that transfers individuals, in Morinis's terms, from everyday profane environments to a sacred place; and that particular sacred place at Pandharpur *is* a recognized *tīrtha* in the traditional sense of that word and it fulfills the functions of a *tīrtha*. But as we have seen, it seems more helpful to our understanding of the *wārī*, the *pālkhī*, and the *Wārkarī Panth* to view them less in the terms of *tīrtha-yātrā* and much more in the terms of *bhaktimārga*. Victor Turner's use of the *pālkhī* pilgrimage as one of his examples of the "liminality" of pilgrimage—specifically as exhibited in the "normative communitas" governing the social relations of the pilgrims during their pilgrimage—seems so apt, I think, precisely because it recognizes, at least implicitly, the *bhakti* heart of the pilgrimage: that is, the community of the *bhaktas*. Since the *pālkhī* pilgrimage is, for this reason, not typical of the broader pattern of Hindu pilgrimage, it is for this same reason not so clear how much Turner's interpretation can apply to our understanding of the broader pattern of pilgrimage in India.

The *Wārkarī*, then, is the representative of a particular tradition. More than a representative, he is a living symbol; in Turner's words, "a total symbol, indeed, a symbol of totality" (208). Heir to a long and very rich spiritual and literary tradition in Marathi, as he sings the *bhajans* of his faith all along the pilgrim road to Pandharpur each year, he becomes the embodiment of that tradition. He is like Turner's ideal pilgrim:

> He is no longer involved in that combination of historical and social structural time which constitutes the social process in his rural or urban home community, but kinetically reenacts the temporal sequences made sacred and permanent by the succession of events in the lives of incarnate gods, saints, gurus. . . . (Turner 207)

That the significance of this reenactment for the *Wārkarī* pilgrim should bear the strong imprint of specifically Maharashtrian cultural values is not inconsistent:

> . . . it is not unnatural that the new "formation" desired by pilgrims should include a more intense realization of the inner meaning of . . . [their] culture. For many that inner meaning is identical with its religious core values. (Turner 208)

In the essay that follows, Eleanor Zelliot examines how, historically, the *Wārkarī* pilgrimage and the *Wārkarī* tradition have become a major part of the core values of Maharashtrian culture. And Mokashi's *Pālkhī*, though certainly not in these terms, affords us a lively and direct access to the very heart of these values.

# *A HISTORICAL INTRODUCTION TO THE WĀRKARĪ MOVEMENT*

*by Eleanor Zelliot*

When Father Deleury began his pioneering study, *The Cult of Viṭhobā*, in 1951, it was with the knowledge that few in his native France, or anywhere outside the Marathi-speaking area of western India, for that matter, had ever heard of Vithoba and his *Wārkarī* sect. The joyous procession to Pandharpur, the outward symbol of the Maharashtrian *bhakti* movement, is now probably one of the better known of Indian pilgrimages. Iravati Karve revealed its all too human quality in her classic essay "On the Road," and the persistence of caste in this most open and egalitarian of events became an example of the caste system in David Kinsley's text book *Hinduism: A Cultural Perspective.* Two other fine Marathi writers' work on Pandharpur has appeared in English: Durga Bhagwat's "The Viṭhobā of Paṇḍharī," an essay on her coming to understand the meaning of Vithoba to Maharashtrians, and Vyankatesh Madgulkar's story, "The Pilgrimage," in which a devout Untouchable pilgrim cannot bring himself to go into the temple and "pollute the god," even though all bars have been lifted.

Victor Turner's important study, "Pilgrimages as Social Processes," drew on both Deleury and Karve in his consideration of the Pandharpur pilgrimage (his only Indian example). He stressed its relatively unstructured *communitas,* Pandharpur as an example of a city on the periphery of the catchment area, and the pilgrimage as voluntary rather than obligatory. Turner also made the error of conflating the name of the god of Pandharpur, Vithoba, with the name of Gandhi's follower Vinoba Bhave, coming up with the astonishing name, "Vithoba Bhave," an error repeated in innocence whenever Turner is quoted.

The pilgrimage has been captured in brief on film in David Knipe's Hindu Pilgrimage videocassette in the Religions of South Asia series.[1] And now Mokashi's moving account adds more characters, more stories, more understanding to what Turner called "the great Maharashtrian pilgrimage."

The Pandharpur pilgrimage is perhaps more tied to one region than any other well-known pilgrimage in India, with the exception of that to the Tamil god Murukan.[2] And yet, the pilgrimage is now as well known to Westerners, or perhaps better known, than the all-India pilgrimages. Indeed the important facet of Hinduism, Buddhism, and Jainism that is pilgrimage has only begun to be studied. There are a number of studies of holy sites, but material that gives a sense of the actual pilgrimage to those sites is still somewhat rare. Agehananda Bharati's 1963 "Pilgrimage in the Indian Tradition" seems to be one of the earliest, followed in ten years by the invaluable *Hindu Places of Pilgrimage in India*, a cultural geography of North Indian sites by Surinder Bhardwaj. E. Alan Morinis's *Pilgrimage in the Hindu Tradition* (1984) looks at three sites in West Bengal. Most like the writing of Deleury, Karve, and Mokashi in its inclusion of personal experience is the lengthy section on the pilgrimage to Lord Ayyappan "who sits on a mountain known as Sabari Malai, in central Kerala," by the anthropologist E. Valentine Daniel in *Fluid Signs: Being a Person the Tamil Way* (1984). Daniel's vivid and moving account of his participation in the pilgrimage is far more analytical of the inner meaning of the pilgrimage, as well as more graphic about the physical problems of mass pilgrimage, than any other account of pilgrimage.

What has made the Pandharpur pilgrimage the subject of so many accounts is certainly not its fame in India nor its "typical" quality. Indeed, even though the god of Pandharpur is worshiped by Kannada speakers, no one from Karṇataka or other neighboring states becomes a *Wārkarī*. And while the Pandharpur pilgrimage has features in common with other pilgrimages—the sense of oneness with other pilgrims (which is also apparent in the pilgrimage described by Daniel), the joyous quality of both the journey and the arrival at the center, the Victor Turner idea of a catchment into which many streams flow, and of course the importance of the site itself—it is in many ways unique. And it is those unique qualities which have made it the center of so much scholarly and creative writing. My reading of those qualities reveals this list: (1) accessibility and openness to all; (2) deep cultural meaning for all Marathi-speakers, whether *Wārkarīs* or not; (3) unbreakable links with the strongest literary tradition in Marathi, a tradition still important and still inspiring to modern writers.

### *Accessibility of the Sect*

The earliest writing on Pandharpur in English is that of the Rev. Dr. Murray Mitchell, who went by pony to the city at pilgrimage time some years before his account was published in 1882. He found welcome, tolerance, *kīrtans*, dancing, the height of emotion followed by "exquisite calm," and the atmosphere he describes seems much like later accounts.

When Deleury became the first Westerner actually to go on the pilgrimage, he joined a *diṇḍī* which had been created in this century. The *pālkhī* of Dnyaneshwar which moves from Alandi to Pandharpur (through the city of Poona) is the oldest in the sect; one of the *diṇḍīs* in that *pālkhī* was formed about 1920 around the figure of S.V. (Sonopant) Dandekar, Principal and Professor of Philosophy at the prestigious and conservative S.P. College in Poona. The welcome of a Jesuit priest as a full member of a religious pilgrimage may be due in part to Dandekar's understanding of the nature of scholarship. But it is also due to the open, sharing quality of the ordinary *Wārkarīs*. Since that time, dozens of Westerners have joined the pilgrims for at least a little way, as have Maharashtrian intellectuals who have no religious connection with the sect. Even American undergraduate students in the Associated Colleges of the Midwest's India Studies Program join the procession at the *pālkhīs'* meeting place at Wakhari four miles outside Pandharpur, and march in, often pulled into a *diṇḍī*, included in the dancing, made welcome year after year without fail.

No writer seems to have made the pilgrimage with lesser known *pālkhīs*, or come with the *pālkhī* from the furthest point, that of Shri Bhuteshwar of Nagpur. Indeed a study of all the *pālkhīs* would be interesting, for in the same way that the pilgrimage is open to all, some *pālkhīs* are formed around saints who seem to have no connection with the original *Wārkarī* cult. Shaiva saints, goddesses, two gurus of the Nath cult, the 17th century political saint who was by no means a worshipper of Vithoba, Ramdas—all are carried symbolically in *pālkhīs* to Pandharpur. Many of the *pālkhīs* have been formed in this century; more are added as more pilgrims join the journey. Mokashi writes in some wonderment of the Muslim woman and other characters who seem inconsistent with the history of the pilgrimage. Only those who wear the *māḷ*, the necklace of *tulsī* beads, are avowed *Wārkarīs*, but all are welcome to join the procession. And yet, in spite of this catholicism, each *diṇḍī* preserves its homogeneity, and I doubt if any pilgrim, true *Wārkarī* or not, escapes the spirit of the journey.

### *The Cultural Meaning of the Pandharpur Pilgrimage*

The word Pandharpur has come to represent the long tradition of Maharashtrian culture. Note, not the *god* Vithoba, but the town, temple, and *idea* of Pandharpur, the center of the streams of pilgrims. Curiously enough, Vithoba is an almost quality-less god.[3] There is the story of the god standing forever on a brick in Pandharpur in tribute to Pundalik's devotion to his parents, but there are no complex myths about Vithoba! Or rather there are many stories, but all telling of the god in some disguise or other, that of a Mahar Untouchable or a Brahman beggar, coming down to help a devotee. True, Vithoba is *not* an avatar of Vishnu, he is a "natural" Vishnu. Some say that Vithoba is the same god as Vishnu, or Krishna, or, a few have said, Buddha; clearly he is associated with Shiva. But none of the complex mythology of most of the Hindu gods or the Buddha has rubbed off on Vithoba. And the iconography of Vitthal is different from any of these. He is shown standing on a brick—that brick thrown him by Pundalik to keep the god's feet from the mud while Pundalik continued his loving care of his parents. John M. Stanley has called this brick Vithoba's *vāhan* or vehicle, just as the bull Nandi is Shiva's vehicle; but the brick makes Vithoba a static god, transfixed by human devotion.[4] Vithoba's arms are akimbo, hands on hips. He is dark, often black, often a naked young boy. On his head is a curious hat, high and conical, a symbol of Shiva, so that the image represents both Vishnu and Shiva, say some.

The god Murugan (Murukan) is identified with Tamil culture in somewhat the same way that Pandharpur is identified with Maharashtrian culture, but no one could write a book on Marathi literature that would be called "The Smile of Vithoba," and one called "The Many Faces of Vithoba"[5] would be short indeed. It is perhaps the very quality-less character of Vithoba that has allowed his cult to assume such identity with the region's culture. One can interpret him as one wishes; he demands nothing but devotion.

Durga Bhagwat's essay on "The Viṭhobā of Paṇḍharī" expresses the larger cultural meaning of Pandharpur and also refers to Vithoba as a "blackish manifestation of Brahman," symbol of the quality-less Absolute:

> Somewhere there exists some inner link between Paṇḍharī [Pandharpur] and every Maharashtrian. Because Paṇḍharī is said to be the home of the blackish manifestation of Brahman. Whether or not one has faith, one not only sympathizes with but feels strongly attached to the principle of equality of the Vārkarī Panth. The kind of innate attachment one has for one's family and ancestors one feels also for Paṇḍharpūr. (p. 112)

Vasant Sawant, a contemporary Marathi poet, ends a poem which suggests spiritual renewal with the lines:

> From afar
> (O so far)
> I begin to see
> The city of Pandharpur.[6]

Irawati Karve not only wrote the much heralded essay about the pilgrimage, "On the Road," but also an essay called "Boy-friend," in which she ruminates about the meaning of Vithoba and Pandharpur to her, a reluctant unbeliever.[7]

The city of Pandharpur is on the edge of the Marathi-speaking area; it has never been an important political center, nor even an important religious center, save for the mass pilgrimage. There might have been a Vithoba temple in Pandharpur as early as 1189, according to S.G. Tulpule,[8] and a copperplate inscription of 1249 mentions the city as the sacred place of Pundarik (Pundalik), but we do not know if the story of Pundalik and Vithoba is as old as this inscription. From the last quarter of the thirteenth century, the place was known as the city of the god Panduranga, and Panduranga is an epithet used for Vithoba in the poetry of the saints and the chants of the pilgrims today. But Panduranga means the White One—a strange epithet for a black god. And perhaps equally strange, the temple of the god Vithoba, a *svarūp* or original Vishnu, is surrounded by temples of Shaivite gods.

The oldest part of the temple of Vithoba at Pandharpur goes back to Yadava times, the 12th and 13th centuries that saw the flourishing of what seems to be the first true Maratha empire, centered in Devgiri near modern Aurangabad. The bulk of the temple probably dates from the 17th century, but additions and reconstruction have continued through the decades up to the present.

There is a Pandharpur *māhātmya* by Shridhar, a traditional song-of-praise for a pilgrimage center, written in the eighteenth century, but it is clearly a traditional Brahman view, not mentioning the *Wārkarīs* as such and bemoaning the turbulence of crowds that become too large. The city *is* a sacred center, situated on a river and filled with temples, although none very impressive. But its importance to the masses is not in itself, but because the pilgrims come *there*. Pandharpur is no Banaras. When the pilgrims leave, it lapses back into a sleepy small town, except for special occasions.

And yet it is in Pandharpur that cultural events which celebrate the traditions of Maharashtra are held. The city is important as symbol of all the good qualities associated with the pilgrimage: moral lives, egalitarian brotherhood and sisterhood, continuing and ever-living tradition, and perhaps more important than any other, the saints and poets that form an important part of Maharashtra's cultural as well as religious heritage. And as we explore the lives and writings of the saint-poets, and the writing about them, we see the identification of the pilgrimage in its broadest extent with the living heritage of Maharashtra.

## *The Literary Tradition*

The pilgrims go to Pandharpur singing the songs of the saint-poets and they feel that the saint-poets go with them. The living and the dead walk together, and all who join the pilgrimage join the company of the saints. There is an extraordinary sense of the living quality of the 700 year old tradition of *bhakti* (devotional religion) in Maharashtra. Even though much of that tradition is new, even though there is constant change—perhaps because there is constant change—the sense of a living heritage is strong.

The *Wārkarī* movement began in Maharashtra in the closing years of the thirteenth century with the fascinating figure of the young Dnyaneshwar (sometimes rendered Jnaneshwar, and often called Dnyanadev or Jnanadeo), who according to tradition was born in 1275 and took *samādhi* twenty-one years later, his work finished. The *Dnyāneśwarī*, a commentary on the Bhagavad Gita, filled with familiar images and idioms, is one of the earliest literary works in the Marathi language. It is also probably the most beloved religious text in Marathi today. The *Amṛtānubhava*, a more philosophical text, and a great many *abhaṅgas*, the poetic form of most of the songs of the saint-poets, are also credited to Dnyaneshwar. These mention the god Vitthal, or Vithoba, although the *Dnyāneśwarī* does not.

Dnyaneshwar's life is known as well to the Maharashtrian as his writing—possibly even better.[9] Legend, fact, and miracle are mixed together in such a memorable way that a simple reference, such as the "Veda-reciting buffalo," is understood by all. Dnyaneshwar and his brothers and sister, Nivrittinath, Sopandev and Muktabai, were born to a Deshastha Brahman woman after her husband had returned to her from a state of *sannyās*: that of a celibate holy man. Although he had been sent back to his unfulfilled wife by his own guru, he was immediately outcasted by his fellow Brahmans, the ritual priests of the Desh area of Maharashtra, and in time his children were also scorned. As a boy, Dnyaneshwar caused a water buffalo, surely one of God's stupidest creatures, to recite a portion from the Rig Veda to prove to his accusers that divinity resides in all things, and in time the children were recognized as especially blessed.

Dnyaneshwar's brothers and sister are vital to the legend. His older brother was his guru, his younger sister was a fine poet in her own right and they lived as a family, although none had proper families of their own. Three elements from this story carry over into the *Wārkarī* movement: implicit criticism of Brahmanical narrowness, egalitarianism in spiritual matters, and family-centered life.

The chief disciple of Dnyaneshwar was Namdev,[10] a tailor who lived on more than a half century after Dnyaneshwar took *samādhi* at Alandi, and who seems to have really begun the actual creation of a pilgrimage to Pandharpur in the company of the saints. In fact, Namdev seems to have created much of the ethos as well as the form of the *Wārkarī* movement. For him, Pandharpur was the center of faith, even though he travelled widely, made the pilgrimage to the famous northern *tīrthas* (pilgrimage sites) with Dnyaneshwar, and spent years in the Punjab. Namdev is credited with the creation of the *kīrtan*, a performance of song, story, text, even dance, which carries the *bhakti* message. Most important of all, Namdev gathered around him the most extraordinary company of saints and poets found in any religious movement. Their names and castes reflect almost the complete range of the populace of Maharashtra in the early 14th century: Changadeva, the yogi turned saint; Parisa Bhagavata, a Vaishnava Brahman of Pandharpur; Visoba Khechara, a staunch Shaivite and guru of Namdev; Gora the potter, who used to test the spirituality of the saints as "baked" or "half-baked;" Savata the gardener; Narahari the goldsmith; Sena the barber; Joga the oilman; Jagamitra Naga, the banker turned beggar; Kanhopatra, the dancing girl; Janabai, the serving maid of Namdev; and most beloved by Namdev, Chokhamela the Untouchable Mahar, whose wife Soyrabai, son Karmamela, sister Nirmala, and brother-in-law Wanka also wrote *abhaṅgas* to the god Vithoba. (Later, even Muslims joined, Shekh Muhammad [1560–1650] the most famous of them.)[11]

There are *abhaṅgas* from most of these *Wārkarīs*, preserved by scribes at Pandharpur through the centuries since Namdev's death. Only a few have been translated in English, although R.D. Ranade gives prose paraphrases in *Pathway to God in Marathi Literature* of some of Namdev, Gora, Visoba, Savata, Narahari, Chokha, Janabai, Sena and Kanhopatra. Perhaps modern English translations of those saints who seem most unusual—the women and the Untouchable—would help give the imaginative, devout, intensely personal quality of the songs of that early circle. Arun Kolatkar, a contemporary poet in both English and Marathi, has translated one of Janabai's *abhaṅgas* this way:

i eat god
i drink god
i sleep
on god
i buy god

i count god
i deal
with god

god is here
god is there
void is not
devoid of god

jani says:

god is within
god is without
and moreover
there's god to spare[12]

Chokhamela is equally god-possessed, but sometimes bemoans the state of his untouchability. A joyous *abhaṅga* can, however, simply refer to his duties as a Mahar; in the poem below, the word *cry* is *dauṇḍī* in the original, which is the proclamation made by the Mahar to call the village people for an announcement from some official:

Clap hands, raise flags, take the road to Pandhari!
The marketplace of Pandhari is the marketplace of joy; there you meet pilgrims in ecstasy.
Uncounted masses of flags fly; the banks of the Bhima resound with shouts of victory.
Unbelievers come; they go back pure!
I, Chokhamela, cry this from my heart![13]

In fact, many of the saint-poets from artisan castes refer to their occupations, using metaphors from their own lifework. And around each of the saint-poets are clusters of stories. While Vithoba is not the subject of myth, save for appearing to his devotees, the saints gathered in his name are the subjects of countless tales, their lives, their doubts, their miracles all recounted.

After Namdev's death in 1350, there seems to be a hiatus in the history of the *Wārkarīs*. The reason usually given is the coming of the Muslims: Ala-ud-din Khalji conquered Devgiri in 1296, and Tughluq moved the court of Delhi to the fort, renamed Daulatabad, in 1327. Later the entire area came under the dominance of the Bahmani kingdom. Whatever the cause, although no saint-poets are recorded for the next hundred and fifty years, the tradition neither died nor faltered. Bhanudas (1448-1513), the great-grandfather of the important 16th century saint-poet Eknath, was so devoted to the image of Vithoba that he went to the Vijayanagar King at Hampi who had taken the statue to enhance his own status and recovered it for the Pandharpur temple.[14] But the full sense of the glorious company of all the saints does not fully appear again until the time of Eknath (1533-1599).

Eknath, a Deshastha Brahman who lived as a householder in Paithan, is a pivotal figure in the *Wārkarī* tradition.[15] He serves as a link between past and present, between high Vedanta philosophy and common religious devotion, between scholarship and popular vernacular *kīrtans*. He edited the *Dnyāneśwarī* that we have today. He translated a book of the *Bhāgwat Purāṇa* which is known as the *Eknāthī Bhāgwat*, and is second only to the *Dnyāneśwarī* as a "text" for the *Wārkarīs*. He wrote amusing drama-poems called *bhāruḍs* which brought the message of devotion in colorful style to the common man. And he carried forward the idea of a company of saints with an *abhaṅga* such as this, which honors the saints of Namdev's circle and which is also aware of the Northern tradition:

> God baked pots with Gora,
> Drove cattle with Chokha,
> Cut grass with Savata,
> Wove garments with Kabir,
> Colored hide with Rohidas,
> Sold meat with the butcher Sajana,
> Melted gold with Narahari,

Carried cow-dung with Janabai,
And even became a Pariah messenger for
Damaji.[16]

After Eknath's death around the end of the 16th century, the tradition again seems to be without saint-poets. Eknath's own son and grandson were totally uninterested in the devotional path to Pandharpur. But the hiatus this time is short and in the 17th century the most beloved of all saint-poets, Tukaram, raises the *Wārkarī* tradition to new heights.[17] Born about the time of Eknath's death, and living until 1649, Tukaram's mature years coincide with the rise of the great Maratha Kingdom founded by Shivaji. Under this Maratha king a state was born which formed something very like the nation states of Europe—an area with a mass ethos of belonging, of unity, of a national spirit. What is the relationship of Tukaram to this burgeoning national ethos? The popular mind makes it very close indeed, with Shivaji a devotee of Tukaram.[18]

Shivaji the King, however, was a devotee of the goddess Bhavani, and a patron, so far as we know, not of Tukaram but of Ramdas, a saint of a more militant and political bent than the gentle *Wārkarīs*. Nevertheless, it is perfectly possible that the unity built by the saint-poets from many castes, the commonality built by the Marathi literary tradition and the pilgrimage itself, formed the underlying sense of belonging which is the hall-mark of the modern state.

Tukaram's fame rests not only on the association of his life with the height of pre-modern Maharashtrian power, but even more on the quality of his life and of his poems. He wrote over four thousand, and many are as fresh and vital today as they were over three hundred years ago. Some modern poets have tried their hand at translations, trying to capture the poetic quality as well as the meaning of Tukaram's songs in English. Arun Kolatkar chooses the most vigorous and unorthodox:

Tuka is stark raving mad
He talks too much

His vocabulary:
Ram Krishna Govind Hari

Of any God save Pandurang
Tuka is ignorant

He expects revelation
At any time, from anyone

Words on him are wasted
He dances before God, naked

Weary of men and manners
With pleasure he rolls in gutters

Ignoring all instruction, all
He ever says is "Vithal, Vithal"

O pundits, O learned ones,
Spit him out at once.[19]

Dilip Chitre has created this version of a poem that deals with the dualism of the saints, a soft-hard approach to life not yet fully explored by scholars:

We slaves of Vishnu
Are softer than wax
We are hard enough
To cut through a diamond

Dead though we live
Aware though asleep
Whoever asks us
The needed thing we give

We strip our own ass
To clothe the worthy
We strike the wicked in the head
With the staff we carry

More loving than parents
When we care

More murderous than enemies
When we flare

No elixir of life
Tastes sweeter than us
No poison can be
As bitter

Says Tuka we are
Sweet as a whole
As sweet
As a satiated soul.[20]

With this poem, we cannot but help entertain ideas about *bhakti* in the modern world—the bhakti poets as moralists, as crusaders against casteism and evil, as agents of change. There is a little more history of the *Wārkarīs* to account for, however, before we see how *bhakti* and the *Wārkarī* movement have become symbols for social reformers in the modern period. Tukaram's own disciples were less iconoclastic than Tukaram. A Brahman woman, Bahinabai, found her Guru in this Shudra saint, and wrote a spiritual autobiography about her struggle for a devout life.[21] Niloba, born in 1635, seems to have been the last of the well-known saint-poets. His songs are sung each day by pilgrims in the requisite order of *abhaṅgas*, even though they are less poetic than those of Tukaram, his master.

In the following century, no *bhakti* saint-poets flourished under the rule of the Peshwas, chief ministers to the then powerless descendants of Shivaji, and rulers of an expanding Maratha Kingdom which reached North, East and South in the 18th century. The *Wārkarīs* were immortalized, however, in the writing of a Brahman hagiographer, Mahipati.[22] In several volumes of lives of the saints, Mahipati, as did Eknath, added the saints of the Hindi tradition. He also included Ramdas, the devotee of Ram, founder of a *sannyāsī* order, writer of religio-political tracts, not songs to Vithoba. And since Mahipati's time, Ramdas has been included among the saints in a sort of generalized mystical tradition of Maharashtra.

The saint-poet tradition is by no means the only literary school in the Marathi language in the pre-modern period, but it is clearly the one most thoroughly shared by elite and common man, by intellectual and illiterate. It also has the continuing capacity to inspire modern creative work, a capacity not shared by the *paṇḍit* poetry, nor by the bardic traditions of *powāḍā* (heroic ballads) and *lāwaṇī* (romantic songs.)

### *The Modern Response to the* Wārkarī *Tradition*

There seem to have been three attitudes toward the *Wārkarī* literary tradition and the pilgrimage in the nineteenth century, as the Marathi-speaking area was coming under the hegemony and ever-increasing influence of the British. In the first Marathi school anthology, *Navanīt*, published in 1854, Parashuram Tatya Godbole, chief translator to the British government in Bombay, presented the work of the saint-poets, Ramdas, the *paṇḍit* poets, the *lāwaṇī* poets and some minor religious poets in the eighteenth century in chronological order and with brief notes on the poets' lives. The anthology was reprinted dozens of times, keeping before the eyes of countless schoolchildren the saint-poets' *abhaṅgas* as worthy literature. At about the same time, John Murray Mitchell was the first Westerner to write about Tukaram, the Pandharpur pilgrimage, and the *Wārkarīs* in an admiring way, finding the *bhakti* cult the closest parallel to Christianity the Hindu world offered.

A third attitude is represented by Mahadev Govind Ranade, a Chitpavan Brahman whose ancestors were in no way connected with the Cult of Vithoba.[23] A moderate, a social reformer and an ardent nationalist, Ranade found in

Tukaram his own personal religious guide, and the Prarthana Samaj (prayer society)—Maharashtra's reformist religious group under Ranade's guidance—chose Tukaram as their master, replacing Vithoba with the non-sectarian word for god, *deva.*[24] Ranade also found the saint-poets to be perfectly in accord with his ideas of a democratic, independent nation-state, and his *Rise of the Maratha Power,* published in 1900, a year before his death, linked the *Wārkarī* saint-poets and the *bhakti* tradition with the Maratha national ethos in a persuasive way.

Two groups of political and religious importance in the nineteenth century ignored the *bhakti* saint-poets and the Pandharpur pilgrimage. Bal Gangadhar Tilak and the whole "extremist" school of nationalists found the *bhakti* movement too weak, too gentle, too apolitical. It must also be said that the extremists were by and large Brahmans and intellectuals, and few of either group at that time had much to do with Pandharpur. The pilgrims themselves were almost entirely non-Brahman, and the intellectual quality of the *abhaṅgas* was not yet fully realized. The discarding of the *bhakti* tradition by the powerful non-Brahman movement of Jyotirao Phule[25], a *Māḷī,* is perhaps more difficult to understand. Phule established the Satyashodak Samaj (truth-seeking society) to try to develop religious institutions not under the power of Brahman priests; he began schools for Untouchables and women; he encouraged rational thought and the rejection of superstition. It may have been that Phule also saw the *Wārkarīs* as too gentle, too weak, perhaps even dominated by the Brahman priests of the Vithoba temple at Pandharpur even though few *Wārkarīs* were Brahman. The Prarthana Samaj, which saw the *bhakti* tradition as reformist, was not radical enough for Phule. His hope was for a priestless, rational, egalitarian, non-Brahman religion, and even so his stress was not on religion but on education and organization.

The twentieth century saw new developments in the *Wārkarī* movement. More and more *pālkhīs* began to be organized; some of the Brahman elite began to take an interest in the movement, even to become *Wārkarīs*; and missionary-translators published volume after volume, bringing the songs of the poets, the stories of Dnyaneshwar, Bhanudas, Eknath, Tukaram, and Bahinabai, and shorter lives of countless other saint-poets as recorded by Mahipati into the consciousness of the English-speaking world. The Rev. Justin Abbott was the chief inspiration of this movement, and his volumes contain notes, glossaries, commentaries, and translations rendered without religious bias. During the twenties and thirties, the history of the movement, and to some degree the movement itself, became part of an intellectual and religious renaissance. In addition to the work of the Westerners and their Indian colleagues, the first scholarly analysis of the saint-poets' thought appeared in English from the pen of a professor of philosophy, R.D. Ranade. More unusual, an intellectual interest in the saints was linked to popular culture in the developing Marathi cinema.

The most interesting sign of this renaissance, and perhaps the instigator of further *Wārkarī* mythology, was the Prabhat Studio's use of the lives of the saint-poets as themes for movies. Prabhat was the young, pioneering, extremely successful company of film makers in Poona who made the early Marathi cinema famous. Tukaram, Dnyaneshwar, Chokhamela and Eknath were all subjects of films, and Arun Khopkar writes: "These films that Prabhat made are intensely humane, warm, simple and expressive. The problem was not so much to glorify the saints—this was unnecessary since they were already revered by the audience—but to make them human and almost contemporary."[26] Prabhat succeeded in making the saints human, so much so that some of the actors were forced into living out saintly lives ever after. It also succeeded, I feel, in adding such a strong visual dimension to the written and spoken records of the saint-poets that the saints' lives and messages took on new life. Tukaram is represented pictorially today as he appeared in the movie. And the leftist message of egalitarianism taught by the young movie makers' depiction of Eknath eating with Mahars, touching an Untouchable child, giving his ancestral feast to the hungry poor, still is felt by the educated who wish to radicalize the common man against casteism.

Four books by intellectuals of the modern period from Maharashtra represent the weight and the importance of the *Wārkarī* tradition today. R.D. Ranade's *Pathway to God in Marathi Literature* brought the teachings of the saint-poets into a universal context of mysticism, and indeed its first edition, and a very recent edition, reflect this in the title: *Mysticism in Maharashtra.* G.B. Sardar in *The Saint-Poets of Maharashtra (Their Impact on Society)* dealt with the various attempts to make the saint-poets a voice for radical egalitarianism. He concluded that they were as egalitarian as their society allowed them to be, but that basically their radicality was on the religious, not the social plane. Ramchandra Dhere, Maharashtra's current premier writer on Marathi religion, has just published *Śrī Viṭṭhal: Eka Mahāsamanvaya*, the most comprehensive work on the temple, the town and the god himself to date.

The fourth book is an indication of the interest of intellectuals in the *Wārkarī Panth* as an indigenous path to social change. *Tradition and Modernity in Bhakti Movements*, edited by Jayant Lele (1981) contains four articles on the Maharashtrian movement, including an extremely interesting one by Lele himself in which he finds a critique of society in Dnyaneshwar which "advocates a revolutionary and critical productive activity within social practice" (111). Bhalchandra Nemade writes on "The

Revolt of the Underprivileged" in the same volume. Jayashree Gokhale-Turner feels that the power of *bhakti* has been changed to the power of *vidroha* (opposition) by the *dalit* movement of the lower castes. Eleanor Zelliot, in the same volume, finds legitimacy for social change in Eknath for new attitudes among the intellectuals but a rejection of Chokhamela by Untouchables, who find him too accepting of his low status.

And as the pilgrims walk and the intellectuals consider, the *Wārkarī* movement itself continues to evolve and change. The most significant change in this century may not be the joining of the *Panth* by Brahmans such as Sonopant Dandekar, or even the literary or social interest of intellectuals, but the presence of a genuinely radical saint from within the tradition itself. Gadge Maharaj (1876–1956) did not remain a householder, as in the *Wārkarī* tradition, but became a *sannyāsī* when he was a young man, and through this century travelled the roads of Maharashtra preaching brotherhood, anti-untouchability, vegetarianism, abstention from drink, and the rejection of idolatry. His was a message of purity, strict devotion, and love of all mankind, ideals very solidly within the *Wārkarī* tradition.[27] He founded orphanages and rest houses for pilgrims; he preached in the traditional *kīrtan* manner, quoting from the saint-poets, telling stories, chanting the names of god. Many see in Gadge Maharaj, the saint whose only possession was a pot, a *gāḍge*, the spirit of Namdev and Tukaram, an assurance that the soil of Maharashtra will continue to bring forth saints worthy of the best of the *Wārkarī* tradition.

## *Notes*

1. Hindu Pilgrimage, Number 11 in the *Religions of South Asia series* of videotapes, produced by David Knipe, is distributed by the University of Wisconsin.

2. See "Pilgrimage Centers in the Tamil Cultus of Murukan," by Fred W. Clothey, *Journal of the American Academy of Religion* 40 (March 1972): 79-85.

3. I was struck with this thought while reading A.K. Ramanujan's translations of poems to Murukan in *Poems of Love and War* (New York: Columbia University Press, 1985). "Murukan: His Places" and "Murukan, the Red One: His Dances" are descriptive of the god and of his worship in a way that *abhaṅgas* to Vithoba never are.

4. John M. Stanley, "The Great Maharashtrian Pilgrimage: Pandharpur and Alandi," paper presented at the International Conference on Pilgrimage, Pittsburgh University, 1980. To be published in *Sacred Journeys: the Anthropology of Pilgrimage,* ed. E.A. Morinis, submitted for publication.

5. Kamil Zvelebil's *The Smile of Murugan* (Leiden: E.J. Brill, 1973) is a study of the Tamil Literature of South India, in which this "youthful god of victorious war" is ubiquitous. Fred W. Clothey's *The Many Faces of Murukan: The History and Meaning of a South Indian God* (The Hague: Mouton, 1978) is concerned with the history, relationships and symbols of Murukan, and includes the poem "Prayers to Lord Murukan" by A.K. Ramanujan. While Murukan has somewhat the same regional place in Tamilnadu as Vithoba has in Maharashtra, and has inspired literature through the ages, as has Vithoba, the comparison between the two gods can go no further.

6. Sawant's poem, "Thou Art the Retreat," appeared in English in "Bhakti in the Modern Mode," by Ashok Kelkar and Sadashiv Bhave, *Vagartha* 21 (1978): 23, and *South Asian Digest of Regional Writing* 6 (1977): 12.

7. A translation of "Boy-friend" by Jai Nimbkar will appear in the volume *The Experience of Hinduism*, ed. Eleanor Zelliot and Maxine Berntsen (Albany: State University of New York Press, forthcoming).

8. *Classical Marathi Literature*, 328-329. See also Charlotte Vaudeville, "Pandharpur, The City of Saints"; the Sholapur volumes of the *Gazetteer of the Bombay Presidency*, 1884, and *Maharashtra State Gazetteers*, 1977; and M.S. Mate, *Temples and Legends of Maharashtra* for descriptions of the temple and the city.

9. For the known facts of Dnyaneshwar's life, see S.G. Tulpule, *Classical Marathi Literature*. A pamphlet entitled *Dnyanadeo* by the *Wārkarī* S.V. Dandekar contains fact and legend as does a longer booklet by P.Y. Deshpande, *Jnanadeva*. A book-length

discussion of *Dnyanesvar, the Outcaste Brahmin* by the Rev. James Fairbrother Edwards includes a summary of the knowledge about Dnyaneshwar, a discussion of all controversy, a long movie review, and considerable Christian commentary.

10. For Namdev, see S.G. Tulpule, *Classical Marathi Literature*; Mahipati, *Bhaktavijaya*; M.A. Karandikar, *Namdev*; and Parbhakar Machwe, *Namdev: Life and Philosophy*.

11. R.C. Dhere discusses Shekh Muhammad and five other Muslims *sants* at length in *Musalmān Marāṭhī Santkavī*.

12. Kolatkar's translations of Janabai appeared first in *Poetry India* 1 .1 (1966) and were reprinted in the *Journal of South Asian Literature* 17.1 (1982): 114.

13. For Chokhamela, see Mahipati, *Bhaktavijaya*; Eleanor Zelliot, "Chokhamela and Eknath"; and Charlotte Vaudeville, "Cokhamela, an Untouchable Saint of Maharashtra." This *abhaṅga* is Number 54 in *Cokhāmeḷā Abhaṅga Gāthā* (Bombay: B.L. Pathak, 1950).

14. See Mahipati's life of *Bhānudās* translated from the *Bhaktavijaya*.

15. For Eknath, see S.G. Tulpule, *Classical Marathi Literature*; Mahipati, *Bhaktavijaya*; Wilbur Stone Deming, *Eknath, a Maratha Bhakta*; Shridhar Kulkarni, *Eknath*; and Eleanor Zelliot, "Eknath's Bharuds: The Sant as Link Between Cultures."

16. Adapted from a translation in R.D. Ranade, *Pathway to God*, 177. A similar *abhaṅga* is credited to Tukaram. The story of Damaji concerns a *bhakta* who was a revenue official for the Muslim Sultan of Bedar. He gave away all the storehouses of grain in Mangalvedhe during a great famine and was arrested by the Sultan. The god Vithoba, disguised as a Mahar whose traditional duty is to carry monies to the capital, brought gold to pay for the grain and secure Damaji's release.

17. For Tukaram, see S.G. Tulpule, *Classical Marathi Literature*; Mahipati, *Bhaktavijaya*; K.V. Belsare, *Tukaram*; Bhalchandra Nemade, *Tukaram*; J.R. Ajgaonkar, *Tukaram*; and the many translations listed in the bibliography.

18. The immensely popular film *Sant Tukārām*, produced in 1937 by Prabhat Films in Poona, contained a sequence in which Shivaji came to Tukaram asking to be his disciple and was told to resume his kingly duties as a Kshatriya. When a jealous Brahman called in the Muslims to take Shivaji as he worshipped Vithoba in

the Dehu temple, the god created Shivajis out of all the worshippers and confounded the would-be captors.

19. Kolatkar's translations of Tukaram first appeared in *Poetry India* 1.1 (1966) and were reprinted in the *Journal of South Asian Literature* 17.1 (1982): 111-113.

20. First printed here by permission of the translator. Chitre's other translations of Tukaram have appeared in *Delos: A Journal on and of Translation* 4 (1970): 132-36; *Modern Poetry in Translation* 32 (1977): 19-20; "The Bhakta as a Poet: Six Examples from Tukaram's Poetry," *South Asian Digest of Regional Writing* 6 (1977): 80-84; *Translation* 5 (1978): 45-46.

21. See *Bahiṇā Bāī* in the Poet-Saints of Maharashtra series and Anne Feldhaus, "Bahiṇā Bāī: Wife and Saint."

22. For known facts about Mahipati, see S.G. Tulpule, *Classical Marathi Literature.* All translations and paraphrases of his work are listed under his name in the bibliography.

23. The Chitpavan Brahman caste includes the Peshwas (chief ministers) who ruled Maharashtra in the 18th century, most of the leading intellectuals of the 19th century (Bal Gangadhar Tilak, Gopal Krishna Gokhale, the poet Keshavsut, the novelist Hari Narayan Apte, etc.) and many of this century. However, Chitpavans or Konkanastas do not appear in literature as a caste until the early 18th century.

24. G.A. Deleury, *The Cult of Vithoba*, 20.

25. For Phule's religious reform, see Rosalind O'Hanlon, *Caste, Conflict and Ideology: Mahatma Jotirao Phule and low caste protest in nineteenth-century western India* (Cambridge: Cambridge University Press, 1985).

26. "Marathi Cinema," *Maharashtra—A Profile*, ed. Achyut Keshav Bhagwat (Kolhapur: V.S. Khandekar Felicitation Volume Committee, 1977) 310.

27. There is little on Gadge Maharaj in English aside from my notes in "Four Radical Saints of Maharashtra," to be published in a collection of papers on Maharashtra edited by N. Wagle. The fullest Marathi biography is *Śrīgāḍgemahārāj* by Gopal Nilkanth Dandekar (1976; Pune: Majestic Book Stall, 1982). A *kīrtan* recorded by Dandekar and published in his biography has been translated by Maxine Berntsen and appears in *The Experience of Hinduism* (forthcoming).

# *WORKS CITED IN INTRODUCTORY ESSAYS*


Ajgaonkar, J.R. *Tukaram.* Tr. R.V. Matkari. Bombay: V. Prabha and Co., 1948.

*Bahiṇā Bāī: A Translation of Her Autobiography and Verses.* Trans. Justin E. Abbott. The Poet-Saints of Maharashtra 5. Poona: Scottish Mission Industries, 1929.

Belsare, K.V. *Tukaram.* New Delhi: Maharashtra Information Centre, Government of Maharashtra, 1967.

Bhagwat, Durga. "The Viṭhobā of Paṇḍharī." Tr. Gunther D. Sontheimer. *South Asian Digest of Regional Writing* 3 (1974): 112–20.

Bharati, Agehananda. "Pilgrimage in the Indian Tradition." *History of Religions* 3 (1963): 136–67.

Bhardwaj, Surinder Mohan. *Hindu Places of Pilgrimage in India: A Study in Cultural Geography.* Berkeley: University of California Press, 1973.

Dandekar, S.V. *Dnyanadeo.* New Delhi: Maharashtra Information Centre, 1969.

——. *Wārkarī panthācā itihās.* Pune: Privately printed, 1957.

Daniel, E. Valentine. *Fluid Signs: Being a Person the Tamil Way.* Berkeley: University of California Press, 1984.

Deleury, G.A. *The Cult of Viṭhobā.* Poona: Deccan College, 1960.

Deming, Wilbur Stone. *Eknath, a Maratha Bhakta.* Bombay: Karnatak Printing Press, 1931.

Deshpande, P.Y. *Jnanadeva.* New Delhi: Sahitya Akademi and Sterling Press, 1973.

Dhere, Ramchandra Chintaman. *Musalmān Marāṭhī Santkavī.* Pune: Dnyanraj Prakashan, 1967.
——. *Śrī Viṭṭhal: Ek mahāsamanvaya.* Pune: Shrividya Prakashan, 1984.
Dnyaneshwar. *Jnāneshvari: A Song-sermon on the Bhagavadgitā.* Tr. V.G. Pradhan. Ed. H.M. Lambert. 2 vols. London: George Allen and Unwin, 1967-69.
Edwards, J.F. *Dnyanesvar, the Outcaste Brahmin.* The Poet-Saints of Maharashtra 12. Poona: United Theological College of Western India, 1941.
Feldhaus, Anne. "Bahiṇā Bāī: Wife and Saint." *Journal of the American Academy of Religion* 50 (1982): 591-604.
Fraser, J. Nelson and J.F. Edwards. *The Life and Teaching of Tukaram.* Madras: Christian Literature Society for India, 1922.
Karandikar, M.A. *Namdev.* New Delhi: Government of Maharashtra Information Centre, 1970.
Karve, Irawati. "On the Road: A Maharashtrian Pilgrimage." Tr. Dinkar Dhondo Karve. *Journal of Asian Studies* 22 (1962): 13-29.
Kinsley, David R. *Hinduism: A Cultural Perspective.* Englewood Cliffs, New Jersey: Prentice-Hall, 1982.
Kulkarni, Shridhar. *Eknath.* New Delhi: Maharashtra Information Centre, 1966.
Lederle, M.R. *Philosophical Trends in Modern Maharashtra.* Bombay: Popular Prakashan, 1976.
Lele, Jayant, ed. *Tradition and Modernity in Bhakti Movements.* Leiden: E.J. Brill, 1981.
Machwe, Prabhakar Balvant. *Namdev: Life and Philosophy.* Patiala: Punjab University, 1968.
Macnicol, Nicol. *Psalms of Maratha Saints: one hundred and eight hymns translated from the Marathi.* Calcutta: Association Press, 1919.
Madgulkar, Vyankatesh. "The Pilgrimage." Tr. Gunther D. Sontheimer. *South Asian Digest of Regional Writing* 3 (1974): 105-11.
Mahipati. *Bhaktalilamrita: Nector From Indian Saints.* Chapters 1-12; 41-51. Trs. Justin E. Abbott, N.R. Godbole and J.F. Edwards. Poet-Saints of Maharashtra 11. Poona: J.E. Edwards, 1935.
——. *Bhaktalilamrita: Eknath.* Chapters 13-24. Tr. Justin E. Abbott. Poet-Saints of Maharashtra 2. Poona: Scottish Mission Industries, 1927. Delhi: Motilal Banarsidass, 1981. Intro. G.V. Tagore.

——. *Bhaktalilamrita: Tukaram.* Chapters 25-40. Tr. Justin E. Abbott. Poet-Saints of Maharashtra 7. Poona: Justin E. Abbott, 1930. Delhi: Motilal Banarsidass, 1980.

——. *Bhaktavijaya: Stories of Indian Saints.* 2 vols. Tr. Justin E. Abbott and Narhar R. Godbole. Poet-Saints of Maharashtra 9 and 10. Poona: N.R. Godbole; United Theological College of Western India, 1933 and 1944.

——. *Bhaktavijaya: Bhanudas.* Chapters 42-43. Tr. Justin E. Abbott. Poet-Saints of Maharashtra 1. Poona: Justin E. Abbott, 1926.

——. *Bhaktavijaya: Tales of the Saints of Pandharpur.* Told by C.A. Kincaid. Bombay and Madras: Humphrey Milford for Oxford University Press, 1919.

——. *Santavijaya: Ramdas.* Tr. Justin E. Abbott. Poet-Saints of Maharashtra 8. Poona: N.R. Godbole, 1932.

Mate, M.S. *Temples and Legends of Maharashtra.* Bombay: Bharatiya Vidya Bhavan, 1962.

Mitchell, J. Murray. "Pandharpur." *The Indian Antiquary* 11 (1882): 149-56.

Mokashi, D.B. "An Experience of Immortality." Tr. Philip Engblom and Vidyut Bhagwat. *Journal of South Asian Literature* 17 (1982): 6-18.

——. *Farewell to the Gods.* Tr. Pramod Kale. Delhi: Hind Pocket Books, 1972.

Morinis, E. Alan. *Pilgrimage in the Hindu Tradition: A Case Study of West Bengal.* Delhi: Oxford University Press, 1984.

Nemade, Bhalchandra. *Tukaram.* Ne Delhi: Sahitya Akademi, 1980.

Neurgavkar, Sadashiv Keshav. *Pālkhī sohaḷā.* Pune: Privately printed, 1965.

"Pandharpur." *Gazetteer of the Bombay Presidency: Sholapur.* Vol. 20. Ed. James M. Campbell. Written largely by Shantaram Vinayak Kantak and Pandit Bhagvanlal Indraji. Bombay: Government Central Press, 1884. 415-85.

"Pandharpur." *Maharashtra State Gazetteers: Sholapur.* Vol. 23. Revised Edition. Bombay: Government of Maharashtra, 1977.

Raeside, I.M.P. "The Pāṇḍuranga-Māhātmya of Śrīdhar." *Bulletin of the School of Oriental and African Studies* 28 (1965): 81-100.

Ranade, Ashok D. "Keertana: an effective communication." *On Music and Musicians of Hindoostan.* New Delhi: Promilla and Co., 1984. 109-137.

Ranade, M.G. *Rise of the Maratha Power*. 1900. Bombay: University of Bombay, 1960. Delhi: Publications Division, Ministry of Information and Broadcasting, Government of India, 1961.

Ranade, R.D. *Pathway to God in Marathi Literature*. Bombay: Bharatiya Vidya Bhavan, 1961. First published as *Mysticism in Maharashtra*. Poona: Aryabushan Press, 1933. Reprinted as *Mysticism in India: The Poet-Saints of Maharashtra*. Albany: State University of New York Press, 1983.

Sardar, G.B. *The Saint-Poets of Maharashtra: Their Impact on Society*. Tr. Kumud Mehta. Bombay: Orient Longmans, 1969.

Shridhar. See Raeside, I.M.P.

*Stotramala: A Garland of Hindu Prayers*. A Translation of Prayers of Maratha Poet-Saints, from Dnyaneshvar to Mahipati. Tr. Justin A. Abbott. The Poet-Saints of Maharashtra Series 6. Poona: Scottish Mission Industries, 1929.

Tukaram. *The Poems of Tukarama*. Trs. J. Nelson Fraser and K.B. Marathe. 3 vols. Madras: Christian Literature Society, 1909–15. Delhi: Motilal Banarsidass, 1981. Vol. 1.

——. *Psaumes du pelerin*. Trans. G.A. Deleury. 2nd edition. Paris: Gallimard, 1956.

——. *Selections from Tukaram*. Tr. Wilbur Stone Deming. Madras: Christian Literature Society, 1932.

——. *An Indian Peasant Mystic*. Translations from Tukaram. John S. Hoyland. London: H.R. Allenson, 1932.

——. *Tukaram's Poems*. Tr. Prabhakar Machwe. Calcutta: United Writer, 1977.

——. For other translations, see footnotes 19 and 20 in Eleanor Zelliot's Introduction to this volume.

Tulpule, Shankar Gopal. *Classical Marathi Literature: From the Beginning to A.D. 1818*. A History of Indian Literature IX:4. Wiesbaden: Otto Harrassowitz, 1979.

——. *Mysticism in Medieval India*. Wiesbaden: Otto Harrassowitz, 1984.

Turner, Victor. "The Center Out There: Pilgrim's Goal." *History of Religions* 12 (1973): 191–230. Reprinted as "Pilgrimages as Social Processes." *Dramas, Fields, and Metaphors: Symbolic Action in Human Society*. Ithaca: Cornell University Press, 1974. 166–230.

Vaudeville, Charlotte. "Cokhamela, an Untouchable Saint of Maharashtra." *South Asian Digest of Regional Writing* 6 (1977): 60–79.

——. "Pandharpur, the City of the Saints." *Structural Ap-*

*proaches to South Indian Studies.* Ed. Harry M. Buck and Glenn E. Yocum. Chambersburg, Pennsylvania: Wilson Books, 1974. 137-61.

Zelliot, Eleanor. "Chokhamela and Eknath: Two *Bhakti* Modes of Legitimacy for Modern Change." *Journal of Asian and African Studies* 15 (1980): 137-56. Reprinted in Jayant Lele, ed. *Tradition and Modernity in Bhakti Movements.*

——. Eknath's Bharuds: The Sant as Link Between Cultures." *The Sants: Studies in a Devotional Tradition of India.* Eds. Karine Schomer and W.H. McLeod. Berkeley: Religious Studies Series. Delhi: Motilal Banarsidass, forthcoming.

# *SALUTATION*

"I've arrived! I've arrived at the *pālkhī*!"[1]

That is the thought that entered my head as, clutching the bag I had hung from my shoulder, I stepped out into the festive ceremony of the *pālkhī* procession.

Every year when the black clouds lowered and the rainy June weather spread across the land I became restless. I kept telling myself, "This year you really must go along with the *pālkhī*." As the day drew near for the *pālkhī* to come through Poona, my restlessness grew worse. The *Wārkarīs* who came ahead of the procession would appear, wandering about the city.[2] If one of them stopped in front of my shop—the pole of his banner over his shoulder, his bundle on his head—and asked for something, I gave him whatever small coin I could find.

To go with the *pālkhī* means you have to close up your business for a whole month. It means you have to make pro-

1. A *pālkhī* is a palanquin, in this case the one that bears the silver clogs symbolizing Saint Dnyaneshwar in the yearly pilgrimage from Alandi to Pandharpur. In many contexts the word also signifies, as a convenient synecdoche, the entire pilgrim procession that accompanies it.

2. *Wārkarīs* are the initiated devotees of Vitthal who perform a regular monthly, semiannual, or annual pilgrimage to Vitthal's temple in Pandharpur.

visions for the month's normal household needs as well as for the extra expenses you incur going with the *pālkhī*. The reassuring thought that any number of other *Wārkarīs* were also going along on the pilgrimage in spite of these very same worries just never seemed to occur to me on these occasions. I fretted and I fumed over it. This year my fretting and fuming became much worse. The black clouds arrived. The rain started pouring down. The air grew heavy. *Wārkarīs* began to appear in the streets. And one day I closed up the shop early, came home, and announced, "No matter what happens, this year I'm going to go with the *pālkhī*."

An idea I had for a novel had given rise in me to this restlessness over the *pālkhī*. It had occurred to me six or seven years ago. The plot would begin at the start of the *pālkhī* procession and would end when it did. A young doctor, the son of a *Wārkarī* who has become too old to go with the *pālkhī* anymore, has to go on the pilgrimage in his father's place—that was the extent of the idea in my head. What would happen beyond that would be impossible for me to know unless I actually went along with the *pālkhī* myself. Year after year I just couldn't seem to manage it. And like an impatient toddler on his mother's hip who clamors to get loose, this idea of mine had kept on pestering me.

I am even astonished now at my devotion to that idea for a novel. At how it could work me up every bit as much as the most ardent *Wārkarī*! At how the cloudy June sky could leave me feeling so restless! I intended just to go along and collect material for my writing—but only as long as it would not feel contrived and artificial. Nor something to regret. My devotion would have to go along hand in hand with the devotion of the *Wārkarīs*.

Fourteen years ago I had written an article that was entitled "What I Saw at the Pandharpur Pilgrimage." The state of mind in which I wrote it no longer existed. On that occasion I set out taking my cudgel with me. I wrote it out of rage at the Railway, which had crammed the *Wārkarīs* into cattle cars; at the stick-wielding police, who had split the *Wārkarīs*' heads; at the priests, who took each *Wārkarī* by turn and snatched his money away as they banged his head down in front of Vitthal; and at these dumb *Wārkarīs* themselves, who quietly bore it all. On that occasion I had just wandered about in the holy precincts of Pandharpur. I stayed overnight at Wakhari. All the *pālkhīs* stop in this hamlet, seven miles from Pandharpur, and stay one night before entering the pilgrimage site. While I was sleeping out in the open fields at that last stopover, somebody stole the water pot and my watch, which I had put in it, from under my pillow.

The funny thing is that once again on this occasion something very similar happened to me. I had meant to meet the procession at Hadapsar, so I first went down to the Poona State Transport bus depot. It was so crowded with *Wārkarīs* that every fifteen minutes or so when a bus came in and carried off a few of them it seemed hardly more than a sparrow carrying away a single grain at a time out of a whole granary. As I stood there in despair watching all this, an old *Wārkarī* woman came up to me. She held out a ticket to me and said, "It's a reservation for Lonand. The people didn't show up."

I took the ticket at once and ran for the bus. As I stood there waiting, I happened to show it to somebody. He looked at it closely and said, "Hey! That was issued for yesterday!"

I looked all around me. There was no sign of that old woman. So I held that very ticket out in front of me and got on the bus. As I was moving toward the front seats I looked up, and lo and behold, there I saw the old woman sitting at her ease in one of the seats ahead of me. Just then she turned and saw me, and she started to laugh with an expression on her face that said, "Did I ever fool you!" I also started to laugh. It no longer upset me that a *Wārkarī* woman would cheat me.

Sixteen years had wrought this important change in my character. I no longer insisted that a *Wārkarī*—or anyone for that matter—should act in any particular way. It wasn't the case either that I had developed religious devotion for the *Wārkarīs* or for the *pālkhī*. My love was only for the writing of my novel. But there were no preconceptions in my mind about what I was going to say in it.

An idea I had some years ago now came to my help in paying the expenses related to going with the *pālkhī*. My idea was to make a survey of the *pālkhī*. I went immediately to meet the people at Gokhale Institute.[1] Pilgrims accompany the *pālkhī* from all classes and districts of Maharashtra. My idea, as I explained it to the people at the Institute, was that if I were to ask the pilgrims selected questions, their answers would serve as a mirror for the whole society. They liked the idea.

D. K. Bedekar prepared the question-sheet.[2] I suggested a few of the questions on it, and then they sent it off for printing. I started getting myself ready to go.

Later on I was to meet *Wārkarīs* who were plying their trades as they went along with the procession. One of them was selling puffed rice, a second was selling bangles, a third had a pushcart from which he sold tea, and a fourth cut hair. When I questioned them about it they replied, "We serve the *Wārkarīs*, and at the same time our expenses get paid along the way." By accepting this work from the

1. Gokhale Institute of Politics and Economics, situated in Poona, is a leading center of postgraduate studies in the social sciences.

2. Dinkar K. Bedekar (1910–1973) was a prominent Marathi intellectual and writer. At the time he was a Research Fellow of Gokhale Institute.

Gokhale Institute I unwittingly joined this category of *Wārkarīs*.

To go with the *pālkhī* means simply to put your bundle on your head and set off, to sleep out in the open fields, and to eat wherever you can get anything. That, anyway, was my understanding of the matter.

But when I started making inquiries, I came to understand that within the *pālkhī* procession itself there are many separate smaller groups called *diṇḍīs*.[1] They take care of all the arrangements for their own members. I even got hold of the address of one of the *diṇḍīs*.

I went and met its leader. Meals two times a day and tea two times. A place to stay at night. Where houses couldn't be obtained, they had an arrangement to provide tents. To carry the bedding and the other luggage there was to be an accompanying truck. "For all this we take forty rupees," he said.

I gave him his money, and he gave me the fifteen-day travel program for the procession. And he gave me two suggestions: "While you're walking during the day, take only a handbag and a water pot with you. Take some simple preparation in your bag to eat along the way. You get hungry—and you get tired."

Later on, when our feet began to ache, that travel program proved itself very useful. We could make our feet ache a little bit less by taking it out and showing each other that the next day we would have to go just five miles.

The walking distance of the procession is about one hundred fifty miles.

In the middle of my preparations I suddenly remembered one very important thing: I went and got my sandals fixed. I rolled everything up in a bundle. A blanket, a quilt, one

---

1. Neighborhood or local groups of Warkaris who worship, sing, and go on the pilgrimage together.

sheet, a cotton spread, and two sets of clothes was all I had.

I also prepared my bag. It included a few things to eat—peanuts, sweets, and so forth—and medications. I took Amritanjan balm, Vasoline, sulpha pills, iodine, and Iodex. But the most important preparations were for public relations. So I included a plentiful store of cut up pieces of betel nut, chewing tobacco, lime to mix with it, and cloves. And then I set off.

371. *Moisture is in water, space is in the sky, sweetness is in sugar; in these there is no separation.*

372. *Flames and fire are one, lotus petals are one with the flower, and the branches and the fruit of a tree are the tree itself.*

373. *The snow which is drawn to the mountain becomes part of it; curds are but curdled milk.*

374. *Similarly the entire universe is but Myself; there is no purpose in stripping the moon; [one would find but the moon itself].*

375. *Ghi is clarified butter, in spite of its solidity; though a bracelet is not melted down, it is still gold.*

376. *Even if a garment is not unravelled, it is still nothing but woven threads; one need not crush a pot to see that it is but earth.*

377. *Therefore do not think that I can only be found through the dissolving of the universe, for I Myself am all.*

378. *To realize Me this manner is called single-hearted devotion; if any sense of difference appears, it is an aberration.*

Jnāneshvari *Fourteen*

CHAPTER ONE

# Saswad

Today it is the eleventh day of the dark half of the month Jyeshtha. According to the schedule, the *pālkhī* had left Poona in the morning and had gone as far as the rest stop at Hadapsar. From there, after the height of the afternoon, when people's meals were finished, it would move on to Saswad. I wanted to meet up with it before it got moving again. But the crowds made me late. Our State Transport bus got to Hadapsar, but there we learned that the procession had left long before us. When the bus set off after it, I told the conductor a number of times, "I just want to go as far as the *pālkhī*."

I had even started to feel important at going along with the *pālkhī*.

We arrive at the foot of Diva Ghat, but there is still no sign of the *pālkhī!* The late afternoon shadows have spread out over the hillside. *Wārkarīs* appear, by ones and twos, climbing up the hill. As our bus also starts climbing, more and more of the *Wārkarīs* appear. A couple of them are pushing a handcart ahead of them as they climb. An elderly *Wārkarī* sits, taking a rest on the retaining wall. Two old women are helping each other as they move along. Now and then, its banners flapping, a loose knot of people makes its way up the hill.

As I watch I am suffused with a sense of well-being. When I was young, I always used to tell myself whenever the curtain in the theater moved a bit, "At last! The play is going to begin!" And now, too, when I see these *Wārkarīs*, I feel, "I'm finally going to see the *pālkhī*—I really am!" A beam of bright sunshine lights up a spot at the bottom of the hill like a color motion picture. Now and then my eyes stray toward it.

❀

The bus arrived at the crest of the hill. Hurriedly, confusedly, the wind bundled up the sounds of the cymbals from the *pālkhī* procession and hurled them in our ears. "The *pālkhī!* The *pālkhī!*" a couple of people shouted. At once they all started to poke their heads out of the windows of the bus to get a look. When our bus passed by the first *diṇḍī* in the procession, one of the passengers cried out ecstatically, "Pundalik's Benefactor Hari Vitthal!"

Everyone in the bus, with one voice, joined in the acclamation, and they all raised their joined palms rapidly in a *namaskār.*[1] But I was struck dumb. My hands didn't even rise in a *namaskār.* My city man's shyness made me shrink back. The conductor rang the bell, and I started to get off the bus. Again the cry resounded throughout the bus, "Pun-

1. A salutation performed by joining the palms, bowing the head and pronouncing the word *namaskār*.

dalik's Benefactor Hari Vitthal! Shri Dnyanadev Tukaram!"[1]

The shout was given rousing support from outside the bus as well. So I too, as I got off, made bold to mutter, "Shri Dnyaneshwar-Mother Tukaram!"[2]

❀

"I've arrived! I've arrived at the *pālkhī!*"

That is what entered my mind as I set foot on the road. The free wind flowing over my body, the fields spreading out on either side, the open, spreading plateau, the hills—I felt as if I were walking through a painting! From now on I would walk and get my feet wet in the streams and gullies. I would go onward with a free, open mind and an unencumbered body. There was joy here. Everything was filled with joy.

I stood at the edge of the road and let my eyes gather in the whole procession. Evening had started to fall. The soft, fresh sunshine gave all of creation a touching tenderness. Full-grown banyan trees stood along both sides of the road, and their leaves were rustling in the wind. The *Wārkarīs* held their banners high, and these seemed to color the very sky saffron and to dance and make merry in the wind. As the *Wārkarīs* moved against the wind they all leaned forward together as one, and their clothes stuck to their bodies. The sound of their cymbals stained each gust of wind.

I didn't even realize it when, right before my eyes, the last

1. "Shri"is a respectful prefix to a name; "Dnyanadev" is another name for Dnyaneshwar.

2. "Mother" is a common endearment used for both Dnyaneshwar and Vitthal.

*diṇḍī* went past me. I started, and running to make up the distance, I entered the procession again.

❀

I run back and forth like a little kid, staring at everything. I stand up on tiptoe to see more of what is ahead of me. I move out of the line of the procession and stand on the side of the road to examine it. Independent *Wārkarīs*, who walk along outside of the procession, pass by me rapidly. Far away the bobbing pinnacle of the chariot in which the *pālkhī* itself is carried moves onward. The cymbals clash. The drums resound. I don't even notice that our pace has increased. The earth falls rapidly behind.

❀

How quickly went the next two miles of the walk! It was past six o'clock, and it was starting to get dark. Suddenly the heavy monsoon clouds began to form. Black curtains covered up nature's windows. And thereupon the rain began. It got to the point where one *Wārkarī* couldn't see another. Even the elephant in the procession started walking more quickly. The clamor in the *diṇḍīs* grew. The echoes of the singing rose above even the voice of Varuna.[1] But only for a short while. The *Wārkarīs* bent their heads under the beating of the rain, and as they were preoccupied thus, the *pālkhī*'s train—each one following right behind the other—came apart. The various *diṇḍī*-carriages were

1. God of the waters.

separated, and they lost all sense of the one ahead and the one behind.

I didn't notice either that the *diṇḍīs* were moving ahead and that I was falling behind. The sound of singing grew distant, and only the drumming of the rain remained around me. I came to myself with a start—like a sack falling out of the back of a moving truck. I suddenly realized just how black the darkness around me was. The chirping of crickets and the croaking of frogs dinned in my ears. How tenuous the boundary of insecurity is! Had I gone back just a little ways, I would have seen the countless glittering lights of Poona from the top of the road up the hill.

For a long time I was walking all alone in the dark. It was simply a matter of walking on until I reached Saswad! The rain kept pouring down. For company I had the bulky State Transport buses. Every ten or fifteen minutes a bus would pass by. When I heard its roar behind me I would rush over to the side of the road—in order that the mud wouldn't fly all over me! A couple of times when I ran to the side, my feet getting stuck in the mud, it occurred to me—what was there left for me to worry about the mud!

Whenever a bus passed by, the whole road in front of me would light up. In that brilliant glare every wheel-rut, pothole, and bump cast a heavy shadow so that a stark lunar landscape seemed to open out ahead of me. But no sooner did the flesh-crawling thought come to mind that I would have to traverse it, than I realized reassuringly that I had already been walking through it that far.

❀

I have to guard each step I take through the mud. My foot twists and I nearly sprain it. I plant it on what appears to be flat and firm, and it lands in holes; I get a taste of Duryodhana's experience in the assembly hall full of illusions built by Maya.[1] Sometimes I go through a heavy thicket of trees, and the darkness presses in on my body. When they see I am alone, the frogs make even more of a racket and the crickets shriek still louder. They are like the sounds that frightened the prince in the fairytale. When he got scared and looked back, he at once turned into a stone!

❀

Just about then I heard somebody calling from somewhere behind me, "Dnyanu! Dnyanu!" From ahead of me came a reply, "*Buvā! Buvā!*" I immediately took heart. With a smile I thought, "With Dnyanu ahead of me and *Buvā* behind me, what have I got to fear?"[2]

The lights of a bus approached from behind me, and I could make out three or four *Wārkarīs* in front of me. Like children who are caught doing something naughty, they were running to the side of the road. I also stepped aside and stood near the road. One of the *Wārkarīs* ahead of me was lame. The second one was an old man; and there was also an old woman with them.

The fourth *Wārkarī* I saw was also elderly. But he was clearly not a peasant. He carried an army bag on his shoulder. On his head he had a black rainproof cap, and over his body he wore an overcoat. As he was moving over to

---

1. This is an episode in the epic *Mahābhārata*. Maya built a resplendent royal hall for the Pandavas in their capital; and Duryodhana was greatly discomfited by the *trompe d'oeil* effects it contained.

2. Dnyanu is a diminutive of Dnyaneshwar. *Buvā* is a title of respect given especially to people of religious attainments.

the side of the road he lost his balance, and when he fell down he threw out his hand into the muddy road to support himself. There he stayed, stooped forward as he was. Half in the wheel ruts and half out! The bus behind me was coming closer. I started running toward him as fast as I could through the mud.

The bus went past me and continued on. I strained my eyes to see. But the bus had turned the corner and gone on. I walked up to the old man, gave him a hand, and pulled him to his feet. Using my arm for support, he started walking again. And while he walked he kept repeating, "What roads! What mud!"

We began traveling together. For quite some time the sandals, off our feet, had been traveling at their ease, slung over our shoulders. Our feet kept slipping and sliding, and the exposed stones in the road cut into our feet with their sharp points. We tried hard to find the easiest way to go. How good it felt if only two consecutive steps fell on flat ground! "Vitthal! Vitthal!" the other man exclaimed from time to time, and occasionally he would have to stop. All his movements were pervaded with fatigue.

I said, "Don't rush! We can rest as we go along."

He must not have believed at first that I was going to stay with him. After some time, without any apparent reason, he came out with the remark, "Nobody waits here for anyone else!"

I asked him, "How old are you?"

He said, "Sixty-eight."

That shut me up. The question that had worried me when I set out was how *I* would walk the distance of a hundred fifty miles.

I felt that I should talk to him, but the road wouldn't let me. I was walking a little ahead, directing him along the best way. We both had flashlights; their two round spots of light fell on the road, and the surrounding darkness seemed only to laugh at us. Repeatedly my old companion stopped, and he kept saying one sentence over and over, "The *pālkhī* must have reached Saswad a long time ago."

His trembling footsteps seemed to be on the point of collapse. I would have suggested that we stop for a rest. But there wasn't a single place that wasn't covered with mud. We had to find a rock or a culvert or something solid. It was all just a desert of mud.

But finally our flashlights revealed a culvert. Our steps quickened. I said, "Let's sit down here for a while."

He said, "All right, let's sit down. But really it would be better not to. Once you sit down here, you really sit down."

I sat on the retaining wall of the culvert, and asked him, "Why do you come on the pilgrimage at your age?"

He replied firmly, "As long as I can move my hands and feet I'm going to come on the pilgrimage. If it's Vitthal's will that I should die along the way, so be it."

We rested only very briefly because he suddenly got up and said, "Let's get going! We can't stay here. It was a good thing though that we sat down. My chest had started to hurt a little."

I said, "Sit here some more if you want to."

"No! No! I don't!"

When we got up and started walking again, he said, "I'm going to reach Saswad all in one piece only because you're with me."

Then, as if he were speaking to himsef, he said, "Here nobody looks out for anyone but himself."

But as we walked onward I couldn't help thinking—what if he really did have a heart attack? I prepared myself for the prospect of having to carry him on my shoulder as far as Saswad. At least they would have carried him like that in the movies. I tried to remember just how it was they did it.

❀

Our feet sensed the Saswad lights before our eyes did. That old gentleman started to walk quite briskly. We arrived and stood in the town square. The shops, with their glittering flourescent lights, dazzled our eyes. But how we enjoyed that dazzlement! What science says about flourescent light not producing heat is all wrong. We could feel its warmth from even quite far away.

The rain had been increasing. Perhaps as many as five hundred *Wārkarīs* were trying to sleep in the open spaces in the square, right out in the middle of the rain—lying stretched out or leaning up against each other. Some of them had wrapped themselves in pieces of plastic. Some had put the clothes they intended to wear the next day on top of their heads.

We entered the town, and that old gentleman and I parted ways. His *diṇḍī* was different from mine.

It took me quite a while to find the place where my *diṇḍī* had put up for the night. It was ten o'clock, and all the shops had closed by then. The houses were locked up tight. I couldn't find anyone from whom I could ask directions. I got to the right place only when I actually met a group from our *diṇḍī*.

❀

The moment I set foot in the house where we were staying I felt like a new boy entering class for the first time. I was all alone there—alone and without a friend! I felt how pointless it was for me to have come along. That I ought to just turn around and go back to Poona!

The chilly, damp air was chilling my spirits. Our wet feet and dripping clothes had made the whole place damp. Some of the people were still stamping the mud off their feet. Others were wringing out the loose ends of their clothes. It looked as if fifteen or twenty people had come. I didn't find any warmth or cheer in the movements all these unfamiliar people made or in their talk.

I washed the mud off my feet, and like all the others I sat down in the outer room and leaned back against the wall. Somebody called out loudly, "Is the tea ready yet?" He had barely spoken when the pot of tea was brought in. We took the tea in whatever receptacles we had brought with us. The hot tea heated them up so they scalded our fingers, but the warmth felt good. We drank the tea by holding our cups or tumblers with handkerchiefs or with the loose ends of dhotis.

❀

Their faces start to perk up as they drink the tea. I look at them one by one, sitting there with their backs against the wall, and I feel better than I did before. The atmosphere is changing. People begin to chat. Somebody complains, "The luggage in the truck won't arrive today—the truck's not coming until tomorrow."

We'll have to sleep the whole night in our wet clothes. Several more complaints on the subject can be heard. But then somebody says loudly, "We complain because we have to sleep in our wet clothes. There are *Wārkarīs* right now at the town's entrance who are sleeping out in the rain.

They're the real *Wārkarīs*. We're just 'Trip'-*karīs*!"

"How true! How true!" a lot of them say. They start to talk about something else.

I appraise each face carefully. They are all a little drawn from the strain of the walk. I don't see one face that is less than thirty. There are two who have passed their sixties. These two are making a special to-do. They appear to be friends. One of them has a sweet, fair, reddish face. While we are drinking our tea he pulls a little bag out of his bigger handbag. In the little bag there is a tiny knotted bundle. He unties it and then goes around and puts a bit of the ginger cake, which is in it, in every person's hand. After walking so far in the rain and mud we all can truly relish the taste of the ginger. As I am eating the pinch of it in my own hand and my belly is warming up pleasantly, I really envy the man his foresight. I've come along here with so many medications. How come I didn't think of bringing along some ginger?

❀

These two old fellows had been playing the game of guru and disciple for a long time. They had made the old man with the fair face the guru. As he was rubbing oil into his "guru's" feet, the "disciple" told us a story about a funny thing that happened to them the previous year on the pilgrimage. Both of them were laughing while he spoke, so the flow of the story was often interrupted.

The old man who played the role of the disciple said, "Have you heard this one, folks? We had finished bathing in the stream at Khadus and had come back up the bank. There was a big crowd all around us. *Aṇṇā*'s fair, reddish body was uncovered.[1] He had a *rudrākṣa* necklace around his neck.[2] He looked like some very important religious personage. In fun I knelt down and put my head on his feet. I hadn't even raised my head before others instantly started dropping their heads down at his feet. I stood silently at one side. All those *Wārkarīs* there were prostrating themselves and putting their heads down at his feet. He was raising them up and telling them, 'Hey, hey! What are you doing? I'm nobody. I'm just an ordinary man.' The more he shouted this at them, the bigger the crowd became. Then somebody fell down at his feet and offered him some bananas. Others offered him other kinds of fruit. Finally, when the people couldn't be controlled, this worthy gent literally began to run for it. The people behind, and he in front. I quietly came along after them, gathered up the fruit that had been offered, and went off to where we were staying."

❀

Today it was *ekādaśī*, the eleventh of the lunar month.[3] A day of fasting. We had finished the light repast we were allowed of fried spiced sago. We all got ready then to give our tired bodies the rest they so much needed.

It was eleven in the evening. We began to look for convenient spaces for ourselves; but we also had to allow room for the others. We spread out whatever we had—a sack, a rug,

---

1. *Aṇṇā* is a respectful title for an older brother.

2. The *rudrākṣa* is a tree sacred to Shiva, from the berries of which is made the necklace that Shiva devotees wear.

3. The eleventh day of both the waxing and waning halves of the lunar months is a special day of fasting and devotions among the *Wārkarīs*.

a dhoti, a shirt—on the cold cement floor beneath us. Some of the men simply stretched out and covered themselves with their dhotis. Some tied handkerchiefs over their ears, while others simply curled themselves up in a ball. I kept on the overcoat I was wearing, lay down, and curled up my legs.

You could soon hear some happy souls snoring away. I was wide awake. The light from the lantern filled the whole room. The rain was crashing down heavily on the roof, and the wind was roaring. If the house had started to sway, it would have felt exactly as if we were traveling in a ship and being tossed about in a storm. The wind blew through a crack in one of the windows like a whistle. How spooky seemed its rising and falling sound!

I looked around at all those sleeping people. Some had turned their backs to me and others their faces. Some had curled up on their sides, while a few had stretched out with their hands flat on their chests. Some were snoring intermittently, and some were even groaning in their sleep. Some of them kept their clothes quite neat, while others were all disarrayed. Some had pulled their dhotis all the way over their heads. I had the feeling that I had entered a veritable jungle of sleep. They all looked so helpless, like warriors who lay aside their weapons to sleep. If I had known any of these sleeping people beforehand, perhaps I would have felt some affection for them. But as it was I found myself filled with nothing but pity.

Finally the last person who was going to sleep there came into the room. It was the man who served us food. As if he had a special reserved seat, he slipped at once into the square space under the stairs, and he curled up and also started to snore.

*July 8, 1961*

❀

In the morning when I woke up it was still drizzling. I had my tea. Then I took out the Gokhale Institute questionnaires I had brought along in my bag. The first experiment with the questionaires at least would have to be carried out in our own *diṇḍī!* I gave a questionnaire to each person, and telling them to read it over, I went out.

I had the whole day and also the evening in which to do my assignment. The *pālkhī* would leave Saswad the following day. But I just couldn't feel any enthusiasm. Where I should go I simply didn't know. The rain had washed out all of the procession's vitality. The streets were quiet. To whom should I ask the questions? Would anybody answer them? And even if they did answer them, what did it matter?

With a down-cast mind I set off walking. I had lost all confidence in my assignment. Why *should* people answer my questions? When we were drafting the questions we had really thought that we were asking something important. It seemed so laughable now. I forced my feet along the road. In order to raise my spirits I started to pose contrary questions to myself. Just what is the meaning behind the *pālkhī* procession then? Why make this long march? When the *pālkhī* sets off, the people simply join it and go along. And the answers would be forthcoming only when I presented my questions.

Asking my way as I went, I arrived at the *pālkhī* of Shri Tukaram Maharaj. I understood that, like the *pālkhī* of Shri Dnyaneshwar Maharaj which I was accompanying, Shri Tukaram Maharaj's *pālkhī* would also stay the whole day here in Saswad. But then it branches off and goes to Pandharpur by another road.

Just as I was approaching the temple where Shri Tukaram Maharaj's *pālkhī* had made its stop and was beginning to inquire about its leaders, an old man came rushing up to me and said, "Come along, Sahib! I'll show you."

He grabbed my hand and pulled me after him. Quite out of the blue he asked me, "You come from the Government, don't you? See, I recognized you!"

He wouldn't even give me a chance to say yes or no. After a couple of steps he exclaimed agitatedly, "Sahib! I've had injustice done to me. Give me justice! I'll tell you all about it. They've gone and messed up my wages."

Inside the temple compound there was a huge line waiting for *darśan* of the *pālkhī*.[1] The old man pulled me along with him through the middle of it all and sat me down right beside the *pālkhī* itself. The *pālkhī's* leaders also thought I must be somebody important and deferentially gave me a squat wooden seat to sit on. And as I was taking my *darśan* they even pressed some of the *prasād* into my hands.[2]

❀

I'm seated just a hand's breath in front of Saint Tukaram's *pālkhī*. Outside in the line, waiting for a quarter of a minute's sight of the *pālkhī*, stand all those *Wārkarīs* who have come trekking so far from so many different places. It occurs to me that if any of them had gotten the chance to see the *pālkhī* like me from so close and in such comfort, they would have gone quite mad with joy. Each *Wārkarī* in the line comes forward in his turn. He deposits his money, and pouring all his devotion into one brief moment he closes his eyes and raises his hands before him in a *namaskār*. He takes his bit of the *prasād* and then moves on.

---

1. *Darśan* is, literally, "vision" or "sight," but it bears the implication of an intimate meeting of the deity and the devotee.

2. Food that is presented to deities or gurus, the remnants of which are distributed among worshipers as a token of grace.

And the person who stands waiting eagerly behind him quickly takes his place. I look at the officiating priest. His face is firmly set. He looks sharply at each *Wārkarī*. Like any other businessman he is in a hurry. Nothing shows on his face except the business. Others can realize the god in his possession. It strikes me as very sad that he himself is deprived of it.

❀

There was such a pressing crowd there awaiting *darśan* of the *pālkhī* that I began to feel it would be impossible to do my work. I had intended to instruct them to tell the people in their *pālkhī* to fill out my questionnaire. But instead, I told them I would be back at a more convenient time, and I got up and went out.

The chawl-like buildings surrounding the temple compound were jam-packed with *Wārkarīs*. Nine-yard saris and dhotis had been hung up together, tied to the pillars to dry. The blue smoke of the cooking fires came out in billows from the rooms and verandas. In the rain and the damp it smelled even more pungent. All about me there were great swathes of red, purple, blue, and green—all the drying saris. And the white dhotis hanging among them looked like lines cancelling out a piece of writing. All the commotion made it seem just like a fair. Scattered here and there were people singing *abhaṅgas.*[1] Others were changing their clothes or tending the cooking fires, and some were in the process of putting the ritual markings on their foreheads. The children were crying and shouting shrilly.

---

1. A traditional form of Marathi devotional poetry, which was used extensively by all the major *Wārkarī* saints.

The rain just kept on falling. All movement to and fro had to be through the covered verandas, right where all the people were lying and sitting, working, or just idly standing around. I set out to make my way through them. It felt more and more like an obstacle course.

❀

The ordeal is not in making a way through them. The real ordeal is within my own mind, as I fully well realize. I want to talk to some of these people. But in the midst of all this confusion I don't know whom I should address. Just when I am about to stop somebody, the person who is making his way behind me passes between us and strangles the opportunity for a conversation. This woman here slapping flat the millet bread. As she is working the dough couldn't she speak to me? That man there who is making folds in his dhoti? Fine! While you fold your dhoti talk to me!

But everything stays in my head. I don't have the courage to talk to anybody. So I finally decide just to wander about and observe things. I banish the questionaire from my head and become a writer.

They are all villagers. From their speech they seem to be from Marathwada. I stand to one side and watch them for a while. I pick out individuals among them to scrutinize. But I drop them one after the other, like a child who throws away unfamiliar dolls. This old man here, this mother with her four children, that naked kid—I can't get beyond this. I'm a stranger, an absolute stranger.

The whole thing has started to feel to me like a vast herd of animals. I'm getting tired of it. I turn around and head for the big gateway, and once I get there I turn back again for one last look.

Through the downpour I dimly see the *Wārkarīs* bustling about. I'm confused. What am I to do with these *Wārkarīs*? What should I be looking at? At their cooking, at the clothes they are washing? At their bathing, the way they knead their chewing tobacco, and how they lounge around and chat? All the same things exactly that they do back in their own villages!

What *should* they be doing? I ask myself. I have to laugh at my own childishness. Should they all appear in the process of getting ready to take *samādhī* like Dnyaneshwar[1] or like Tukaram absorbed in making *abhaṅgas*?

It hits me, "You don't even know what you have come to see."

I quickly turn my head and go out.

❀

I went out, and I didn't even ask anybody where the road went. The rain had increased still more. The very stones in the road protruded, washed clean of their cover of mud. I heard the screeching of the country Ferris wheels turning. And then I saw the fair that had gathered there on account of the *pālkhī* procession. Two crude Ferris wheels were whirling around, and there was a merry-go-round also revolving nearby. Vendors selling sweets, spicy and salty snacks, and tea were shouting their wares. The balloon-men were blowing their reed whistles. The children in the Ferris wheel were screaming. The whole carnival was dripping in the rain. But nobody even paused in the middle of all the

1. *Samādhī* is the rite of burying a *sannyāsī* in earth and also the commemorative ediface erected over the site. Dnyaneshwar ended his earthly career in this manner at the site now marked by the main temple at Alandi.

fun to think of anything like an umbrella. The women ran laughing and shouting from the Ferris wheel to the merry-go-round, then from the merry-go-round to the bangle-seller, stopping only now and then to wring out onto the ground the rain that had gathered in the folds of their soaking saris. The younger girls would wring out their long skirts in the same way. People were wiping their faces with their hands in the manner of windshield wipers.

I passed right through the middle of the fair and walked out to the edge of town. In front of me I saw three low hills. Mother Dnyaneshwar's tent was at the top of one. A tall Hemadpanti temple occupied the second hill.[1] But the third hilltop was empty. I climbed it and stood up there on top.

The large open space before me was filled with the bullock carts and the tents that were accompanying the *pālkhī*. The tents looked thoroughly soaked and black. It seemed to me more like an army camp than anything.

I suddenly noticed that there *was* a tiny temple behind me. Not any higher than my waist. As small as an alcove in the wall of a house for keeping the images of the household gods. A banner was standing there leaning up against the temple. I looked more closely. In the recess of the temple there sat very quietly an old man.

I thought it was rather funny. This old man's way of taking shelter from the rain was certainly clever. He couldn't have found a drier spot in any tent or in any of the houses either. I went up to the recess and said, "Grandpa, you've sure found a nice place for yourself."

His eyes twinkled with laughter. Eyes that had pus gathered in their corners. He must have been very nearly eighty. It was really perfectly all right if, after all these

1. "Hemadpanti" is a distinctive temple style that is prevalent in Maharashtra, dating from the thirteenth-century Yadav kingdom. The style is ascribed to Hemadpant, prime minister of the last Yadav king.

years, these minor bodily concerns didn't trouble him. He didn't bother either to wipe away the spit that occasionally dribbled out of his mouth. He laughed at first—but on second thought he looked at me suspiciously. I sat down right at the mouth of the recess and asked him, "Did you come all by yourself or did you come along with the *pālkhī*?"

He bobbed his head noncommitally. He was still perplexed over why I would come up and talk to him, and like all peasants he was suspicious. I took out the little tin of tobacco and asked him, "Do you chew?"

He nodded his head and moved forward a bit. He took the tobacco in his hand and tossed the piece of betel nut and the clove I gave him into his mouth.

I said, "I've also come along with the *pālkhī*."

He asked me, "Where you from?"

I said, "From Poona. Where are you from?"

"From a village near Alandi."

"Why did you come along at your age?"

He said, "I went out to tend the cattle, and I couldn't herd them. So I got mad and just took off."

It was certainly a curious answer. I purposely kept quiet.

He asked me suddenly, "You got four annas to spare?"[1]

I asked him, "How did you come along without bringing any money?"

He said, "My son will just have to send me some. Let me really tell you. I came along with the others from the village."

I asked him, "Does you son know about it?"

"They'll tell him—back there in the village."

"What are you going to do for money right now? If I do give you four annas, how far will that reach?"

"Vitthal will just have to take care of that."

After a short pause he said, "Let me really tell you. My

1. In the old currency an anna was one sixteenth of a rupee.

son sent ten rupees along with the other people from the village. I'll get it at the next stop."

He was laughing slyly to himself the while.

"Let me really tell you. I ran off. And that's the truth. I ran away, and so people are bound to tell my son, 'The old man's gone off to Pandhari.' They'll ask if the old man took any money with him. So out of shame, if nothing else, my son will just have to send the money. What do you think?"

I asked him, "If you had just asked him for it, wouldn't he have given it to you?"

That really irked him, and he exclaimed, "That son-of-a-bitch! He'd certainly give it to me! Let me really tell you. I've fallen on hard times."

"How's that?" I asked.

"Let me tell you. Only the good Lord and I know the way my son and his wife treat me. What more can I say!"

After saying "Let me really tell you" so many times, the old man had finally begun to tell the truth. Once again we both took a fill of tobacco. He spat out a stream and said, "I never in my life spoke an angry word to *my* old man. I really took care of him. And look at my kid! Let me really tell you. It's not my kid who's the culprit either. The real culprit is my wife."

I naturally asked, "Your wife is still alive?"

"What do you mean 'wife'? She's not a wife—she's a penance. Even so, my father kept telling me that with a wife like that I'd end up with nothing but penance to pay. Let me really tell you. Right from the day of our wedding my wife couldn't stand me. But being a manly sort, I beat her and beat her and made her behave. I treated her fondly too. Every day I'd throw her two or three rupees. I trusted her with all my daily earnings—'Go to hell, do what you like!' I was her master only when it came to eating and sleeping. Son, let me tell you. She's had something against me all my life. I finally just blew up. The last five years I've stopped sleeping with her. When night comes I go out and sleep on the porch. 'Go to hell,' I tell her, 'you, your son, and your daughter-in-law.' Let me really tell you. When a man gets old like me there's nothing left but penance. The wife, the kids, everyone—they all turn against you. Now you tell me! Am I at any age to scrap and fight? My wife and kid gang up and beat me up. They don't let me say a single thing about anything. They don't let me do anything. I finally just got fed up with that penance. I saw the *pālkhī* setting off. I joined it. I didn't leave a trace behind me for anyone back home."

He paused for a moment.

"Let me really tell you. See, it's fine when you're young. I had a bullock cart. In season I would never get less than ten or fifteen rupees a day. Now I'm just worn out. I'm going to die right here on the road to Pandhari."

He suddenly fell silent. I sat there wordless watching him. He drew an arm around his knee, and with his chin sunk down on it he sat staring at the ground. He forgot my presence there in front of him. His lips trembled occasionally, and the wrinkled skin below his eyes moved. Glittering tears gathered in his eyes. Even as I watched, a stream started flowing down from them. I got up very softly and drew four annas out of my pocket. I put them in front of him and left.

❀

I set off for the other hilltop. A tea-seller passed by me lugging tea in his portable bucket-stove and shouting, "Tea! Tea!" Immediately behind him came a woman who stopped and asked me, "Will you buy me some tea? My husband has gotten a chill."

When I didn't say anything, she followed after the tea-seller babbling the same words. A tiny hut stood in front of me. Under its roof a woman was taking shelter. A little beyond her I also stopped and stood with my back against the wall of the hut. And I asked her, "What place are you from?"

She said, "From Latur."

"How many of you came along?"

"A whole lot of us came."

"What's your occupation?"

Unwittingly, I had begun asking the questions on the questionaire. As one question followed another, she suddenly clammed up. I told her, "I'm gathering information about the *Wārkarīs*. May I ask you some questions?"

She said, "Why do you ask me? The men-folk are over there. Ask them."

As politely as possible I said, "Lady, they're very simple questions! When did you accept the *tulsī* necklace?"[1]

She suddenly shouted, "So you catch hold of women who are alone and ask them questions, do you? Get going! Or else I'll start screaming."

I didn't tarry there another second.

The tea-seller had come wandering back by then. Behind him was the same woman asking for tea, babbling the same words. Upon seeing me again she broke off her sentence midway.

But now I needed some tea myself, and I took some from the tea-seller. I told him to give some to the beggar woman too. The cup had hardly entered her hand before her "chill"-beset husband, as if lying in wait, suddenly appeared. I just don't know where he had hidden himself. Husband and wife, they both greedily seized the cup.

---

1. The holy basil plant, the *tulsī*, is held in veneration by Hindus as sacred to Vishnu. A necklace made of its wood is one of the obligatory tokens of a *Wārkarī*.

❀

After I had drunk my tea I went over to the Hemadpanti temple on one side. I walked right up to the temple and peeked inside. The inner sanctum may have been about fifteen feet square. Warkaris were simply jammed into it. Women, children, and men sat all huddled together. Their bundles were piled up in the middle.

Just then a Marwari man who was sitting over on one side came up and stood beside me. I asked him, "Who are these people?"

In a responsibility-laden tone he said, "I've brought them from Warhad."[1]

I asked, "You came walking?"

"Oh no, no! We came by train up to Alandi. I'm a priest. Every year I bring a few people—just as many as will come."

"At your expense?"

"Indeed no! Everybody is paying for himself. What's the point of acquiring somebody else's merit?"

I asked him, "Being as you are a Marwari, how did you become a member of this sect?"

"Does God stay separate and apart? It's been twenty years since my guru gave me the necklace. My guru gave the necklace to a whole lot of folks up where we come from. He is a great saint!"

"Do you worship your family god too?"

"We acknowledge only Vitthal:

> 'For us he's enough, just Vitthal alone,
> How vain to let some other in your heart!' "

Just like that he tossed off a stanza from some *abhaṅga*. And then he proceeded to talk excitedly, "Everyone comes here—the fun-lovers, the vow-keepers, the profit-seekers.

---

1. In British days, the district known as Berar.

It's only a very few who come out of real devotion—"

But that was the point where my attention wandered away from what he was saying.

During my last visit to Pandharpur I had heard of this same threesome of the fun-lovers, the vow-keepers, and the profit-seekers so many times! The very same words he was going to say had already begun to echo in my mind. The very same proverbs, the very same similes. How many times do you have to hear all of this? The way he just tossed off those very same *abhaṅgas*! Why? So he wouldn't have to say anything in his own words? The same thing ten years ago, the same thing a hundred years ago! Hasn't there been any development in the human intellect since then?

But it struck me then: what about the fact that the well-educated do the very same thing? They throw Shakespeare or Shaw at you—they are always quoting references. It simply wouldn't do, even for them, not to call upon some authority in support of what they say.

One of my dreams rose up before me. In that dream there are no leaders, just as there are no followers. No saints, no devotees. Neither missionaries, nor converts. No businessmen struggling to climb the ladder of success, and no laborers. No ivory tower scientists, and yet no one ignorant.

In this dream it isn't left to the lonely individual alone to strive and struggle, not the lonely individual who must always sacrifice himself and who must break his back working. Everyone, no matter who, has the strength and the fortitude to master his own mind. The strength to work and to think and to be creative.

❀

My dream came to a sudden end—in the same way that trifling causes break all dreams. My attention had

wandered off to a glass display case that was leaning against the wall. It was filled with cheap imitation jewelry—bangles, rings, children's earrings. Such things here in this place!

A fellow of about twenty-five was standing with his hand resting on the case looking out into the rain. I edged over to him and started asking him questions. Name? Town? Total number of people in his home? The state of his business?

At home he had only his mother, a sister, and a younger brother—that was his whole world. His business was to wander from village to village selling bangles. He didn't much like it when I started to ask him questions such as how much he made from his business. He looked pained as he said, "Business is a day-to-day thing. Sometimes you sell more and sometimes less. Just see how slow the business is in this rain. But I don't worry about it. To tell the truth, I come here to see the beauty of nature."

I asked him straight-out, "What do you mean you come to see the beauty of nature?"

He looked at me as if he was surprised. I didn't understand the beauty of nature? He threw out his hand and said, "All this is what I look at. The rain, the green countryside, the hills. But what I like even more than that are all the carvings in the temple—so skillful, so lovely. I sit looking at them for hours on end."

He drew his hand feelingly over the carved pillar near him. It totally astonished me. I asked him, "Do you yourself draw or paint?"

He replied coldly, "No."

"Then why do you look at all this?"

"For the joy of it."

Now I'm a practiced writer! Someone who exploits each and every experience for the sake of my writing. His answer cut me to the quick. Just for the beauty of nature! Just for the joy of it! It was like recalling something forgotten long

ago, but I suddenly remembered that feeling. I thought that he must be deliberately trying to provoke me.

But how ingenuously, without ever looking at me, he was telling me these things. Sometimes he just stopped speaking and stared out into the rain. I kept probing him with my questions, trying to get him to explain what he meant by "beauty." Eventually he just shut up. He stared straight in front of him. It was a clear hint: "Leave me alone." I gathered my overcoat about me, and I went down the steps and out into the rain—whether it was to subtract from or to add to that beauty he was still looking at.

❀

A little farther on I reached the tents where they had put up the *pālkhī*. It started to feel as if I was in a military encampment. The poles of all the banners had been stacked upright like spears at the mouths of the tents. Inside I saw heavy brass cymbals and two-headed drums hanging from the roof poles. I walked past, dodging the tent ropes and the pegs.

Suddenly, a stench, borne on the wind, assailed my nose, and it increased with every step. On both sides of my path there began to appear the signs of the "morning rituals." They increased until they filled the entire road. The faeces and mud made a veritable slough. The other *Wārkarīs* there were going right through the middle of it—holding handkerchiefs or the ends of their saris to their noses, their faces set, determined to ignore evil things.

I had gone down to the river in the morning. Then too I had seen the *Wārkarīs*, by the hundreds, sitting there defecating. When the procession moved on this stench must envelop the entire town. Wherever the *Wārkarīs* camped there certainly would never be any lack of filth or mess. All those stones for the cooking fires, the smoke-blackened walls, whole areas reddened with the spit of *pān*,[1] scraps of food, clotted paper—it occurred to me that I ought to stay behind the *pālkhī* once and observe these festivities too.

Everywhere I looked in the bazaar I saw squares of plastic sheeting being sold by the yard. The normal four-to-six anna price for one piece had gone up to a rupee-and-a-half. The price had shot up because of the rain. The same thing also for milk and vegetables. In the morning I went down to the riverside for milk and vegetables. The prices had doubled. The organizer of our *diṇḍī*, who was with me, kept issuing a steady stream of oaths.

❀

It is just past noon. My stomach has begun to rumble. My steps automatically turn toward the place where our *diṇḍī* is staying. Along the way I bought a pair of short pants. I put them on in the store where I bought them. This is the first time since I was in school that I have put on this abbreviated version of trousers. See my bare calves and knees! How strange it feels when the breeze brushes them. I look at them again and again. They just don't seem to be mine! How unshapely! How flabby! They have quite cast out all the hero in me. No! Really! I ought to have taken exercise more regularly. I should have kept my body in better shape. I find it amusing—and embarrassing too—that I should have to think about my body this way after so many years.

❀

1. The piper betel leaf folded up with betelnut, lime, spices, etc., which is chewed, especially after meals.

We finished our lunch. The women in our *diṇḍī* had also gathered by then. Even here, after lunch was over, everyone was trying to keep to his normal habits. Some took out *biḍīs* or cigarettes and were puffing away contentedly.[1] Others simply stretched themselves out right there on the cement floor. One of them was absorbed in kneading his chewing tobacco in the palm of his hand. Another man was pacing back and forth, and still another was picking his teeth. There was that after-meal drowsiness in most eyes. A couple of them, with their eyes strained wide, sat fiercely awake. And they seemed like our sentinels.

After some time, people started to perk up enough to begin chatting. Somebody produced the question, "Why isn't there a railway concession ticket for the Pandharpur pilgrimage? There is for the Kumbhamela, and there usually is for the Nasik pilgrimage."[2]

So a discussion about round-trip tickets got going. Somebody complained, "A round-trip ticket is useless, because at Pandharpur you have to go get the date stamped on it. You can't avoid having to stand in a line."

Somebody else said, "We're *Wārkarīs*. Nobody is going to complain about it."

Once again the question came up, "Are we really *Wārkarīs*?" The ordinary *Wārkarī* goes along out in the rain getting drenched. If the cooking fire can't be lit because of the rain, he simply fasts. We were staying in a building. We ate comfortably. Took naps. No, indeed! Ours wasn't a pilgrimage. It was merely a trip.

Once again they all began to berate themselves. They started to entertain doubts about whether those who go along with the *pālkhī* so comfortably could really be said to

1. *Biḍīs* are tobacco rolled in a leaf and smoked like cigarettes.

2. The Kumbhamela is the gigantic twelve-yearly pilgrimage festival on the Ganges at Prayag. The Sinhasta pilgrimage at Nasik also takes place every twelve years.

have faith. But then, neither could they accept the notion that they didn't have faith. Without faith would they have come along at all? They also left difficult problems behind them in order to come along. Each person goes with the *pālkhī* after making the necessary adjustments with his own particular circumstances. It shouldn't have any connection with either comfort or faith.

Immediately thereupon they took up the subject of the thefts that invariably accompany the *pālkhī*. One of the men displayed his slit-open pocket. Just that morning in the bazaar, as one man was asking directions from him, another one came from behind him had cut open his pocket. He knew it was a robbery. He put his hand on the pocket that was being cut open and beseeched them, "Brothers! Why are you cutting open my pocket? I have only four annas. And that's in my upper pocket." He tried to catch hold of the thieves, but they ran away.

We were laughing as we listened to him. And then everyone took his own turn to tell about thefts on previous pilgrimages. It appeared that the methods employed in the thefts were all the same. Some poor woman entrusts her bundle to somebody while she goes down to bathe in the river, and that person runs off with it. Or the thief comes along distributing sweets, and he calls to some woman who is sitting beside her bundle. Then his accomplice comes up behind her, picks up the bundle, and disappears with it.

In the course of just one pilgrimage there must normally be about two hundred thefts. That is just an estimate. On one occasion even the *pālkhī*'s collection box was stolen, so they say.

I was a newcomer! So everyone warned me, "Don't keep anything on you. And when we get to Baradgav, well, be extra specially careful."

Just then the women folk inside the house started singing

a *bhajan.*[1] Everyone felt uneasy about our having sat out there enjoying our friendly chat so much. We all picked up cymbals and sat down to sing.

This was my first *bhajan* with the *pālkhī.*

When I was young I used to sit in the *bhajan* group trying hard to match the slow rhythm of my brass cymbals with all the others. That is when the *bhajan* melodies had become fixed in my head. When I heard the *bhajan* melody those women inside the house began to sing, I was shocked. They were singing in the style of popular romantic songs! But to convey the proper sentiment of a *bhajan* this manner was ineffective, passionless, and meaningless.

They had started the *bhajan* inside the house, and those outside gradually joined in. The *abhaṅga* came to an end, and it was decided that everyone should sit together for the *bhajan.*

The women are singing another *abhaṅga.* Their manner of singing it confuses the other men even more than me. Each line of the song is supposed to be sung twice by the leaders before the others join in to sing it, but all the men start to sing the line after they have heard it only once. The leaders stop, explain their manner of singing, and again begin the *abhaṅga.* But the habit-bound men join in again too soon after hearing the line only once, and the upshot is one tremendous confusion and a great deal of laughter.

The moment the *abhaṅga* is over I tell the women that I think their melody for the song is artificial.

One of them replies, "That's how the *bhajan* groups sing in Poona. They sing like that even in the *bhajan* classes."

I say, "Maybe they do. But all you're doing is making a

---

1. A traditional devotional song—usually an *abhaṅga*—which the devoties sing together as a group to the accompaniment of drums and cymbals.

romantic song out of the *bhajan*. The established melodies are the real melodies."

Another woman shoots back, "No, certainly not! These men do nothing but complain."

*July 9, 1961*

❀

Today is the thirteenth day of the dark half of the lunar month, Jyeshtha. At the very crack of dawn the bustle of leaving Saswad begins. There is a concerted rush to wash faces, have tea, answer the call of nature, and bathe. The bedding rolls are tied and ready, and they are all piled up into the truck.

I throw my bag over my shoulder and come outside, and I stand in the road waiting with the others for the *pālkhī* to move. Our ears are all attuned for some sound from the *pālkhī*, but we can see no sign of it. We stand where we are, shifting from one foot to the other. We march in place as it were. Somebody yawns. A few of the others get tired and sit down on the low parapet in front of a store.

And suddenly the news reaches us: the *pālkhī* is going to leave late. A woman who was accompanying the *pālkhī* had died giving birth. The *pālkhī* wouldn't move until after her funeral rites were over.

We stand in little groups and talk about the news. The rain falls on us from above. The mud splashes up from below. Somebody says, "What a pointless delay this is."

I move from group to group and listen to what they are saying. The remarks I hear are various.

"She died accompanying the *pālkhī*—how truly blessed she is!"

"She really shouldn't have come along with the *pālkhī* at all."

"How can you say a thing like that? She had to keep the rule. A *Wārkarī* never breaks the rule about going on the yearly pilgrimage."

They begin to ask each other how long it is likely to take before we get going. In no uncertain terms, each one states his own best estimate. The question before everyone is whether to stay here or to go back to the place where we stayed overnight. The question that presents itself to my mind is, "How can we call the place where we *were* staying ours anymore?" It was all nothing but an illusion.

I begin to see a symbolic similarity between that woman "leaving her body" and our leaving that place where we were staying. Like us, she will never be able to go back to the dwelling she had left behind.

I walk back and forth on the road, and I feel disturbed. Is it the fact of the death that has made me so uneasy? Or is it the way these *Wārkarīs* are talking, the way they comment so coldly about it and think only of their own distress, that makes me so restless? Or is it the pouring rain, the flies buzzing about my head, and the constant itching of my calves that upset me. Once more I start to feel how pointless it was for me to have come. I feel more and more like a rain-soaked crow.

❀

Somebody pulled the sleeve of my overcoat. I turned around to look: it was the manager of our *diṇḍī.* He said to me, "Come on, let's go get some tea."

Together we went into a tea shop: a godown-like affair,

blackened with smoke, the cashier's table at its door, some snacks arrayed on a metal plate on a bench, and a strong smell of frying from somewhere inside. We sat on one of the benches and started on the tea.

It turned out that our manager knew the boy who served us the tea. I wasn't surprised. The previous morning I went with the manager to buy milk. Whether anyone paid attention to him or not, he called out cheerfully to one and all. While he was drinking his tea he asked the boy, "Hey, what do you say! When did you quit your job at the movie house?"

Scarcely had he asked the question when the boy burst out angrily that the owner of the movie house hadn't paid him for several months. He had been making him work for nothing.

The boy had to break off his story abruptly to serve another customer, and the owner of the tea shop told us then, "He sure is a fresh kid! Don't listen to him. He broke things. That's why he wasn't paid."

But the boy came back to us and started to tell us his sad tale. His mother was sick at home in the village. They desperately needed some money. His home was twenty miles away. Since he couldn't afford the bus fare, he had to walk the whole way.

A new customer came in. As soon as the boy turned to wait on him the owner said, "Nobody was sick in his home. It was all just an act to get an advance!"

The owner's words, the boy's tale, and the smoke-filled atmosphere of the teashop—how they made my heart sink! No matter what small town I've gone to in Maharashtra I've always gotten this same sad feeling. When I see kids slaving away for five rupees a month, my skin crawls. I begin to think of my own situation as pretty good, and this well-being of mine seems something to be ashamed about.

That's exactly what happened this time, too. I felt the same shame-facedness along with the satisfaction that I was at least better off than this poor kid. That is the way satisfaction usually works. There is really nothing more to it.

Somebody came shouting for us, "The *pālkhī* has started."

At once the two of us left the shop. I asked the manager, "You're going to go on with us, aren't you?"

He said, "No. I've got to get back to Poona. I just came this far."

❀

The news about the woman dying had come to us just as unexpectedly as it now transpired that she was actually alive and had given birth to a boy. Both the baby and the mother were doing fine. And now I overheard quite a different kind of remark.

"Just see! Panduranga never fails us along the *pālkhī*'s path."[1]

" 'Who can kill, against God's will?' "

The depressed atmosphere immediately livened up. We stepped forth vigorously, warding off flies and trampling down the mud.

The townspeople who had come out as far as the gate to see of off turned back. The *pālkhī* set off on its way to Jejuri. There came a mighty roar, "Pundalik's Benefactor Hari Vitthal!"

*July 10, 1961*

---

1. Panduranga is one of the popular names of Vitthal.

380. *O Pārtha, as gold is one with the ornament made from it, so thou shouldst not regard thyself as different from the Self.*

381. *A ray may be emitted by light, but the ray is the light itself; in such a way shouldst thou conceive of Me.*

382. *Like an atom of dust on the earth, or a particle of snow on a snowy mountain, so thou shouldst realize that thou art in Me.*

383. *However small a wave may be, it is not different from the ocean; nor is there any difference between Me and the Universal Self.*

384. *When the vision is illuminated by the experience of oneness, we say that this is devotion.*

Jnāneshvari *Fourteen*

CHAPTER TWO

# Jejuri

The march to Jejuri had begun. I gradually started to become acquainted with the *pālkhī* procession. The word "*diṇḍī*" no longer remained just a common noun to me. I was walking in "our" *diṇḍī*—in the Shedge *diṇḍī*.

For a little while I made my way alongside of the *diṇḍī*. I stood on the roadside and let the other *diṇḍīs* that were behind us walk past me. The *Wārkarīs* were walking in lines, five abreast. My eyes were brimming over with everyone's bare legs: coal black or merely dark; fair, reddish, or pale; hairy or smooth. Their concerted movement seemed to be like that of a herd of animals on the move.

If this had been a military expedition, we would have been described as "making the very earth tremble." But all those bare legs produced instead an entirely gentle feeling. It seemed as if they had come up out of the earth itself. They were adding something to the beauty of nature.

I have come walking quickly ahead along the side of the road, right up as far as the *pālkhī*'s "chariot." It is a bullock cart with wheels—that run on automobile tires! It hurts somewhere deep inside of me to see them. Take them off! Take off those tires! Put on wooden wheels! That ancient, heavy-timbered, red *pālkhī* up there on it and the even more ancient *pādukās*[1]—let them go clattering along on wooden wheels! Not so long ago Saint Tukaram went walking with them hung around his neck. Don't you remember? Take off that silver on the decorated frame. Rip off the silver plating on the *pādukās*—after heating it and pounding it on an anvil. Don't forget: Dnyaneshwar himself baked the *kānavalās* on his own back.[2]

I am irked. I don't even bother to take *darśan.* I fear that a solemn voice might issue from out of the *pādukās* and say to me, "You're just one of them too!"

Is it modernity that so irks me? I can't understand what it is I am feeling. At one time, after all, even bullock carts were modern. Once even Dnyaneshwar's philosophy itself was modern. Or am I just angry that a writer whould be overlaid with silver after his death?

❀

I counted the procession. All told, it comes to twelve hundred.

I was walking alongside of the *pālkhī.* A farmer brought some green sorghum fodder with him and stood waiting at

1. A type of wooden clogs worn by ascetics, which are worshiped as a relic of a god or a guru.

2. This refers to one of the stories in the Dnyaneshwar hagiography, in which he heated his back by yogic means and baked the *kānavalās* (a kind of stuffed pastry) in order to confound the disbelief of the brahman priests.

the side of the road. When the *pālkhī*'s bullock cart came in front of him he fed some stalks of the fodder to the bullocks. The rest of the bundle he shoved into the fodder bin underneath the cart. Then he took *darśan* of the *pālkhī*.

Every time a State Transport bus passed by, it would approach the *pālkhī* slowly. The passengers would raise their voices in praise and acclamation, and the driver would lift his hands for an instant from the steering wheel to make a *namaskār*. Occasionally a private touring bus would come and stop by the side of the road. The family group that had come in it would get off and run up to the *pālkhī*. A young fellow came along on a shiny brand-new bicycle. He leaned the bicycle up against a tree, then took the wallet that contained his offering out of his pocket and pressed into the crowd around the "chariot."

Not a single person ignored the *pālkhī* or simply passed by it. The farmers out in their fields threw aside their hoes and rakes or stopped the great leathern buckets of their irrigation wells and washed their muddy hands. They threw down their bullocks' reins, and they all came running to the *pālkhī*.

As for the women and children, how they came running pell-mell! Mothers clasped their infants on their hips and ran for the road. Even quite a distance away they started making their *namaskārs*. The woman who reached the road first called back to the other women, who were more burdened with their babies, behind her, "Come on, you girls, run!" She started jumping impatiently where she was, with her baby on her hip, because she thought the others weren't running hard enough and might miss the *pālkhī*.

As they ran to the *pālkhī*, the boys and girls clapped their hands and shouted loudly. They were cuffed and slapped when they pushed in ahead of the adults. And when they got up to the *pālkhī*, they reached out and hung on from the chariot.

Four or five children came along carrying a toy paper *pālkhī* suspended from sticks on their shoulders shouting, "Dnyanoba's *pālkhī*!" And they stood it up so solemnly beside the chariot that for a moment you couldn't decide from which *pālkhī* to take *darśan*.

Our afternoon stop came at the temple of Shivari Yamai. When we had finished our afternoon meal there, the *pālkhī* set off once again for Jejuri.

I ran into the same old man who had been my companion on the way to Saswad. As we were walking along together, he put his hand on my shoulder and said, "Really and truly, when I met you day before yesterday I met Vitthal!"

I said, "Don't make such a big thing out of it! I still think that at your age it would be better for you not to come along."

Just like that he replied, "This month is the happiest one in the whole year."

When I heard the tone of his voice I kept silent. He went on, "Old people just don't have any value left in the home anymore. The kids have gotten smart nowadays. And their wives even more than they. They always have money for the movies. But they don't have any left to give me for the pilgrimage. They think it's just some craze of mine that I go. How can I convince them? They'll understand when they get old. For the present, at least, it is ordained that we should have to put up with our sufferings."

I asked him, "How much does the pilgrimage cost you?"

"It costs thirty rupees to have meals in our *diṇḍī*. Any extra expenses are determined according to what we can afford. I rarely take tea. If I went with some other *diṇḍī*, the expenses would be still less than that. But there they have only rough millet bread, and I can't digest that anymore. I save up money all year long here and there as best as I can. I'm usually five or ten rupees short. So I have to ask my son for the rest. He answers me with oaths and curses. There isn't anything very enjoyable about that. Which *diṇḍī* are you with?"

I told him the *diṇḍī*'s name, and he said, "They're all big people."

I said, "I wouldn't know. I went with them because they don't follow the purity-pollution restrictions."

"They have wheat bread and rice every day in your *diṇḍī*. And they also have snacks from time to time."

I said, "I have yet to find that out. What does it matter here whether there are snacks or not? They are all good people, that's for sure."

"Yes! They're good people. But the fee they charge is higher. People like us can't afford it. We have to struggle hard to get as much money together as we do."

"How many years have you been going along with the *pālkhī*?"

"I've been going to Pandharpur for twenty years. But along with the *pālkhī* it's been only seven years. I started having trouble at home with my son. I told myself, 'I can spare myself this trouble for at least that many days.' Life is hard."

❀

I had walked the road to Saswad groping my way through the dark. Now with my eyes wide open I am on my way to Jejuri. For quite some time now we have been able to see the temple of Khandoba on the hill above Jejuri.[1] Even though we can see the exact place we are headed for, it doesn't seem to come any closer. It's like trying to run after the moon—which just gets farther and farther away. At one curve in the road it seems as if you could almost reach out and touch it, and then as you move onward it recedes far away again. We are conscious of nothing but our tired feet.

We finally reached the town. The day's trek was over. I felt relieved and happy. My stomach was begging ravenously for food, and my feet needed to be rubbed down well with oil. I kept reassuring them, "We've arrived, we've finally arrived."

There were approximately fifteen hundred *Wārkarīs* who were going with the *pālkhī* and at least an equal number of people from the town who had come out to meet us. We made our entry into the town together amid the tumultuous noise of all the *abhaṅgas*. The crowd kept on growing. People were walking all pressed together. As we came closer and closer to the place where the *pālkhī* was going to stay our pace grew slower and slower.

I suddenly realized that we had gone in a great circle, but I had no clue that we were turning. *Abhaṅgas* came surging from all the *diṇḍīs* with greater and greater force. We progressed step by step, endlessly stopping and moving, stopping and moving. All of a sudden, as if a curtain were being

1. Khandoba of Jejuri, a pastoral and warrior god identified with Shiva, has had a long-standing and very major importance as the family deity for many castes in Western Maharashtra. Jejuri is the primary pilgrimage site for Khandoba devotees.

opened, a space appeared on my right. I could see the *pālkhī*'s tent right ahead of me.

We came to a stop. Right in the middle of the crowd a circle opened up, about thirty feet across, and we were left standing along its perimeter. The enthusiasm of the *bhajan* singing was still increasing. The *pālkhī*'s chariot was standing some twenty-five or thirty-five feet in front of the tent. The attendants were taking the *pālkhī* down. Even as I watched, there was a sudden din of shouting. The bearers had taken the *pālkhī* on their shoulders and set off running for the tent, and hundreds of *Wārkarīs* were hanging onto it for *darśan.* With each step the bearers sank down under the load. The ponderous *pālkhī* itself was swaying like a ship on a stormy sea. The police were pushing the people back—trying to restrain them.

The *bhajan* singing rose in a pinnacle, higher and higher, until the *pālkhī* came and settled on the ground in front of the tent. But the very moment it touched the ground all the cymbals were arrested in midair and all lips were clamped shut. There was a sudden hush everywhere. As when a teacher brandishes his cane.

One of the attendants stood forth and announced the time the *pālkhī* would be leaving the next morning. The very moment he stopped speaking, the *āratī* for Dnyaneshwar began, sung out of all those thousands of mouths.[1] Extremely direct and lively.

> This *āratī* is for Dnyanaraja, the Light of great Final Liberation!
> All saints and holy ones serve you; you have captivated my heart.
> Understanding is hidden in this world; no one knows the genuine Good.

1. *Āratī* is the ceremony of waving a burning lamp on a platter before an icon or a person, as well as the verse chanted on the occasion.

Avatar of Panduranga, you are called by name the
 "Wise One."
You made the Mystery known; you made out of all the
 world the One.
Rama-Janardana gazes riveted at your feet.[1]

To my tired feet and my famished stomach the lively tempo of the *āratī* seemed especially delightful. All along the way I had been encouraging them with the thought that I would be able to go to the place where we were going to stay just as soon as the *pālkhī* entered the town. How could I know that it takes an entire half-an-hour to establish the *pālkhī* in the place where it would stay overnight?

As soon as the *āratī* was over, everyone turned quickly away. The place where we were going to stay was at one end of the town. The town itself was packed and swarming like a house during a wedding. *Wārkarīs* had camped even out on the porches of the houses. Smoke had started rising already from cooking fires under the trees and inside the tents. Here and there people could be seen carrying great jugs of water on their heads.

In the big square in front of the town the snack carts were doing a roaring business. The sweet shops were filled to overflowing. You could hear from out in the street the clatter of cups and saucers and the shouting of the waiters in the teashops. A hatha yoga ascetic lay right there at the side of the road with a giant stone on his chest. The *Wārkarīs* were

1. Rama-Janardana, the composer of this sixteenth-century *āratī*, was, along with Eknath, one of the five major disciples of Janardana Swami, a Sufi from Daulatabad in Marathwada.

passing by and looking at him with curious eyes. Some naked kids from the town were standing around him.

How strange this hatha yoga spectacle seemed in this *Wārkarī* ambience! Incongruous. He was trying to sell his wares to customers who were not very likely to buy from him.

❀

When I got to our place, the first thing I did was to alleviate my fatigue with some tea. I sat down then and stretched out my legs, and I started to massage my tired feet.

One of the members of the *diṇḍī* came in from outside just then. When he saw me there, he said, "Go take a look outside! They're feeding the *Wārkarīs*."

I felt better now, seeing that my role as only an observer had been accepted. That had been precisely one of my fears. So even though my feet were still complaining I got up—in order that I might fulfill my role.

I went outside. Immediately in front of me—on the road itself—two long rows of people were seated. No utensils, not even leaf plates, were provided for them. Each one had sat down there with whatever he had: a bowl or a pan, a wide aluminum dish or even a tin can! Every one of them had on old patched clothes, and they guarded their little bundles under their crossed legs. The town itself had undertaken to feed these poor *Wārkarīs*.

I went back inside for a moment and fetched my camera. I stood leaning on one foot and started to focus it.

The camera was really just a pretext. As I was trying to decide what to photograph, I kept forgetting to take the picture. And I was simply observing the people.

Here and there I could hear occasional loud voices—"Take your sandals off!" The people who were serving out the food were running back and forth and shouting, "Bring the pan over here."

One of the *Wārkarīs* had been overlooked, and he was saying, "Hey, brother, don't forget to serve me!" Somebody else was complaining about him, "He just sat down to eat a second time." Every person there got one large ladle of sweet thin wheat porridge. The bowl one person had was even smaller than the ladle. He was saying, "Brother! Just let me drink off a little of it first. Then give me the rest."

Just then one young fellow sat bolt upright, looked toward my camera, straightened his shirt, and smiled. I immediately pressed the button.

I go back inside, and I sit down to eat too. What a joy there is here in eating! They are all like hungry and impatient children. Their eyes are all fastened on the hand of the man who is serving the food. The only difference here is that nobody is shouting, "Me first, Mommy, me first!"

One individual among us cannot restrain his hunger any longer. The slightest hitch in the serving of the food upsets him. "Serve the food quick!" he shouts. But in all the commotion the group is making nobody pays any attention to him. His impatience finally reaches an extraordinary pitch. Our leaf plates are being filled with food, but as yet nobody has invoked the name of Vitthal. The custom is to clap your hands and sing a *bhajan*—"Vitthal, Vitthal"—before you start to eat. No one is clapping. This person becomes so impatient that he starts to clap his hands all by himself, but nobody else responds. His face becomes distraught. At last our host starts reciting loudly, "Vitthal, Vitthal!" The others start to clap their hands, and the tempo begins to increase: "Vitthal" turns into something that sounds like "thala-Vit." Then comes the final shout, "Pundalik's Benefactor," and the distraught expression on his face starts to dissipate.

They all attack their food greedily. The pungency of the hot mustard seed in the pickles makes our noses start to run. A sharp sibilance echoes all around the room as people cool their mouths. The man who is serving the food has a very generous hand. The food keeps pouring down and filling our leaf plates. And how still more importunate our host is! If someone says, "No more! no more," he is given a stock answer: "We've got a long way to go yet! You don't want to lose your strength. Don't worry about your digestion here."

No one feels the least bit shy about asking for whatever he wants or about blessing the host when he belches. Here food really and truly is *pūrṇabrahma*—perfect fulfillment.

*July 10, 1961*

❀

We are leaving Jejuri today.

It is six o'clock in the morning. We have caught up our bags and left the house where we have been staying. We are heading right through Jejuri town on our way to the main road. There is still half-an-hour before the *pālkhī* leaves.

How different this town seems, built as it is, inclined along Khandoba's hill. The entire town lives under Khandoba's shadow. The yellow of turmeric and the oiliness of copra permeate everything. These two items, which are the specified ritual offering to Khandoba, appear to be the chief merchandise in all the stores. If Pandharpur strikes one as red and black, then Jejuri is all yellow and white! The gaudy tint of the turmeric has blown over everything—hands, clothes, temples of every size, and the houses.

And how small these houses under the hill seem. And the people also. I walk along bolt upright and look around me, and sometimes I stretch myself to see. But I seem rather to be sinking into the earth. The hill and the temple at its top climb up so high—and look down upon this tiny life of mine.

If I were a devotee of Khandoba, perhaps this feeling of humbleness would increase my faith. Like the Khandoba devotees who are among us, I might feel that we were under his protective shade of grace and mercy.

I can't help wondering about the townspeople here. They are always going to live like dwarves under this hill. They will continue to show the temple to the pilgrims. Offer places for them to stay. Sell them the materials for worship. They are never going to get away from it. Like a great man's children who turn out stunted.

There is really nothing to the climb up the hill to Jejuri's Khandoba. If you climb slowly, you don't even lose your breath. Along with my companions, I also went up the hill. I had come to Jejuri once before, but there was a big difference between the way I simply wandered about the temple that time and seeing it again now. Then I had thought that the entire temple and the customs and rites surrounding the deity were very strange. I had always been acquainted with Ram, Krishna, Vishnu, Narsimha, and Shankar. I felt somehow uneasy, however, about the offerings here of turmeric and copra and about that shapeless image.

But when one of the devotees who was accompanying us recounted Khandoba's whole interesting story, I understood a lot more this time about this god. We know so little about one another's gods and about their stories and customs. We say, "Your Khandoba! My Narsimha! In the end all the gods are One." And that is where we drop the subject.

Our *darśan* of Khandoba is over. We are standing on the southern fortification of the temple. The road to Pandharpur has disappeared somewhere into the maw of the hills on the horizon. It is drizzling. The *pālkhī* procession has reached the main road. The bullock carts in the van fill the entire road, and behind them the people have formed a long line that reaches right up to the distant hills. From so high up you can hardly distinguish the movement of the procession. It looks rather like when a movie projector stops in the middle of a film. All around us spreads the green countryside, dripping with the rain, the hills that appear as if they are stuck to its edges, and the iron gray sky above it all! And tiny man, who seems caught between the earth and the sky. But even though they find themselves between these two vast elements, the people's mile-long doggedness, pressing ever on and on, makes my chest swell.

*July 11, 1961*

*348. So long as he is like a fish in the waters of earthly existence, naturally he has to experience pleasure and pain;*

*349. nevertheless he disregards them both, being established in his true nature, as the seed is separated from the husks.*

*350. As the river Ganges, having run its course, merges itself in ocean and leaves behind its turbulent flow,*

*351. similarly, O winner of wealth, pain and pleasure are equally accepted in bodily life by him who has begun to dwell in the Self.*

Jnāneshvari *Fourteen*

CHAPTER THREE

# Walhe

We climbed down the southern side of the hill and joined the procession. Upon reentering it I bent down like all the others, touched my hand to the road, and made a *namaskār*.

Once previously a Frenchman had gone along with the *pālkhī*. When he saw all the people touching the road with their hands before entering the procession, he became flustered and didn't know what to do.

In order to count the procession I hastened on ahead and then let all the *Wārkarīs* in the procession pass by me. I added up all the numbers I had noted down in my notebook. It came to three thousand.

❀

We constantly encounter streams now that go across our path. Streams that gush, with their bellies swollen, through the culverts across the road. In some places the water comes up to our thighs. The current pulls at our feet, and I avoid looking at how fast it flows.

❦

We come across another stream. It is running wildly out of a thicket on our right, and after crossing the road, it plunges down in a cascade. The right bank is covered with sand. The bits of flint in it are flashing like a white design printed on a black sari. Trees stand on the bank dipping their hands into the current. The thickly-grown bushes hide the source of the stream.

As I look at it I am thinking—peacocks most likely come and dance here. They would spread out the brilliant feathers of their tails and cry, "Me--ow! Me--ow!" If you went and searched in the sand, you might very well find their footprints. You might also find a fallen peacock feather staring up at the sky with its single eye.

I always think of peacocks when I see a stream and sand and bushes together in one spot. I was staying at my brother's home in Ahmednagar District when I was very young. There it was for the first time that I saw a herd of antelopes bounding across the landscape. I felt then as if I had somehow found my way into a fairy tale. One unrestrainable antelope among them was leaping higher than all the rest, and as it hung for an instant in mid-air, what a picture it made against the blue sky! That was also the time when I sat on the bank of a stream and saw the tracks of peacock feet in the sand. The peacocks I imaginatively created from those tracks I still remember exactly the same way! And the peacock feather I looked for then I am still looking for now!

We have come upon another creek that flows across the road. The water moves with terrific force. The *Wārkarīs* pull their clothes up around their thighs and pass right through it. Their feet slip. They laugh and shout and show their fright. They cling to one another's arms and try to keep their balance. Occasionally somebody will lose his footing, and his bundle falls into the water. Everyone laughs.

Suddenly there is an outcry, "A woman has fallen in! A woman has fallen in!"

I am startled. Everyone is startled. They ask each other, "Where? Where?" I hurry forward. Struggling to keep my balance, I wade out into the water. To our left the stream is falling in a cascade. The water is foaming and splashing and churning in a whirlpool.

Somebody says, "Here's where her feet slipped. When she fell she just disappeared. She shouted, 'Vitthal! Vitthal!' And then she was gone."

I look far out over the stream. Her body would eventually have to come up somewhere, and then something could be done. But the stream has its own ideas. It feels itself under no obligation to let the woman's body come up.

I turn and look at the *Wārkarīs*. They are all moving on just as they were before, trying to keep their own balance in the current. They seem to have forgotten about the woman. They seem to have become as cold and unconcerned as if nothing had happened.

Had a woman really fallen in? Are the *Wārkarīs* really so cold-hearted that they could quietly go on their way after a woman had drowned right before their very eyes? Wasn't there anyone with the woman? Didn't anybody even cry for her? Had she come along purposely in order to give up her life on the road to Pandharpur and so be eternally blessed? Or hadn't there even been a woman who fell in? Even now, at this very moment, it all remains a mystery to me.

When we were crossing over the next stream there was another outcry, "Run! Run!" I saw a man with a bundle on his head running far off along the sandy bank of the stream. "Run! Catch him!" bawled a woman who was running after him. The thief had already gotten a head start of about two hundred feet. A couple of men set out after him. But even as we were watching them, the thief disappeared among the bushes. His pursuers gave up the chase. The woman started crying very loudly and beating her head with her hands.

❀

Walhe is seven miles from Jejuri. There were just three miles left. Both the afternoon and the overnight stop were to be there.

I smiled to see an eight-year-old boy trotting along trying to keep up with his father. I talked to the father as I was walking beside them: "How can you expect such a little fellow to walk so far?"

He said, "The boy insisted that I take him along."

I asked him, "You don't care if he misses school?"

"So he misses fifteen days—what's that?"

He went on after a short pause, "I carry him on my shoulders if he gets tired."

As we walked on I came to realize how very fond they were of each other. If the father *had* come alone, it would have been harder on him than on the boy.

I saw a number of mothers who had come along with their babies tied to their backs. I was impressed by their stamina. Those of us who were walking alone and unencumbered were having enough trouble as it was. I even asked one of these women, "Why did you come along when you have such a little child?"

She replied, "I'd said I'd go on the pilgrimage with my child. This year I managed to do it."

She didn't use the word "vow."

❀

I go up to people and talk to them, and sometimes people also come up to talk to me. I try to make little events happen, but sometimes events just come along and happen.

A woman came and pushed right through the middle of our group, dragging and beating a little child. Three or four of us ran and tried to stop her. But she just kept on beating him, and the boy just kept on sobbing. His chest was heaving violently, and he was screaming with what breath he could get between his sobs.

The woman said, "This kid is nothing but a pest! I've told him a dozen times to keep hold of my hand. But he just lets go and runs off into the crowd."

One of the men ran his hand over the boy's back soothingly and said, "Why do you go and run off into the crowd, sonny? You should hold on to your mother's hand while you're walking. How will your mother find you if you get lost?"

Somebody else said, "Lady, give him something to eat. He looks hungry."

The woman answered angrily, "Should I give him my head to eat then? He's gobbled up everything I brought with me."

Somebody took half a piece of flat millet bread out of his bag and gave it to the boy. As he started munching the bread, he took hold of his mother's hand, and they set off walking. He had stopped crying, but his dry sobs kept on even so.

We may have gone another mile since that happened. That very same boy is returning from somewhere ahead of us, all by himself, crying for all he is worth. "Mother!

Mother!" he is shouting as he runs here and there and looks wildly around him. He doesn't even remember to wipe the tears streaming down his face.

I run forward quickly and try to grab his hand, but he jerks it away and runs into the crowd. I plunge in right behind him. I shout to the people to stop him. He dodges all of them and goes on. You can see how frightened he is by the way he runs—as if he fears that by stopping he will lose his mother forever.

The boy has disappeared into the crowd, so now I start to look for his mother instead. I am almost running as I go back and forth searching people's faces. Every woman there seems to look like that boy's mother. I ask some of them, "Have you lost your child?"

They just stare at me, and I run on. I can imagine what despair must be written on the face of any mother who has lost her child! So I start to search everywhere for signs of this.

I have now run the entire length of both sides of the procession. I still can't find the woman. Somebody asks me, "Hey, what's happened?" I don't know whether to tell him that it is a woman who is lost or a child.

Now I start to look for the boy again. I can at least put him in the safe-keeping of the police. I ask everyone I meet, "Have you seen a lost boy?"

I have circumambulated the palkhi procession twice. There is no sign of either the woman or the boy. I have to admit that I have lost them both.

My feet got tired from all the running around. I went back into the *diṇḍī* and started walking with it. I tried to forget about the mother and her son, but my eyes went on searching for them.

Just then a Ramdasi man, who was walking along the edge on the road, caught my attention.[1] He was wearing a long loose ochre robe. His beard was as solemn as a sage's. I stepped out of the *diṇḍī*.

There is at least one good thing about being here! You don't have to know a person in order to talk to him. Everyone has that sense of being fellow travellers. You simply walk along beside a person and start talking about anything at all. And when the conversation appears to be at an end, you just have to fall back a bit. As I walked along I made a *namaskār* to him, and he returned a *namaskār* to me. I asked him, "Do you come along every year?"

He shook his head and said in a gloomy voice, "Oh, I just come. There's no rule about it."

His lack of enthusiasm dampened my own. I decided that therc probably wouldn't be much of a conversation with him. I walked along silently. Just when I was thinking of falling back, he threw out his arm and pointed all around him. He said, "They're all corpses. We're all corpses. The Muslims are getting out of hand."

He stopped as suddenly as he had begun. His face was working with his emotions. What agonizings and despair! He was shaking his head to himself as he walked, and he stared with mournful eyes at the ground.

I pulled one of the questionnaires out of my bag and gave it to him. He read it, handed it back to me, and said, "We'll see! We'll see! Who am I to be doing this? There's still a long way to go. We'll see about it later."

I fell back, but I kept on walking not far behind him. I was watching him the rest of the way to Walhe. He didn't

1. The Ramdasis are followers of the seventeenth-century Marathi saint-poet, Ramdas, whose strong Hindu nationalism is credited with helping the establishment of the Maratha Kingdom under Shivaji.

raise his head once the whole time, and there was no spirit in the way he walked either. Occasionally he would send a stone flying with a blow from the stick in his hand. His indignation over the state of society and his deep disquietude pervaded every movement he made. The *bhajans* kept right on going meanwhile. Before and behind us the *Wārkarīs* were pressing on. And his solitariness was standing out disquietingly from it all.

We arrived in Walhe in the afternoon in time for lunch. We are to spend the rest of the day and this night here. In the morning the *pālkhī* will set off for Lonand.

There is a river right at the entrance to Walhe. Somebody pointed out the temple that was in the riverbed as we were passing by and said, "Don't forget to take a look at that temple. It's Valmiki's temple."[1]

But I did forget it. A strange resentment settled in my mind. I couldn't bear it that the poet Valmiki should be tied down and made into a god like that.

The moment we set foot in the house where we were going to stay somebody asked me, "How large was the procession?"

I said, "When we left Jejuri there were three thousand."

He laughed—at my ignorance. At Jejuri he had laughed in exactly the same way when I told him that upon leaving Saswad the procession numbered twelve hundred. I had begun to realize even at Saswad that some of the people didn't like that I was making a survey of the procession. Why make a count at all? This is a devotional path. Those who will come will come!

1. Valmiki is the putative author of the epic, *Rāmāyaṇa*.

Others would characterize the *pālkhī* pilgrimage's numbers as "growing." Nobody had actually bothered to count. But out of their love for the *pālkhī*, they felt that there must be lots of people. When I told them the figure "twelve hundred" as we were leaving Saswad, they got angry. They were sure it must be ten or twelve thousand. At Jejuri their figure had increased to more than fifteen thousand.

They got upset again today when I told them my figure of three thousand. They felt it was an insult to the *pālkhī*. Their chief question was how it was possible to count so many people. I explained to them that when we left a town I would go on ahead and sit down and let the entire procession pass by while I counted it. But they still wouldn't believe me.

Counting the procession certainly is difficult. But I had adopted a certain method. The *Wārkarīs* who go along the sides of the procession normally go one behind the other. Those within the *diṇḍīs* walk in ranks arranged one after the other. At Saswad each rank consisted of four people. At Jejuri it had become five. I determined the number of people in each *diṇḍī* by counting the ranks. I agreed that it was a rough method and that I might miss two or three hundred people. At the start the *Wārkarīs* who walked independently were about equal on either side of the procession, so taking both sides, there were two extra people for each rank.

At Walhe I had a lot of free time. I wandered about and got people to fill out my questionaire. In the evening before dinner I neatly arranged all the information that I had noted down roughly beforehand. And then I went out and wandered about the town.

The place where we were staying was at the very edge of town. There was a Maruti temple right in front of it where we had our meals. As you enter the town there is a culvert across the riverbed. Farther out was the *pālkhī*'s tent, around which a bazaar had sprung up.

I wandered around there for an hour before I headed back. Along my way I noticed a *Kaikāḍībuvā* giving a *kīrtan* in a temple by the roadside.[1] I am particularly fond of the loud, vigorous clatter of the *abhaṅgas* in the *kīrtans* given by the *Kaikāḍībuvās*. The original *Kaikāḍībuvā* used to say about himself:

> What an amazing fellow, this *Kaikāḍībuvā*!
> He drove me wild and then ran away!

I don't think these words of his are false. Of all the various preachers in the *Wārkarī* movement, I don't think any of them sing such spirited and pungent *abhaṅgas* as do the Kaikadibuvas. In the month of Kartik on the sandy bed of the Chandrabhaga at Pandharpur, you can always find a number of these *kīrtans* going on right next to each other. They tie an ochre banner on a long stick and plant it in the sand, and with his accompanyists the Kaikadibuva starts to sing his *abhaṅgas*. The *Wārkarīs* gradually gather around. And when they think the group is big enough, the real *kīrtan* begins. I once jotted down some ten or fifteen of these *kīrtans*, and I made my own *kīrtan* based on them. I still remember one stanza that kept recurring in all those *kīrtans*:

> Don't ridicule and mock;
> The stain will fall on you.

I stood for about half an hour at this *kīrtan* in the temple. The *buvā*'s clothes were all colored ochre. His coal-black hair swept down over his shoulders. He was tall and he had black skin. And what gestures he made! How far he could fling out his arms! How he threw back the curls of hair on

---

1. The *Kaikāḍīs* are an itinerant caste who are apparently of tribal origin. Formerly they were included among the "criminal tribes." A *kīrtan* is a religious performance combining song, dance, and narrative for the exposition of a devotional theme.

his forehead with a toss of his head! His companion was a girl—dressed in a nine-yard sari drawn up between her legs. Neither one of them would allow their listeners even a moment to rest. When one *abhaṅga* came to an end they would speak a few words in prose and immediately start on another *abhaṅga*. It was the style of this *kīrtan* to include the audience in the singing of the *abhaṅgas*. So when an *abhaṅga* was approaching its end the two would shout, "Ho! Ho!" while raising both their arms, and exactly on the right beat they would stop all the people who were singing with them. Their skill at this was most exemplary. *Abhaṅga* after *abhaṅga* came and went. They wouldn't let anybody take even a moment to rest. Even so, here and there a woman might stretch out her cramped legs or lean back against something, or one of the men—overcome by sleepiness—might rest his head against the wall. Then the *buvā* would wax strong, given this new subject matter for the short two-sentence speeches he interspersed throughout the *kīrtan*. He chastized the people who were sleepy or who were yawning or stretching their legs.

"Hey, woman! You sit there sprawled out on your behind—aren't you ashamed?"

"You there! You're sleeping during the *kīrtan*? You're heading straight for hell—"

There was just one point that they repeated over and over throughout the *kīrtan*: "No matter who you are—blind, lame, deaf, or dumb—take the name of Vitthal. Whether you're brahman, shudra, rich, or poor, this is the one and only way that's open to everyone—and that's the way of Vitthal's name."

*July 11, 1961*

314. *When the sherds of a broken pot are thrown aside, the air which was contained in the pot is absorbed by the ether,*

315. *and in the same way, when bodily awareness passes away, if a man remembers his true nature, he experiences nothing else but this union.*

316. *Therefore I say that such a man has transcended the qualities, having received this great illumination even while still in the body.*

Jnāneshvari *Fourteen*

CHAPTER FOUR

# Lonand

I'm an outsider in the *pālkhī* procession. Minor disagreements are unavoidable. Someone sets forth some doctrine as the indisputable truth, and an argument ensues.

As we are talking, along our way to Nira, one of the *Wārkarīs* says, "The *Dnyāneśwarī* is the very crown of all books.[1] All the world's mysteries are revealed in it."

I roll up my sleeves to do battle. I tell him that I simply can't agree with this kind of book-worship. I can't believe that any single book can solve all the world's problems. That is just blind faith. That is precisely why the *Wārkarī* sect has stopped thinking and stagnated. I speak vehemently.

But no debate emerges from this. In such a press and crowd as this no debate can expand and grow. Although the debate comes to an end, the train of thought continues in my mind. What would happen, I wonder, if the problems

1. The *Dynāneśwarī*, composed by Dnyaneshwar in 1290 as a Marathi commentary on the *Bhagavadgītā*, is one of the classic texts of Marathi literature.

the world faces were all solved? If that happened, the world would simply come to a stop. Nothing would be left. Or would all creatures live in that Bliss that Dnyaneshwar desired? But what would being in that Bliss mean? Just suppose everyone were to become a *karmayogī.*[1] All passions were to go and dispassionate duty were to remain. The effect it would have would seem to be merely a social one. What would become of all these *karmayogīs* later? Where would they go after death? And where, indeed, did they come from? And just what is this magic and mystery that we call the Universe?

It strikes me then that the *Dnyāneśwarī* and all the other books like it have avoided all the important questions. Or else they have taken certain things simply for granted, as their foundation; and all their thought flows out of a simple belief that these things are true. Take a simple thing: Krishna says, "I am both the one who does the deed and the one who makes one do the deed." I can't agree with that. If I were Arjuna who was listening to him, I would have stopped Krishna then and there and said, "Prove it!"

I realize finally that it all boils down to one thing. It has to be taken as a matter of faith. He who has faith, let him hear.

❀

Our afternoon meal at Nira is over. We have set out again in small groups. We intend to go on ahead for a couple of miles and sit under a tree until the procession goes by and we can join in.

---

1. One who seeks spiritual liberation, not through renunciation, but through the performance of his duty without any expectation of reward.

The sun is hot. The meal has made our eyes heavy, and our footsteps drag. It really would have been better if instead of stopping we had just kept on walking.

Along the way we come and stand on the bridge that goes over the Nira. The river is in flood. Great rolling masses of water go jostling past. The water strikes the arch of the bridge, breaks into foam, and leaps back. The waves seem to be in a race over which one can leap the highest. I don't let my eyes dwell very long on the flow of the water: they feel as if they are pouring along vertiginously with the current and will carry off both me and the bridge. I shake my head and the movement of the bridge stops. It is like waking up from a nightmare.

Occasionally a tree comes tumbling along in the flood. I can't bear to watch it being tossed so violently about. I marvel at how I stand here firmly, simply because of the bridge, above this furious flood of water. I marvel at the bridge, and I marvel at the designer of the bridge and at the builder. One doesn't often experience such pure and simple wonder. I experienced it once as a child when I read a certain poem. The wonder expressed in that poem was in seeing with one's eyes, hearing with one's ears, walking on one's feet . . .

Coming to Saswad I had had an experience of the rain. Now it was the sun I was experiencing. We crossed over the bridge at the Nira River and continued on beyond it. I was terribly thirsty. Sip by sip, I drank the water I was carrying in my bag, and I tried to make it last. The sweat was pouring off my body.

I saw some grass at the side of the road, and I lay down on

it. It had seemed at first so cool and green, but then the vapors started rising from it. When I looked up at the sky my eyes hurt. The sun had prostrated me, both body and mind.

I somehow put up with it for a while. But then I got angry and sat up. In the end everything depends on one's own mind. So with that same anger I looked up at the sun and said, "Your warmth gives me such pleasure!" I told the grass, "Your vapors make my body feel so light and free!" To the streams of sweat that were pouring off me I said, "How cool you make my body feel!"

With these taunts some alertness returned to me. Meanwhile, three other *Wārkarīs*, whom I didn't know, came by and sat down with us. When I first saw one of them, I told myself, "There's a *Koṅkaṇastha* Brahman for sure."[1]

This caste-related thought occurred to me, and I felt as if the joke were on me. Whenever we meet someone, why do we invariably think of his caste? But more than that, it was I, I who had stopped recognizing caste distinctions when I was still in school! I had even refused to write down my own caste on the required school form.

This *Koṅkaṇastha* Brahman was talking about trucks. It was clear that he had to be in the trucking business. As we were talking, the subject of walking came up. And he started to tell us a story—about himself. Once he had gotten a telegram telling him that his brother was sick. He took a servant with him, and that very night they set off to walk the distance of thirty miles. The servant who went with him was a strong man, but halfway there he got tired and stopped. This man went on without him. The next morning he

1. *Koṅkaṇastha* (of the Konkan) is a common name for the Chitpavan Brahman caste, one of the two major Brahman castes of Maharashtra, members of which have made exceptional contributions to Maharashtrian intellectual and political life during the last three hundred years.

brought his brother home in a bullock cart and began to take care of him there.

What intense feeling he showed when he told us about his thirty-mile trek through the dark! As I was listening to him it quite naturally occurred to me why that servant had gotten tired and given up—it wasn't *his* brother who was sick. It was the one whose brother was sick, of course, who would go the whole way, as he had in fact done.

But I still felt moved as I listened to the story. I noticed that the other men were also listening very intently. The pain and turmoil the one brother had gone through for the sake of the other! I think everyone must have thought the same thing I did: what happiness it would be to get a chance to do this for a brother!

Something else also occurred to me then. If one of the listeners happened to be on bad terms with his brother, this story would have affected him still more. Or could it be that some wouldn't even believe it? They might very well tell themselves, "At the time he may very well have acted in one way, and now when he is telling us about it he is making it all up so it looks good. The two brothers probably don't have anything to do with each other."

My feeling was that it really isn't right to judge what anyone says as true or false. Our confusion comes from looking through our own particular point of view. In fact, nothing is ever altogether false. Everything is true—after you have looked at it from all points of view.

Once again, quite fortuitously, I thought, "He is a *Koṅkaṇastha*."

❀

Ever since we left the Nira River, things have become pretty tiresome. Our thirst is pursuing us, crying, "Water!

Water!" The government water tanker is accompanying the procession. People take whatever containers they have with them and crowd around it.

Actually, I have begun to feel better now that I have been walking for a while. The hot sun has gone somewhat lower in the sky. As the sweat that covers their faces begins to dry, the *Wārkarīs* are perking up like gradually reviving flowers. Their weary steps move more steadily. The afternoon fieriness of the earth has subsided and is giving way to the shadow's chiaroscuro.

When we were approaching Lonand, the distance had seemed to diminish foot by foot. Now it diminishes by furlongs. In every *diṇḍī* the vigor of the *abhaṅgas* is increasing. In our own *diṇḍī* there is one short, dark man who has completely lost himself in the music. He has assumed the role of Radha, and keeping one hand at his waist he is dancing, jerking his hips, as he sings the *abhaṅgas.* In one way, the fact that he is in his sixties makes it look very incongruous. But the way he has lost all consciousness of his body and has merged himself with the beat of the cymbals and drums casts its own spell. His companion, a very tall, fair-skinned man, who wears a fine-textured shirt and turban, gazes at him through Krishna's enraptured eyes. The entire *diṇḍī* stops and watches them. Now and then the two of them clasp hands and whirl about each other, and as that finishes they squat on their heels and move in circles keeping time by clapping each others hands. The sound they produce—"pak-pak-pak-pak"—resounds like the drum. Now and then "Radha" stamps with bells tied at his feet. He puts his hand to his waist again, glances coyly over his shoulder at "Krishna," and then whirls around. The white stubble on his chin disappears. With his one hand at his waist and waving the other in the air, "Krishna" bobs and reels. He jerks his waist and struts and starts. He whirls around and around "Radha"—and how he smiles!

The entire procession is immersed in the gaiety and liveliness of the *bhajans.* The *abhaṅgas* pour out with ever increasing vehemence. Even men and women in their fifties and sixties jerk their bodies ungracefully as they dance to the rhythm of the music, and they look at one another and laugh with happiness. Just look! This is the joy of the *pālkhī*! This is why we come along.

All the problems of the world have been forgotten in the sound of the cymbals and the drums. There is no atom bomb; no inflation; no worries about hearth and home.

The *Wārkarīs* who are carrying banners have unfurled them. We are approaching the town. We have arrived at Lonand.

❀

How many words I could have written in my diary about the stop at Lonand. But all I wrote was, "A terrible stop."

❀

The very moment we entered the house where we were to stay that night we got the news: "The Panshet Dam has collapsed. Poona has been swept away." We were all struck dumb.

One of the women finally sobbed and the fence gave way. Our feet had felt nailed to the ground but now were loosened. We were standing staring at each other, but now we looked away and avoided each other's eyes. As if *we* were the ones who were to blame. In the end nobody could bear to stay there. And by twos and threes we ventured out to try and get news about Poona.

We went into the center of town and tried to get the owners of the various teashops to get Poona on the radio. To that end we bought one cup of tea after another. Finally somebody listened to our anguish, and through the indistinct growl of the static we tried to hear the news. But even as we were sitting there listening, as if our very lives depended on it, the waiter came along and turned the dial to Radio Ceylon.[1] I felt at that moment like picking him up and hurling him out the door.

In this way we made our way through at least five teashops. But we couldn't learn anything beyond the bit of news that the dam had collapsed but that Poona wasn't in very great danger. Out of desperation we just kept wandering around. Whatever paltry bit of news we occasionally did hear we would go and tell to those who remained at our overnight camp, and then we would go back for more.

We went to meet the last train coming from Poona that night. We didn't learn a thing. We tried phoning. But the telephones weren't working. The radio station was also closed. We heard one bit of news from Bombay: the water was rising and the army had been called out to help.

Poona's connections with the outside world had been severed. And along with them, its connection with us as well. It was hard to accept the fact that in this age of technology any place could be so cut off.

We were wandering around the town until twelve that night. All the various programs in the town went right on as planned. A large fair was in progress. All the lights were glittering brightly. Over the loudspeakers the film songs were adding in their clamor. And the movie theaters issued

---

1. Radio Ceylon used to be the one commercial "pop" station of South Asia, with a staple fare of Hindi film-song music.

appeals, over their own loudspeakers, to come see their movies. The film song records went on and on, and we were going wild from the shrill voice of the woman singer.

The streets in the bazaar were flowing with people. Now and then we heard the screech of the soda bottles being replenished. The shopkeepers were hailing their customers. All these sounds created the most horrible background music for the state of mind in which we found ourselves.

That whole night passed by uneasily. We got the news that all roads to Poona were closed. It was after midnight when the leader of our *diṇḍī* got up. He had decided to go back to Poona by whichever train he could get. He enjoined us before he left to stay right where we were until he could get back and not to be unnecessarily afraid. We went and saw him off as far as the station and then returned to the house.

❀

We are on our way back from the station. Along the way we see the huge crowd at the Jaitunbai *kīrtan.*[1] All those people enjoying themselves at the *kīrtan* and the crowds rushing to see the movies and all the others who sit eating and drinking in the teashops! Does our anguish mean absolutely nothing to them? There has been a terrible flood and hundreds of houses washed away—right in one of the neighboring towns. Doesn't that move their hearts the slightest little bit? When a tiger gets into a barn and carries away one of the animals, even cattle in the neighboring stable become agitated. I remember now how in

1. A Muslim who adopted the *Wārkarī* way, Jaitunbai had her own *diṇḍī* and a group of devotees. For a fuller account see pages 219–22.

Germany, when the Jews were being burned alive in the neighboring death camps, the German townspeople carried right on peacefully with their everyday business.

❀

When we got back to the house, we found everyone there speculating—on the basis of the location of his house—as to whether the flood waters could have reached it. I live in Natubag. I was quite sure that even if the Final Deluge arrived, the waters wouldn't reach that far. But as I listened to the others' fears I started to grow anxious. Doubt also began to infect me. But then I felt ashamed of myself. Many of those who were talking had their homes right along the river bank. How enviable their peacefulness seemed! Some of them were even saying, "Let the house go. I'm not going to turn my back on Vitthal now. Whatever it is his will to accomplish, that's what will happen!"

We kept talking until late in the night. Each one of us had his own speculations about the matter, and we also listened to what the others said. Nobody really *knew* anything. How high would the water have risen? How much of the city would be submerged? Everyone felt some fear. They were finding solace in each other's reassurances. "O, your house is far out of the way." "Your house is on high ground—" But every now and then they would all fall silent and stare straight ahead with empty eyes. One of the women would start to cry. And then they would all start trying to comfort her.

Finally, toward dawn, out of sheer exhaustion, we fell asleep.

*July 13, 1961*

❀

In the morning immediately after tea we set out in search of a newspaper. We went to the newspaper seller's shop, but none of the papers had come as yet. The man there said, "A man just came here from Poona. The entire city was swept away. Why inquire about Poona—or go there?"

When we head these words we were just set back on our heels. At last I said, "Mister! That's no way to talk to us. All of us have come here from Poona with the *pālkhī*. You didn't even stop to think what effect your words would have on us."

He threw his arm into the air and said, "Poona has been swept away. I told you what I heard."

A couple more people entered the shop, and with equal nonchalance he told them the "hearty" news of Poona being swept away. Before I left him I said, "Mister, there's no way the whole of Poona could have been simply swept away. And even if it is, we'll build it again. And even if all the rest of the world goes, Natubag will stand. Like Baby Krishna on his peepul leaf or like Manu's boat in the Great Deluge. We'll create the whole world again."

After I left the shop, I realized that it was wrong of me to have gotten angry. I ought to have tried to enter into his feelings and probe why he harbored such anger against Poona.

❀

We returned without getting our newspaper. At the house they were discussing once again whether to go back to

Poona or to go on. They were worried most about the likely shortage of drinking water in Poona after the flood. Most of them decided to continue onward and not to turn back. They left to Vitthal the problem of whatever had happened back at home.

By afternoon the news gradually started coming in. We got hold of a Bombay paper. Based on the news it contained we came to know what the flood's waterline was, and we decided that most of our houses were safe.

While we were talking, a bunch of monkeys was dancing on the tin-sheet roof of the house making an unholy din. Very suddenly, the thought came to me that *I* ought to go back and pay a quick visit to Poona.

Our part of the city was safe. But my mind remained uneasy. I spent the entire day trying to settle on my plan for going back to Poona. I just couldn't make up my mind whether I ought to leave the work I had undertaken half-finished. But I couldn't bear it either to stay away when my town was in such danger. In the end I decided that I would just wander around until I had settled on what to do.

I hung my bag over my shoulder. Should I perhaps work at getting the questionnaires filled out? The hand that I put into my bag began to falter. It seemed like such a terribly petty thing to do, when such a calamity had befallen Poona, to go around like some idiot asking, "When did you first undertake this pilgrimage? Did you approve of the Harijans being allowed to enter the temple?"

It struck me how quickly a city like Poona can disappear. And what remains behind? What importance is there to things like economics and statistics? What things in this world do make sense still? Everything begins to seem ridiculous. Just like the way I am feeling now!

I kept wandering around, through one street after another, like a person dazed. Nothing seemed important to me. I myself included. I had turned into an ignorant, stupid lame-brain who couldn't even decide for himself what to do anymore.

What should I do? What should I do? Once more I went into a teashop to hear the news. It had started to drizzle again. I sat down on a bench on the veranda of the teashop.

A *sannyāsī* came and sat down beside me, but I didn't really notice him.[1] It was only when the waiter asked him, "What more can I bring you?" that my attention turned to him. The waiter and he had started a conversation.

The *sannyāsī* must have had some tea earlier. When he tried to hand over his money the waiter asked, "How can I accept money from a *sannyāsī*?"

The *sannyāsī* replied, "Well, you're a *sannyāsī* too. Are you married yet? No? And you're already getting old!"

The waiter said, "Who's going to go asking for trouble if he can help it? You aren't married either."

The *sannyāsī* laughed and said, "But I *am* a *sannyāsī*. You know, you really must get married."

"I feel better not getting married."

The waiter turned to me then and said, "He's been coming here with the *pālkhī* now for eight years. He has some tea and pays for it, but I don't accept the money."

The *sannyāsī* said, "But your boss will get mad at you."

"That skin-flint! What will he lose? I pay for you out of my own pocket."

And saying that he dropped some coins from his pocket into the empty cup, and he took the cup and saucer inside. I asked the *sannyāsī*, "Do you regularly come along with the *pālkhī*?"

The *sannyāsī* said, "Yes! Wherever I happen to be in India, I make sure I don't miss the *pālkhī*."

"How many years has it been?"

1. A *sannyāsī* is one who has renounced worldly life to become a religious mendicant.

"Seventeen years."

"How old are you?"

"I must be fifty-five. Who can tell for sure?"

The hair in his beard and on his head was largely white. His whole body seemed as if it was dried up; but it was tough and wiry. The veins in his ankles and feet stood out. I found myself wondering what these single wandering *sannyāsīs* do when they get old. Who is going to look after their needs when their arms and legs grow weary?

And I asked him just that, "Who's going to look after you when you get old?"

He replied, "Vitthal."

"Don't you have a disciple or somebody like that? Married people have their children or their grandchildren. It's sure not going to be easy for you."

As we were talking his fingers kept pushing aside the hairs of his mustache and beard that covered his lips. He was doing this when he replied, "Well yes—yes, I am thinking of adopting a disciple."

When I was young I used to be full of curiosity about *sannyāsīs*. Did a *sannyāsī* always wear these clothes—right from birth? And where did he sleep? He would of course have no relatives—either father or mother, or brother or sister. All alone he would be born and just go wandering about. That is what I used to believe.

When I learned later on that anyone can become a *sannyāsī* by taking initiation, I found myself drawn more toward finding out about their lives before they took initiation. And that is what I asked him now: "Why did you become a *sannyāsī*? Where are you from originally?"

He said, "I'm from Alandi. I became a *sannyāsī* when I was twelve. I was a stepchild. My stepmother used to provoke my own father into mistreating me. One day I got angry. I burned the clothes I was wearing and put on a loincloth, and I ran away.

"Later on I met up with this *sannyāsī.* I stayed with him. I would press his legs, massage his body, and wash his ochre robe, and he would feed me on the alms we got. I wandered all over India with him. Sometimes we went by foot and sometimes on the train without tickets.

"I finally got tired of just wandering around. I wanted to become a *sannyāsī.* But he wouldn't initiate me. So when we got to Banaras I left him. I found a monastery where the *sannyāsī* let me stay with him. I asked him if he would initiate me. He told me to stay a while and see.

"The monastery had a lot of cattle. I was given the work of taking care of them. I took them down to the water, washed them, milked them, and cleaned the cowshed. There were always plenty of good things to eat at the monastery. So I worked, drank milk by the pitcher, and ate the sweets that were offered for the rituals. It was a good life.

"But after four years I started to get tired of it. When I spoke to the 'Baba' who ran the monastery about giving me initiation, he would only tell me to stay on there as I had been. He would make me his disciple, and I would be able to look after the monastery after him. But I was fed up with it all. I had been away from my hometown for so many years. I felt myself being drawn back there."

As I was listening to the *sannyāsī*'s story I really started to pity him. What a life! I made up my mind then to leave him something when I got up to go.

The *sannyāsī* went on, "I had never intended to stay there. I became stubborn about having my initiation, and finally the 'Baba' gave it to me."

I asked him, "How is the initiation done?"

"It's a very complicated affair. You have to receive a *mantra.*"[1]

1. A *mantra* is a mystical formula sacred to a deity, which is given at initiation into a religious order.

I asked, "Which *mantra*?"

He said, "The *mantra* is a secret. You're not supposed to tell anyone. I assumed the name Shankargiri. I lost my former name."

"So you had your initiation. Then what happened?"

"As soon as I had my initiation I left the monastery. I had it very much on my mind to go back to my hometown. But I didn't have any money. And if I did go home, what would I do there? Just then I happened to meet some *sādhus* who were heading off for the Himalayas.[1] They told me, 'Come along with us. We're going to Prayag first.[2] That's where they give secret gifts.' I listened to them and decided to go along."

I asked him, "What are secret gifts?"

"The Bengalis are very devout. They give secret gifts. And other rich people from all over India who are devout also come to Prayag to give secret gifts. All the *sādhus* sit at the side of the road. Those who are giving secret gifts come along and distribute sweets to them. The gifts are hidden in the sweets. Out of a hundred sweets that they distribute like this, maybe ten might have pieces of gold or silver or gems hidden in them. During that one season I accumulated six hundred fifty rupees worth in secret gifts.

"So then I decided to go back to my hometown. Along the way I visited all the holy places, and after subtracting my expenses I ended up with a thousand rupees. I arrived home, and I asked for my share of the property. The land is our ancestral property. So I must get my share of it.

"I had it out with my step-brother and my father. And then I left Alandi. It was just when the *pālkhī* was supposed to leave. So I told myself I might just as well go along with it and see what this festivity was like. Along the way we came

1. *Sādhu* is a respectful term for holy men, saints, and sages.

2. Prayag is the sacred confluence of the Ganges and the Yamuna and the site of the twelve-yearly *kumbhamelā* pilgrimage.

to Jejuri. I liked the place a lot. I decided to stay there permanently. I managed to get a bit of land and built a small hut there. I had brought *śāḷigrāms* with me, which I had collected from the rivers of India at many different places.[1] I had also brought twelve *liṅgas.*[2] I decided that I would set up the *liṅgas* and build a temple of the 'twelve *liṅgas.*'

"I made a small shelter. The twelve *liṅgas* I set in marble. And I also set out the *śāḷigrāms.* I started a daily ritual of worship, waving oil lamps before the shrine and singing *bhajans.* People gradually learned about it. The yearly fair at Jejuri was a tremendous advantage. Even those people started coming. They offered their small coins and grain. They even began helping me with the building of the temple. I started the work after I had been there two years. It was all completed in one year. I got people to make contributions and I had a celebration, and that is when I made the sacred resolution to give a feast for at least a thousand people every year.

"Once the temple was built everything became easy. People would send me bags of rice, while others would send bags of millet or lentils. Then the problem arose of where to keep it all. So then I undertook to build five rooms next to my hut. And I was able to collect enough money for that too."

He sighed happily, and looking at me with distinct satisfaction, he said, "Nowadays I'm satisfied. The property amounts to some thirty thousand rupees. There are two or three thousand rupees in cash too."

He had his satisfaction, but my own had quite disappeared. The eight annas I had taken out to give him had long since dropped back into my pocket. I had to say

1. *Śāḷigrāms* are river pebbles, normally from out of the river Gandaki, which are worshiped as a representation of Vishnu.

2. The *liṅga* is the phallic representation of Shiva.

something still, so I said, "Your labors have yielded their fruit."

"Yes! It's all Vitthal's goodness. Now there's only one thing left to do. Just the other day I went to Alandi and arranged once again to have notice served on my brother. When I get my land I'm going to build a hall for the *Wārkarīs* there."

I asked, "How much land is it?"

When he told me the amount, I realized how very difficult it would be for his father and his brother to get along on the land that was left.

I asked him, "Why are you going after your brother? You already have so much."

"I want to teach him a lesson. Him and his mother."

I really began to pity that stepbrother of his, and I said, "Why go to court over it? Try settling something with him."

Fondling his beard he said, "I'm thinking about that too. If you take into account thirty-five years with interest, it easily comes to twenty-five thousand rupees. That's how much he has to give me or else I'll have the land seized."

I pitied that man still more.

"Seized! What are you going to get out of having the land seized? How much do you think they have left after having to support the family all these years? Take however much your brother willingly gives you. That would suit your conduct better. People will wonder what kind of *sādhu* you are. What would be your worth then?"

He sat silent for a while thinking. Then he said very suddenly, "What you just said is right. I'm going to withdraw the suit."

What he actually did afterward I have no way of knowing. But it is true that now and then I do give others unsolicited bits of advice.

When my conversation with the *sannyāsī* had ended, I suddenly remembered that one of the men in our *diṇḍī* was going to take me around and introduce me to certain people.

I made a *namaskār* to the *sannyāsī* and got up, and I went back to the house. I found the man there, and we set off together. Along our way he said, "For some time now I've been meaning to tell you. These days a lot of things are in a real mess in our *Wārkarī* Way. The really dedicated ones who remain you could almost count on the fingers of one hand. If you want to get genuine information, you have to see these people. Others will tell you whatever tall tales they feel like telling. They're out to make a name for themselves. You couldn't bear to see the way they actually behave."

When we were approaching the *pālkhī*'s tent he pointed with his finger at another little tent nearby, "Here is a godly man. A true *Wārkarī*. Pure in speech and in deed. But he's been shunted aside. Good people are often lackadaisical. They don't strive enough. Bad people are always scheming after something or other. In order for the good to be able to win, you have to have the will to fight for the good. We are the ones who are really to blame for it. This good man was a school teacher. He has been going with the *pālkhī* now for fifty years."

I made the teacher's acquaintance, after which my companion told him, "Let him meet some of the good people. He has started a very good work."

The teacher said, "Let him come back in the afternoon. That's when they all meet."

As we were going away my companion kept admonishing me, "He is a very good man. Don't let go of him. Come along now! We'll go see another one of the good people."

We set off and made our way right through the ropes that were supporting the little tents all around the *pālkhī*. the horses that always accompany the *pālkhī* were there, and a line of people had formed to take *darśan* of them. The rider of one of the horses, who was wearing a large silk kerchief, was standing there holding the horse's bridle. A dhoti had been spread out in front of him, and the people who had come for *darśan* dropped their money into it. Each person would touch the horse's face with his hand and make a *namaskār*. With each touch the horse would rear back its head.

My "next acquaintance" we found slicing vegetables in a little room. All around him he had piled great heaps of potatoes, eggplant, carrots, and various leafy vegetables. How tiny the slicing blade looked when compared with the stupendous body of the man who was slicing the vegetables with it! We made our *namaskārs* and sat down. My companion told me, "All the arrangements for this *diṇḍī* are in his hands."

I wasn't able to accomplish my work here either. He put aside the form I gave him—and said he would sent it to me later after he had filled it out. But I did make a mental note of his story. This man had gone wandering all over India many times. At first he went alone. Then he started doing it as a guide. From Nepal to Ceylon, he made all the pilgrimages. His acquaintances were sown across the whole of India.

Toward the end of the afternoon I went back in the direction of the *pālkhī* and met the teacher. He told me, "You go on over to the *pālkhī*'s tent. I'll be coming very soon. The leaders have a meeting there every evening. They discuss the problems that have come up along the way."

As I was going there I stopped to hear a sermon someone was giving at one side of the tent. Four or five hundred *Wārkarīs* were listening to him. I also stood there and listened.

The speaker was trying to convince the audience of the worthlessness of education. He made one young fellow stand up, who, as he was getting up, caught his foot in his floppy pajama pants and stumbled. All the people started laughing. The speaker asked him, "How much education have you had?"

"I've finished high school."

"Do you know English?"

"Yes."

"So if I ask you a question in English, you have to answer in English too."

"Yes."

"What-fruit-to-mash-tash-cash?"

The boy's face fell. When the audience understood that the speaker had made the boy stand up to make a fool out of him, they burst out laughing. He wiped away the sweat that started to cover his face.

The speaker also laughed when he saw how successful his trick had been.

"That's all right! I just made a little joke. I'm only an old man—forgive me. Now I'll ask you some real questions. How much is five times four?"

"Twenty."

"How much is nine times ten?"

"Ninety."

All the people could easily see that such simple questions had to be leading up to the coup de grace. Some of them had already started laughing. And sure enough, at the right time he popped the question, "How much is sixty-seven times three-and-a-half?"

The boy became flustered. Faltering, he asked, "What?"

"Sixty-seven times three-and-a-half."

In utter confusion he asked again, "What?" He moved his lips and muttered as he tried to remember the multiplication table for three-and-a-half. The speaker told him to sit down then, and he went on,

"That's the way it is with knowledge. When you keep getting more and more knowledge, where do you stop? Is there any satisfaction in that? You get a B.A., an M.A., a Ph.D.—you go off to England. Say you even go off to America. What have you gotten for yourself—anything? Go to the moon. Go all the way to Mars! There's no satisfaction there. More education only makes you more ignorant. It's only through devotion that knowledge becomes complete."

The entire sermon was one violent assault! Why should women need liberation? Socialism is the worst possible thing. The eradication of untouchability is against all religion. He blasted other religious sects. He blasted their leaders.

Until then it had been my innocent belief that the *Wārkarī* sect was all upright and straightforward, a sect that would not meddle with anyone's way of belief. But this was an official sermon right in front of the *pālkhī* itself. The only thing that is true in the end is that no religious sect is really upstanding.

I listened for a short while and then moved on. I went into the leaders' meeting. They were discussing whether they should even start the meeting or not. The chief man in the *pālkhī* had gone to Poona because of the flood. I handed out my questionnaire to each one of them. Some muttering to themselves and some right out loud, they read the questions.

"There's something fishy about this."

Somebody else said, "What do you mean? He only wants some information. Just give it to him."

A third one said, "Read it carefully. Let's think about it

before we decide. Do we really want to give him the information?"

I told them, "There's nothing to be suspicious about."

I showed them Dhananjay Rao Gadgil's letter of reference.[1] I explained to them what the Gokale Institute was. I realized then that it wasn't a very easy thing to do. They not only did not know who Gadgil was, they could not grasp the purpose of an institution that conducted statistical surveys and gathered information. They couldn't understand the motivation behind that.

In the end, after some debate, they decided that they would wait to fill out the forms until after their leader came back from Poona. They folded up their forms and put them all away in their pockets.

❀

We have finished our evening meal. I have announced that I am going to go back and visit Poona. I am taking each person's address down in my diary. As they are telling me their addresses I can sense how unsettled their minds have become. Some of them draw me maps of the streets where their houses are. Others instruct me in great detail on how to find their rooms after I enter their courtyards—where I'll find the stairs, how the galleries have been designed. Someone tells me about the telltale rope that hangs from his balcony. They all tell me, "Tell them to write." Yesterday all of them had already sent letters. Somebody asks me, "Why don't you bring back a note from them?"

1. Dhananjay Ramchandra Gadgil (1901–1971), one of India's preeminent economists, was director of Gokhale Institute at that time.

In the middle of this, one man who has already given me his address comes forward again. He tells me where his son might be if I were to go to his home sometime in the morning, what his daughter would be doing, and what work his wife would be busy doing. Everything they tell me—addresses and messages—somehow seems inadequate to them.

"Tell them to go and stay with our niece in Khed if there's no water there in Poona."

"They have a well there. Just tell them our name, and they will give you water if you need."

As I am busily noting all this down, midnight comes and goes.

❀

When I had finished writing down all the addresses, I took my flashlight and my waterpot and went down to the river.

The darkness was such that it made the very light look deformed. The hard rock looked like mud. The water looked like rock. On my way back I saw a boy leaning back against a haystack crying bitterly. I stopped and asked him, "Hey, why are you crying like that?"

A man who was standing nearby told me, "He's crying because the flood is going to reach Pandharpur now."

"Is that a reason for him to cry?"

"He thinks now that Poona is gone, Pandharpur will be the next to go. His home is right on the riverbank. He's from the *Koḷī* caste."[1]

The boy wiped his eyes and looked up. He blew his nose, and then he said, "I came here all by myself. If Pandharpur

1. The *Koḷīs* of Pandharpur have the traditional caste occupations of boatmen and priests in the town's Shiva temples.

goes, I won't have anybody left."

He broke down again and started crying. I told him, "The water won't reach as far as Pandharpur. This isn't a natural flood. It's all the water from the dam. By the time it gets to Pandharpur it will dissipate. Go to sleep now. Don't cry."

I told him simply what I had heard everyone around me saying. It's true at least that it made him quiet.

❀

I climbed up to the upper floor where we were staying. In the large hall where we slept a sermon was being delivered. A new *buvā* had joined our *diṇḍī*. As I sat listening to his sermon, I kept waiting for him to make some reference to the catastrophe in Poona. There were a lot of parables. But no mention of the flood.

I certainly felt that he ought at least to have mentioned it. Nothing even so formal as a moment of silence, but at least something. We needed something to relieve the pressure of our feelings. Just what are these *Wārkarīs* like then? A woman gets swept away in the water—cold! We hear about the flood—cold!

The sermon was nothing very special. I started to doze right where I was sitting. Afterward, just when I had lain down to sleep, somebody called me, "Mokashi! We wrote down our address on a separate piece of paper. If you lose your diary, we don't want you to make a mistake. Go to our house before three o'clock so you can see everyone. After three my wife goes out to hear the *purāṇas*—"[1]

1. The *purāṇas* are a class of sacred literature in Sanskrit, which treats of the creation, the gods, sages, heroes, sacred places, etc.

But I heard the rest of what he said half in my sleep.

At three o'clock in the night I woke up with a start. I had had a dream that something horrible had happened at home. In actual fact the chances of that were very small. This was nothing more than an upsurge of all the tensions on my mind. I went back to sleep.

423. *Even after an arrow is shot through a target it continues its flight until its momentum is lost.*

424. *When a potter removes from his wheel the vessel which he has made, the wheel continues revolving with the force of its spinning.*

425. *So, O conqueror of wealth, even when the sense of individuality of the body comes to an end, its inherent activity still promotes action.*

426. *A dream may arise without any previous thought, trees may grow in a forest without being planted and castles in the air may appear without being built.*

427. *So without the participation of the Self the five physical causes by their very nature initiate all kinds of activity.*

428. *Owing to the result of actions in past lives these five causes, with their accompanying motives, bring about manifold activities.*

Jnāneshvari *Eighteen*

CHAPTER FIVE

# Poona

I am standing this morning at the State Transport bus stand in Lonand. Two of the women from the *diṇḍī* are also going to Poona. Both of them have their homes right on the river-bank. One of them had just recently spent ten thousand rupees to have her house fixed up. She can hardly expect that her house will be standing still. But the reason she is crying is whether she will at least find her family alive or not.

The bus has started on its way. I wonder what scenes I will see in Poona. Collapsed houses and heaps of mud? Everything familiar vanished? All the people I had known start to come before my eyes. Who will still be there—and who won't? Wherever the bus stops I get out and try to find out more about the situation in Poona. I hear them talking everywhere about little else than the water problem there. Poona has lost its water supply. Water is gushing out of an open tap right in front of me. I wonder if I should find a can and take some of the water with me. There is no milk available in Poona either. Our little girl is still just a baby. Should I also take along a can of milk for her? I keep asking people about the water situation. Finally someone says, "Look here! There are still lots of cisterns and wells left in Poona."

I start to laugh at myself and my fears. Somehow my thought had been that no water in the pipes must mean no water at all. But so there is water outside of pipes?—I felt as happy as if I had made some great discovery.

From the moment we enter Poona I prepare my eyes for the awful scenes they are about to see. We arrive at the bus depot at Poona Station. The crowds there do seem to be somewhat less than usual, but everything else looks just as it used to. So at least the news of the water reaching as far as the station was wrong!

Our bus sets off again from the station to the Swargate bus stand. I press my forehead against the bars in the window and look out over everything. I can even see people in the teashops. And the really surprising thing about it is that they are drinking water!

I get off at Swargate. Nothing seems to be any different. We walk down Tilak Road from the bus stand, and still there is nothing different. It does seem a little quiet. But this part of town is always quiet around this time of day.

I enter Natubag. Everything strikes me with wonder. The houses are all still standing. The trees are all where they always used to be. Wonder of wonders! I reach our chawl.

I step into the house, and I start slightly—I almost feel a little guilty. What an uproar there would have been if I had come home at the end of the *pālkhī* procession! My wife and my niece come out and meet me. For a moment we just look at one another without saying a word. Just one short moment. But that one moment tells me all about the flood. I understand the chasm that separates their state of mind from mine. I know I shall never fully be able to appreciate what these people have gone through. The moment ends, and my wife starts talking rapidly. I don't pay attention so much to her words—but more to their speed. It is a dam breaking, and the built-up tensions are dissipating. I can see that from her face.

There were really two floods that came through Poona. Two times a dam broke, and two times the water rose. In the first flood the area of Poona along the riverbank and adjacent to it washed away—my wife is telling me—and then the second flood that came through was a flood of rumors. The rumors started in the morning about ten o'clock. It was just about then that a man on a bicycle came flying into the compound of our chawl. He leaned the bicycle against the wall and asked, "May I leave the bike here?"

My wife asked him, "What if somebody steals it?"

He replied, "What does the bicycle matter when it's time to run for your life? The dike has broken and the water has reached as far as S.P. College. Everyone is running away."

Thereupon he abandoned his bicycle and scampered away. And a tremendous uproar arose in our chawl. Some of the people quickly pulled out their trunks and ran over to the third floor of the neighboring school. My wife and niece also started preparing to leave the house. But they decided not to go at least until the water reached the steps. Their preparations involved little more than putting some milk in a bottle for the baby girl. They got together a few diapers and shawls for her to sleep on. They didn't even think about what the rest of them might need. Then they remembered that the two trunks under the bed would get wet when the water came, so they lifted them up as high as they could—which was no more than on top of the bed. Then the four of them—our two daughters and my wife and niece—sat down in the doorway and watched the road to see if the water was coming.

My wife was laughing when she told me this—she was laughing at the memory of leaving those trunks on top of the bed.

❀

When I had changed my clothes and had a bite to eat, we went out together. We were going out to see the damage the flood had done. But everything I had heard since I got home had already given me the feeling that I knew all there was to know about the flood. We set off for the quarters of town that are along the riverbank. We didn't see anything until we had crossed Laxmi Road. But then a rotten stench began to assail our noses. The street started to be filled with sticky mud. We saw heaps of rotten grain, which had been thrown out of the stores onto the sides of the street. Rotten paper and sacks and straw. Then everything became virtually indistinguishable. The houses looked like mounds of mud, and you could see the household things poking out of them. We started to feel as if we were wandering around a battlefield. In one place nothing remained but the foundation of a house. Elsewhere a portion of the walls or a roof had collapsed, and all the inner parts of the house lay scattered in the street like spilled intestines. I felt stunned looking at it. I got the fortuitous feeling—if only I had been here, I wouldn't have let this happen.

We went as far as the police station in Shaniwar Peth. They were allowing only those people who actually had homes there to go into the lanes beyond that point. From where we were standing we could see one entire family digging through the mud and bricks on the spot where their house had been: an old man, a son who was near twenty, two teenaged daughters, the mother, a sixteen-year-old boy, and a little girl still in skirts. The old man was pushing aside one of the rafters and poking around in the mud below. The older boy was wearing short pants. Whenever he saw some household object he would rapidly bend down and pick it out. We could see a wooden barrel, a bucket, a few pots and pans, and a couple of glass bottles, which they had piled up on one side. All these things were completely coated with mud: you could recognize them only from their shapes. The clothes these people were wearing were likewise just full of mud. They had mud on their faces and even in their hair.

Just then the little girl held up her hand and showed the others a spoon she had found in the mud. And she laughed. When they saw that mud-caked spoon in her hand, everyone around her started to laugh.

The road was filled with people coming and going, not only those who were bringing the household effects out from their flooded homes but also spectators like us who had just come to see the spectacle.

Some people had brought hand carts along with them, as far as the main street went. They carried their belongings from their homes down the narrow lanes and loaded them on the carts. They brought anything and everything they could: little shelves, rusted barrels, clothes all wadded up with mud, and even mattresses! Swollen with mud as they were, these mattresses looked especially horrible. And to see this in the middle of the all-encompassing soddenness, you had to wonder if any of it would ever get dry again. The older people were coming out maybe clutching some little box or some odd pot or pan. They walked wearily, and the expression on their faces showed what they were feeling: everything was lost and nothing would ever rise up again. But the young people were running around here and there with determination and zeal. In the lanes farthest down toward the river the army men were working with equal vigor. It was such a reassurance to see!

Actually, there were more people like us, who had just come to look, tracking through the streets than those who were trying to retrieve their things from the mud. The bleached white clothes of all the people who had come from outside Poona just to see the flood especially caught our eyes. These people would point at the walls and tell each other loudly, "See that line? That's how high the water rose!"

My attention was suddenly drawn to a man who was sitting on a mud-covered chair on our right. All his clothes were full of mud, but I had no trouble recognizing him. I saw instantly that he was that very same Ramdasi man who had been in the pilgrimage procession. He was sitting there staring vacantly before him. I stepped forward and made a *namaskār*. And I exclaimed, "Maharaj! What's happened here!"

He waved his hand and said, "What's happened is—I've lost everything. All the things in the house are gone. But what really makes me feel bad is that my entire collection of books was lost. I'll be able to rebuild everything else. But all those rare books I lost—how can I ever replace that knowledge?"

❀

When we got back home I had to face the question: should I go back and join the *pālkhī* or not?

It really was my duty to stay in Poona. I could have made myself useful somewhere. But I had the feeling that I shouldn't abandon the *pālkhī* pilgrimage halfway either. The fact that I hadn't been there during the actual flood also had a peculiar effect on me. I couldn't look at this calamity as subjectively as I might have. It was like having to complete a job someone had left spoiled and half-finished. The picture I had of the flood was all from the outside. I had to collect the news, like a newspaper reporter, after the fact: the daring deeds during the flood, the people who were left with just the clothes on their backs, the people's anger against the government officials, the bitter caste feelings between the brahmans and the non-brahmans, the stories about certain people pilfering the relief supplies sent for the flood victims, and even the parasitical, selfish behavior of some of the flood victims themselves at the relief centers.

This is why I couldn't wholeheartedly enter into the feelings of the city. Or was it that even after living here for twelve years I still hadn't developed any real love for it? Could it be so? Do I still have to think of myself as living here only for the sake of my livelihood? Why should the mere memory of my home town make my heart feel so full and disdain city life as squalid? And make me think of the place where my whole life is being lived now as friendless and loveless? I began to feel appalled at my own feelings.

I finally turned over to my wife the decision of whether I should go or not. It was her opinion that I should go.

*July 14, 1961*

1079. *As waves in water, atoms and grains in the earth, rays in the sun,*

1080. *as the limbs of the body, feelings arising in the mind, and as sparks in the fire,*

1081. *so are all created forms rooted in the One. When this vision of unity is awakened, a man finds the ship of the riches of Brahma [for crossing the ocean of life].*

1082. *Wherever he looks he sees only Brahma and enters into the infinite bliss.*

Jnāneshvari *Thirteen*

CHAPTER SIX

# Phaltan

I spent two nights in Poona. During the time I have been away I have missed the *pālkhī*'s stop at Taradgav. It left Lonand on the fourteenth and was at Taradgav that night. It left from there on the fifteenth and was to continue on to its overnight stop in Phaltan.

The time is early afternoon. I have slung my bag over my shoulder and set out walking to the State Transport bus depot. My steps feel heavy. My heart is dejected from everything I saw in Poona yesterday. I didn't want to take the bus or a rickshaw. It wouldn't seem right somehow to be riding in a vehicle in the middle of all the surrounding suffering. So I am walking. Inside me I sense countless cracks and tears. Is the shell starting to break open? Is the seed of friendship that is down there somewhere finally beginning to grow—for this city I only came to make a living in?

On my way I run into the son of a master carpenter I know. I remember when I met the master carpenter in Lonand. With tears in his eyes he had told me, "I've spent my whole life building up the business, and now it's been destroyed." But even as he was speaking he had felt ashamed of his tears and he had said, "What's gone is gone—and we'll just build it up again."

I remember it all very distinctly now as I listen to the message his son is sending back with me for him, "Tell the master there's no reason for him to come back home now. He should come back after the pilgrimage is over. Tell him not to worry about things here. The shop was destroyed, but we've found all the really important things."

According to the pilgrimage program, the *pālkhī* has left Lonand and gone as far as Phaltan. I'll arrive in Phaltan this afternoon. And the *pālkhī* will be leaving Phaltan tomorrow.

While I am traveling along in the bus to Phaltan, I keep seeing all the familiar places we had passed previously in the pilgrimage procession. We had walked step by step right along this very same road. Did we pass by this tree here? We must have. Did we see that hill? And didn't we stop here for a rest?

On this side of Jejuri the bus is forced to stop. Ahead of us there is a small bridge across a creek, and on either side of it there are twenty or thirty vehicles backed up along the road. A tree has fallen across the bridge.

I get out of the bus and walk up to the bridge. A roaring wind is blowing. The cap of another passenger who has gotten off goes flying away, and he goes running after it. I get some idea of what a tremendous wind storm it must have been earlier. I reach the bridge. About a dozen men are busy cutting up the tree and pushing it aside. Just as I get there the last branch comes crashing down. I grab hold of it and throw it to the side of the road. As if they had all been waiting just for me.

*July 15, 1961*

❀

In Phaltan we are staying in a large apartment in the old palace. The moment I arrive there is a loud cry, "Mokashi is back!" As I enter in among them, they all start making a fuss over me: "Mokashi! Come and have a bath. You'll want to eat something, won't you? The bathroom is over there."

To each one of them I convey whatever comforting news there is from home. But that isn't enough to satisfy them.

"You're sure you found the right address? Who did you meet? How did the kids look? Who all was at home? How were they all doing? Did they give you some tea?" I have to answer these questions too: "How bad is the water shortage? When will the electricity be restored?"

I ask them in turn about the part of the pilgrimage I missed between Lonand and Phaltan. It was a very difficult walk I learn. One person's feet had swollen up, and somebody else had gotten sick with a fever.

I spent the rest of the day wandering around in Phaltan. I met a couple of *Wārkarīs* with whom I passed a whole hour most interestingly. They were an uncle and his nephew. The uncle was well over sixty, and the nephew was about ten years younger. I asked them how they made a living. They were both farmers. Next I asked them how much it cost them to go on the pilgrimage with the *pālkhī*. They laughed and told me, "Two rupees!"

"Just two rupees!" I said in astonishment. But then they gave me an even bigger surprise: they had made the pilgrimage all the way to Banaras on fourteen annas!

I sat down then and there and listened to their fascinating description of their Banaras pilgrimage.

They had walked some of the way to Kashi on foot. But

for most of the journey they went "without ticket" on the train. I learned for the first time that it can take a year-and-a-half to travel ticketless by train to and from Banaras. You have to add in the days you spend seeing the religious fairs and famous places along the way and the days you have to spend in jail. The police or the ticket checkers force you off at small stations, and days might be lost waiting to get the next train. If you get too hungry along the way, you have to get off anyway and find something to make a meal with. So many hindrances!

I told them, "It takes only fourteen annas for the Kashi pilgrimage you say but two rupees for the Pandharpur pilgrimage—you've got your accounts all backwards!"

The uncle sighed and said, "What can you do? In the North everybody gives to the pilgrims, and here you have to travel a little ways by bus."

We have the chance today to sleep in the old palace. We are sleeping in the great hall right next to the street. It has broad, spacious windows. The ceiling seems to rise as high as the sky. My sleep is very uneasy.

I don't remember what time it was. I woke up from my sleep with a mighty start. People were waving their arms in the air and shouting all around me, "Hey! Hey! Hit him! Beat him up!" The sounds were ringing in my ears. What kind of horrible dream was this? Where was I? What on earth was going on? Had the whole world gone mad? I couldn't understand a thing.

It took a while, but I finally realized that these were the people in my own *diṇḍī*, and it wasn't a dream. But even then I continued to feel the initial shock for a long while.

heavy blows. Whatever is brought along here should be brought along on the understanding that it belongs to Vitthal—or else it shouldn't be brought along at all. They are spoiling all the joy here on the pilgrimage this way. Not just their own but everyone else's too.

*July 16, 1961*

One of our people leaped over to the window j and started to pound at something with his fists. Sor else shouted, "Thief! Thief!" I got up on my feet. Ar person ran to the window yelling, "His turban! See, t his turban!"

The uproar has finally quieted down. They are all telli each other now how they saw the thief's turban through th window as he was trying to climb up into the room. I hear people remarking, "The thieves are really getting insolent!" And a lot of abuse is heaped on the security arrangements the police have made.

We no sooner go back and lie down again than a man comes striding in through the door. He stands right there in the middle of all our beds. He looks around him sheepishly here and there. One of the women in the *diṇḍī* screams. A male *diṇḍī*-member leaps up and starts to pound the man who has just come in.

"Why are you hitting me?" the man asks.

"A thief is a thief! And you ask me why I'm hitting you!"

"I came here only because I thought this was a place where *Wārkarīs* could sleep."

"So, now you're a *Wārkarī*, huh? I've seen plenty of *Wārkarīs*! You come here to steal and then tell us you're a *Wārkarī*! Get out of here—or do I have to throw you out?"

It is none other than our newly arrived *buvā* who has gotten so angry!

Everything is quiet again. It all begins to strike me as very funny—this fear the *Wārkarīs* have about thieves. Half of their attention they give to Vitthal and the other half to the thieves. If something they own gets misplaced, they become distraught. Anyone in tattered clothes who happens to come near them is driven away with harsh words. Be he educated or a peasant—this is the manner of all *Wārkarīs*!

I can't get to sleep. My expectations about how the atmosphere of this pilgrimage would be have taken some

1102. *The spirit is neither divided nor whole, neither active nor inactive, neither slender nor gross; for it is without attributes.*

1103. *It is neither perceived nor unperceived, neither shining nor dark, neither small nor large; for it has no form.*

1104. *It is neither void nor full, neither with nor without possessions, neither with nor without form; for it is the void.*

1105. *It does not experience joy nor is it free from it, is neither one nor many, neither free nor bound; for it is the Self.*

Jnāneshvari *Thirteen*

CHAPTER SEVEN

# Baradgav

In the morning the *pālkhī* went on to Baradgav. Two of us stayed behind in Phaltan—one of the organizers of our *diṇḍī* and myself. He had to stay behind to do some work for the *diṇḍī*. He said, "The two of us can follow along later." And I said, "O.K." This also was an experience for me.

This part of the pilgrimage turned out to be a very different experience. His work was finished around noon. I had already gotten some lunch by then, but he was on a fast. Our two-man pilgrimage got started at twelve.

The *pālkhī* had a scheduled stop for the afternoon meal three miles away at Vedhani. We had figured that we could meet the *pālkhī* there. But when we got to Vedhani, the *pālkhī* had already moved on. We had imagined that even if the *pālkhī* did leave before we got there, at least somebody would be waiting for us with a little something to eat. But there was no sign of anyone. The country fair was still there. But the people in our *diṇḍī* had forgotten us.

We continue on our way. I've had something to eat at least, but my companion is still fasting. That is all I can think about. I tell him he should at least have some tea. But his fast won't allow him to have even tea outside the *diṇḍī*. I buy four sweet limes for myself, and with much persistence I give him four sections of one lime to eat.

He *is* a little upset that they didn't leave anything for him to eat. But he has a rather unusual way of showing it. As he is walking along he tells me, "Those rascals! They probably think they've taught me a good lesson. But how could they have known that this would only allow me to earn the merit of a fast without even water! God works everything out for the best for those who are worthy!"

We have eight more miles to walk ahead of us. I suggest to him, "Why don't we go by bus?"

He says, "Come on, come on! We'll see about that farther along."

As we are walking on I feel the belches rising up inside me—and the man walking beside me is still fasting. Each time it happens I feel as if I should be ashamed. I offer him some more sections of the sweet limes. But he refuses them.

❀

I have gotten used to walking along with hundreds of people every day. I feel strangely at a loss today. My attention wanders constantly to the mile stones and to my feet. Without the noise of the cymbals and the drums everything feels very, very vacant, and when I look ahead at the road I can only wonder—what is the point of such a big road?

We discuss whatever subjects we can find to talk about. There is no danger that we will run short of subjects. My companion is quite addicted to story-telling. He knows the

*Dnyāneśwarī* by heart. For every incident in his stories he makes use of one of the verses from the *Dnyāneśwarī* to draw the moral. As I listen to him I keep wondering at how he has packed the entire world neatly into the *Dnyāneśwarī*. His whole world is made up out of the *Dnyāneśwarī*, just as in the Konkan everything they eat—whether cooked rice, flat bread, or even relishes—is just another form of paddy. It was from the *Dnyāneśwarī* alone that he had taken the rafters, the lathing, and the thatching to construct the hut of his life; and if a rafter ever rotted away or the lathing cracked or the thatching leaked, it was with the *Dnyāneśwarī* that he repaired it.

❀

We went on walking for another three miles. His storytelling began to subside. Like a child who won't let the adults talk, our tiring feet kept us from talking.

The flat open plateau land all around us spread dark green all the way to the horizon. The road too was a good one. But nothing could hold my attention. Now and then there would be a downpour. After each mile of our walk we would sit down and rest for a few minutes. We would each take a plug of chewing tobacco. At intervals along the way we encountered other *Wārkarīs*, and that helped to alleviate our boredom and relieve our weariness.

It was here on this road that I met the oldest *Wārkarī* on the *pālkhī* pilgrimage. Supported by a servant, moving forward a half-step at a time, was this ninety-year-old Marwari. His arms and legs were trembling, his head was shaking. His entire body was wizened and wrinkled, and little but his skeleton was left. When we saw him my companion said, "You want to see faith, don't you? Then go talk to him."

The Marwari didn't have enough strength *left* to talk, so we spoke with his servant. His master came from Marathwada. He was a big merchant. He had put his faith in the *pālkhī* when he was still very young. Ever since then he had gone along on the pilgrimage every year. People who drove by in their cars tried to get him to ride with them. But his master always said no. He wanted to lay his body to rest right there on the Way.

We finished our talk, and after we had gone on a ways I turned around to look back. He looked like a dried-out old branch that had fallen in the middle of nature's freshly blooming garden.

A *Wārkarī* man with a bundle on his head and a banner over his shoulder got up from under a tree and started walking with us. He also looked back, and he said, "Just look at the kinds of people who come along! Once you lose yourself to Panduranga—" and just like that he began to tell us the story of his own life. He was a tailor by trade. He had lost his only child. And then he had lost his wife. That is when he had adopted this faith. Now, the whole year round he kept walking, from Alandi to Pandharpur, and from Pandharpur to Alandi! The people in the house on the porch of which he dropped his bundle at night would feed him. Sometimes he got a few small coins. He met his other expenses out of that.

This must be a road where you get to meet the most unexpected people. During the next half mile I met a woman who sometimes comes to my shop to beg for alms. Some five months later she came back to my shop to tell me, "What can I tell you? After getting wet so often on the pilgrimage I got the chills and a bad fever. When I got back from the *pālkhī* I brought with me four months of illness."

As we move across the high open plain I feel myself exposed and shelterless. There are trees but very few. Now and then we get a shower. There is nothing for us to take shelter under. Baradgav is still four miles away. The fair we saw at the last rest stop has folded up, and the vendors are passing on ahead of us. Before I know it the whole road in front is lined with them—some shoving their handcarts along before them and some on bicycles, holding their crossed display sticks up in the air on which they have strung various braided string ornaments. Every once in a while it really pours. The pushcart wallahs stop. Through the downpour you seem to see them as if through a piece of oily paper. One of them might find shelter under his cart. Another might pull a piece of plastic over his head. And the plastic covers they have thrown over the carts look for all the world like big chunks of ice.

But compared to the rain at Saswad this seems positively dry. Like a flower-seller who sprinkles his heap of flowers with water to keep them fresh. When the shower goes away you feel that same sort of freshness here. And the clouds don't smother the sky as at Saswad. The dome of the sky is so enormous here that there still remains at least onc open square on the azure checkerboard for the clouds to make another move.

❀

We have walked another two miles. There are still two miles left to Baradgav. Nature no longer draws our attention at all. Our conversation has completely ebbed away. My legs are worn out. They keep moving ahead for no reason but that I lift them. It occurs to me in a flash—this is no pilgrimage of devotion. This is a pilgrimage of bodily mortification.

Somebody had told me that the name "Baradgav" is derived from "town of the *Beraḍas*."[1] He said, "That's the stopover where you have to be most wary of the thieves."

But as Baradgav approached us I was feeling happy instead of fearful. From this town onward all our stopovers would be in tents. I can't understand myself why I have such a fascination for staying in tents.

At the far edge of the town you cross a stream. The *pālkhī* makes its stopover in the open fields beyond this stream. Going through the transparent, gurgling flow of the water, up to my knees in depth, my weary feet felt so much better. Large areas of the sandy riverbed were bare. Scattered here and there were bushes, rushes, and slate boulders. Evening had begun to fall, and birds were flying about over the stream. As soon as we crossed over we came across a giant banyan that stood, arched and buttressed, on its countless descending roots. On the masonry platform around the main trunk someone had set up a shop to sell firewood. They had hung a giant scales for weighing the wood from one of the branches overhead. As if that great old banyan itself had set up shop to sell its own body!

Immediately across the stream the *pālkhī* procession's camp began. First there were various shops. Then the tent of the god. And beyond that the tents of all the *diṇḍīs*—white triangles wherever you looked! When we got to our own tents everyone there rushed about getting us *kicaḍī* and tea.[2] If anyone tried to explain why they had forgotten to wait for us with the special food for this day of fasting, my companion told them, "Hey, it was only natural you would forget. That's how it was written down in my fate. It was my destiny to be allowed this waterless fast."

---

1. The *Beraḍas* are another caste that used to be designated a "criminal tribe."

2. On days of fasting special foods, such as a fried mixture (*kicaḍī*) of sago and peanuts, are eaten in place of the normal rice and breads.

Although my feet are tired, I don't yet feel like lying down in the tent. I am standing outside. They have marked off a square in the middle of about twenty-five square feet, and they have pitched the tents along its edges. The tent right in front of me is serving as the kitchen. Along the remaining three sides of the space there are eight more tents. One of them is reserved for the women.

I peek into the other tents. There are seven or eight bedding rolls in each one. They have unrolled them from the middle outward to the left and right sides. Everyone has his pillow placed toward the middle. They are all sitting or lying on their own beds, chewing tobacco or smoking *biḍīs* while they chat. Their hands massage their tired legs. One of them is stringing up a line on which to dry his clothes. Someone else is trying to fix a way to hang up the lantern.

In the kitchen tent the evening meal is being prepared. Just outside it the low, clay stove is blazing. The truck that is accompanying our *diṇḍī* is standing nearby. I remember the advice somebody gave me—"If you get lost, just bear the truck in mind." Along one side of it there is a piece of cloth with the *diṇḍī*'s name written on it in characters big enough to be seen hundreds of feet away.

I wander over to the truck and peek into it. It is crammed full of stuff: large tins of grain, leaf plates, sticks of firewood, sacks of charcoal, pots and pans. All our earthly needs are included there. We must be about sixty or seventy people in our *diṇḍī*. Daily provisions for so many—two meals a day—would have to include salt, chili pepper, spices, firewood, pots and pans . . . I try to figure out just how much would be required for all of us over a period of fifteen days.

❀

This evening we have our meal outside the tents—in the open space between them. We sit out in the open on the damp green grass like the children of the cowherds picnicing in the forest with Krishna. We have plates before us made of leaves stitched together.

The enormous sky above my head gives me a very strange feeling. It seems as if my crossed legs have spread out into the whole earth leaving just the points of my knees poking out. Before me is set food that is *pūrnabrahma*—complete fulfillment.

I feel like laughing when I remember our mealtimes back home: the squat wooden seat, the wide metal plate, the brass pitcher with water from the tap, and the asbestos sheets or concrete slab overhead.

During the meal an occasional cow or bullock noses past us, and someone throws them a piece of their flat bread. A dog comes by wagging its tail. They shout him away, but he also gets a quarter piece of bread. There is a poor *Wārkarī* standing nearby in a corner, and they serve him a leaf plate full of food. They don't close the doors here at mealtime as at home. There is no fear of the evil eye. Usually the first mouthful is offered right there to the five great elements themselves.

❀

When our open-air feast was over, we threw away our leaf plates, washed our hands, and came back to the tents. Chewing *pān* and tobacco we soon became absorbed in our talk. The topic of conversation was the *buvā* who had just recently joined us.

The *buvā* had demanded a separate tent for himself and his male and female disciples. At mealtime we had all sat down to eat from leaf plates. The *buvā* had used a metal plate (which appeared to be made of silver). Everyone else had picked up his own leaf plate at the end of the meal, but one of his disciples picked up the *buvā*'s plate. He had received a special towel to wipe his hands on from one of his female disciples. Our clothes had become stained rusty from all the mud and the water of the monsoon. The *buvā* and the group of people with him all wore clothes that were as clean as if they were visiting Bombay.

The *buvā* has created a bad feeling in everyone. They say that he even rides in the truck, and when a town approaches he gets out and joins the procession again. I could sense their ill will toward him in the unpremeditated comments they all made. They couldn't stand to have anyone in the *diṇḍī* act special. I was there to see it too. All of us, whether great or small, acted on friendly and equal terms.

I also heard some of the complaints the women were making. Both men and women were sleeping in the *buvā*'s tent. The fragrance of powders and of attar emanated from it.

After a while I got up and went off to take a turn down by the stream.

There are cooking fires burning everywhere. The smell of the smoke is drifting in the air. They are deep-frying vegetable fritters in the shops. The perforated ladles used in making *jilebīs* are banging and clattering, and the frying *śev* is sizzling.[1] The sound of the *bhajans* comes from every direction. The owners of the little shops open up their knotted bundles wherever they happen to be sitting and eat their meals. The little bells tied around the necks of the tethered bullocks are tinkling, and I can hear them munching their fodder. I reach the stream.

I remember the pleasing atmosphere here when we arrived early in the evening. Now the trees and their shadows have become as one in the darkness. I can't even distinguish the water from the sand. I hear the shrill grating of the crickets. I feel suddenly very alone (without any companion now) but also very peaceful. I almost want to sit down right here and do meditative austerities. And then I have to ask myself what it must feel like to sit here in the middle of the afternoon with the hot blast of air from the burning sand on my eyes.

On the other side of the stream, Baradgav is completely quiet. The kerosene lamp at the top of its pole at the entrance to the town is throwing off a reddish light. Like an older brother who looks with fond amusement at the eager hustle and bustle of a younger brother who has just come home after a long absence, Baradgav looks with an elder's indulgence upon the tumult and commotion of this "guest town" that is the *pālkhī*.

And it occurs to me—the *pālkhī* really is a sort of town, isn't it? What effect must the *pālkhī* have on a town where it makes its stopover? The townspeople get some business. They also have *darśan* of the *pālkhī*. The town must seem pretty deserted and empty when the *pālkhī* moves on after just one day's celebration there. The people must simply go back to living with their same old sorrows and pleasures and their everyday business.

1. *Jilebīs* are a sweet made of fermented dough extruded into pretzel-like shapes, fried, and soaked in sugar syrup. *Sev* is a noodle-like string of gram flour extruded through a press and deep-fried in oil.

Is that the only effect the *pālkhī* has? When the circus goes through town, the children all start playing circus games. One of them might even try to become a circus performer someday. After the *pālkhī* of Dnyaneshwar has gone through the town, is there any likelihood of some boy giving up the keeping of accounts of profits and losses and taking up this path of devotion? And might it even occur to the adults that going through their town is the embodiment of a principle that is quite different from that of merely making a living?

❀

I have come wandering back from the stream. It has started to drizzle. Through the rain I can hear the cymbals and drums and *bhajan* singing. I go from one tent to another. The standard roles of the women taking care of the kitchen and the men earning the keep also seem to apply here. Some are taking care of the work, and some are singing in the *bhajans.* Both acquire exactly the same merit.

I am standing beside a couple of the tents listening to the *bhajans.* I am getting tired of hearing them. Hour after hour, the same *bhajans* in the same melodies—from which all the spirit has been lost. Is this simply because the words can't be heard?

For a *Wārkarī* the *bhajan* takes the place of *pūjā.*[1] Isn't it also possible to do a *bhajan* by yourself? Once the drum is added and two or three people join in the singing, the *bhajan* turns into a group performance. The melody and the in-

1. *Pūjā* is all the ritual of worship done, often individually, before the iconic representations of gods, which involves prostration or bowing before the image and the offering of flowers, coconuts, or other specified offerings.

struments then become the predominant things. The words get lost—and with them, reflection too?

Let it be as it may. I don't feel any enthusiasm for these *bhajans.* It has all become for me just as it might for a child. He doesn't like the toy he has been given, and he can't think of any other.

After a long while, I return to the tent.

I had been asleep for some time when I woke up in the middle of the night. I groped my way out of the tent, trying hard not to step on the other people's hands and feet, and stood up outside.

There was a great stillness everywhere. The entire *pālkhī* was sound asleep. The sky was twinkling with stars. Underneath that vast open sky my mind began to fill with joy. I started to feel lighter and lighter. I felt as if my body was pervading the wide open atmosphere. For that instant I wasn't standing on this earth. I was pervaded by the feeling of unbounded space.

1109. *Beloved Arjuna, those who declare that this Self is confined in the body are like those who say that the ether can be confined in the shape of a pot.*

1110. *O wise Arjuna, it neither assumes nor abandons bodily shape; it is eternally the same.*

1111. *As day and night appear and vanish from the sky, so do bodies come and go by the power of the spirit.*

1112. *So in the body it neither acts nor causes action, nor is it the promoter of spontaneous events.*

1113. *Thus of itself it is not subject to the less or the more; it may be present in the body yet is untouched by it.*

Jnāneshvari *Thirteen*

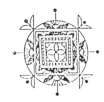

CHAPTER EIGHT

# Natepute

The rain often comes along as far as the edge of town to see the *pālkhī* off. Today it did that too as we were leaving Baradgav.

The afternoon meal was to be near the temple of Sadhu Buva. The stopover for the night: Natepute.

When we left Baradgav, I counted the *pālkhī*, and it came to seven thousand.

The *pālkhī*'s meal stop is usually different from the stop it makes for the night. At the meal stop they don't take the *pālkhī* itself down from its cart, nor do they do an *āratī*. The line of people taking *darśan* is always there, of course. When it is time for a stop, a horn is blown. It is an embossed brass horn, a good ten spans long. Two men hold it up, and one man blows it. They turn its mouth in all directions as it is being blown. When the time for the stop has come to an end, they blow the horn three times at intervals. At the third sounding of the horn the *pālkhī* begins to move.

During the afternoon stop the *Wārkarīs* are usually all spread out. Some of them might erect a tent just to do the cooking in. But for the most part they do their cooking and eat the meal itself right out in the open—after taking care to see about the availability of water. That is the reason why some of the *diṇḍīs* go on a whole mile beyond the *pālkhī* for their stop.

I happened not to know that, so I had a lot of trouble at this particular stop finding our *diṇḍī*. As usual I had gone out of the *diṇḍī*, and I was wandering about here and there. I came up to the temple of Sadhu Buva. And I went onward wandering along the stream there. The *Wārkarīs* had crowded into the water to bathe. Nobody eats without bathing. They will bathe wherever they find water, no matter how it looks. They all stood here in the stream, crowded and pressed together. The water had long since become utterly filthy. In one place it had turned red like blood. Maybe because of some disinfectant or because somebody had rinsed a new sari in it that had bled its color!

I crossed over and went beyond the stream. The area there was raised quite high. Far off over the fields I could see where the bullock carts and the trucks had stopped. Saris and dhotis had been spread out to dry here and there right on the ground. It looked like the fields had been painted with wide swathes of color. To one side just about all I could see was trucks. I counted at least twenty-five of them.

Our *diṇḍī*'s truck was not among them. I looked on the other side of the road where ten more trucks had been parked. It wasn't among them either.

I turned back—having gotten the idea that our people must have stopped on the near side of the stream.

I was in no hurry at all. I was just walking along enjoying myself. If I didn't get my meal, I still had peanuts in my bag. I must have looked strange walking along there simply enjoying myself: a camera over my shoulder, my bag hung around my neck! People would turn and look at me.

Everyone who comes along here is for sure a *Wārkarī*, or failing that, a shopkeeper. Occasionally I would scribble something down in my notebook. That must have seemed even more peculiar. Even I felt it to be rather strange.

I have taken a seat here on a rock. A *Wārkarī* has come and sat down beside me: white cap, long shirt, and pajama pants. His body is gaunt; his skin color, black.

I try to guess who he might be, rather in the manner of trying to describe unseen someone riding on a camel. What must his occupation be? Definitely not a farmer. His face is very sharp and quick. But he doesn't seem to be a teacher either. I can't see any pen or pencil stuck in his pocket. He must be an artisan or a small shopkeeper.

I feel amused at myself for playing this game. But I go on with it. I notice the dirty cloth bag in his hands. It has a little bit of embroidery on it. It is not too likely his wife did it. Probably it was a daughter who goes to school. His situation in life must be just so-so.

He must be talkative by nature, but also obstinate. I can see how his expression might change if he were to be crossed. His fingers are tapered. He has got to feel more at home in the world of imagination than in dealing with practical affairs.

While my inspection is in progress, he pulls out his tobacco. He kneads it skillfully. He slaps one palm against the other and flourishes his one hand. I'm convinced—he is an artisan.

He stuffs the tobacco in his mouth before he asks me, "You from Poona?"

When I tell him yes he says, "They say there was terrible damage done in Poona."

Once again, as soon as I tell him yes, he says, "I'm from Pandharpur."

I ask him in surprise, "Do people from Pandharpur go with the *pālkhī* too?"

He said, "Lots. There must be fifty of us at least. They go along right from the start at Alandi."

That struck me as being just about as improbable as someone from the Konkan coming up to the Desh to get coconuts. I asked him, "How many years have you been going along?"

"It's been at least twenty years."

"Where do you live in Pandharpur?"

He told me the name of a lane. I asked him, "What's your business?"

"I'm a carpenter."

I was happy that one of my guesses had turned out right.

"When you come along here on the pilgrimage, who looks after your business?"

"My uncle, my nephew, and my brother are all there. They let me take the time off."

Another one of my guesses had been proven right. The carpenter went on to say, "Only, this time I met the *pālkhī* at Phaltan. Some people had invited me from the neighboring town to look for water."

"To look for water?"

"I know how to find water."

"You take a forked branch and look for water that way, huh?"

"That's not how I do it. No matter how deep the water may be, when I reach that spot it's like I become possessed."

"How many times have you predicted correctly?"

"How many times? Every time. I don't go looking for

water with some machine. It's a supernatural power behind me."

And so the carpenter started telling me stories about finding water. A Gujar from Marathwada invited him once. He had just built himself a new house. He wanted to plant an orchard. He had already dug one dry well and given it up. The carpenter went there. He inspected all the likely places in the neighborhood. Then he stopped in one place and fell silent. The Gujar asked him urgently, "What's happened?" The carpenter couldn't speak. But finally he said, helplessly, "You'll find water here. But somebody is going to die as a sacrifice."

I broke into the story to ask, "Who was to be the sacrifice?"

But the carpenter knew the exact technique for telling his story. He made as if he hadn't heard me and went on to tell the rest.

He had been on close terms with the Gujar's father from the time he was a boy. What fabulous style they lived in then! And the old man himself was a godly person. And what a way he died! He had prepared a feast to serve to the entire village. He instructed his sons to paint the house. The old man himself settled on the day for the feast. Somebody asked him, "What's the reason for the feast?" The old man said, "Because it's a happy day—the Lord is going to give *darśan* of himself."

On the day of the feast all the villagers came. Right away that morning the old man himself had gone out to his farmhouse in the fields. He walked around the whole house before he left. In various places they had drawn *rāṅgoḷī* designs on the floor.[1] The brahmans had prepared

1. *Rāṅgoḷī* is a powder made of soft white stone used to draw figures by hand before an icon or on a floor where entertainment is to be given.

everything for an important *pūjā*. He took some of the *prasād* and went out to the farmhouse.

The villagers came and ate. The feast was over. From the farmhouse in the fields one of the servants came beating his chest—crying that the old man had died. Everyone went out to the farmhouse. The old man seemed as if he had gone to sleep with a smile on his face. How mightily meritorious! He had known the very day he was to die.

I asked him once again, "Who was to be the sacrifice?"

Without giving an answer to my question, the carpenter started to tell me about the engineers from Poona and Bombay. Some bigshot engineers had come to look for water; but they had all failed. The reason for their failure was this—the goddess who dwelt there. She was the one who had fooled them. And their machines too. She had done to them just what had befallen the Kauravas in Maya's assembly hall. Where there *was* water she had showed on the instruments that all was dry. And where there wasn't any she had indicated there was a great abundance.

I made one last effort, "But who was to be the sacrifice?"

The carpenter went on telling his story as if he were in a trance. He had shown them the place. They had dug down a good twenty feet. They couldn't find any water. Everyone started to look at him suspiciously. The carpenter already knew for certain what was going to happen. He showed them a place in the well and said, "Put some dynamite there. But be sure to get the digging tools and the men out first. If somebody gets killed, don't blame it on me."

The Gujar was standing nearby. The carpenter told him, "Don't stay here when they do the blasting. Go home."

"But I want to see."

The carpenter said, "Don't put the blame on me afterwards. Go home."

The Gujar didn't go home. The explosion went off. A

spring of water the thickness of a man's thigh came writhing out of the earth like a snake. The Gujar started to dance. The carpenter's attention was directed instead toward the house. The Gujar had barely raised his head upon seeing the water when a loud cry came from the house. The Gujar's wife had vomited once and fallen down dead. They all ran to the house.

The Gujar said, "Why didn't you tell me beforehand that it was my wife who would die? What's the point of doing all this without my wife here?"

The carpenter said, "I wasn't allowed to tell you. I did tell you that somebody was going to die as a sacrifice."

The Gujar broke down and sobbed, "Lord! I don't even have a son. What shall I *do*?"

The carpenter had compassion on him. He said, "Don't cry! You'll get married again in six months. You'll still get your first son."

The carpenter had ended his tale. He said to me, "That's how it is. God gives us one—and takes another. In all this world who is completely happy?"

I asked the carpenter, "So you read the future too?"

"The goddess who demands the sacrifice tells me."

"Which goddess is she? Is she your family deity?"

"Oh no! Vitthal is our family deity now."

The carpenter held up the *tulsī* necklace around his throat and showed it to me. I asked him, "Well then, how can you believe in this goddess too?"

"What can I do? She takes possession of my body."

"How much money do you get for finding water?"

"I'm not allowed to ask for money. Whoever invites me pays me for my coming and going. He takes care of my food and lodging. When I leave he honors me with a dhoti and a sari for my wife. I don't ask for them. There are those who do ask. Usually they are the ones who have lost their art."

The moment we had finished our talk the carpenter stood up and said, "So long." And swinging his bag he went briskly away.

I also got up—in order to take a look at the temple of Sadhu Buva.

❀

It is a Hemadpanti temple. Fortified walls on all four sides around it. There are small rooms in the walls. *Wārkarīs* are sitting in these rooms eating their meals. I make a circumambulation of the temple.

Exactly half way around the circumambulation I notice a gentleman standing with his back up against the temple. He is wearing a good wool coat. Also a pure white shirt and a white dhoti of the same kind—tucked up above his knees. He has a cap on his head, rings on both his hands, and a wristwatch with a gold band.

There is no mistaking that the man is rich. But the way he stands there all alone is what seems especially striking. You normally encounter the higher class *Wārkarīs* each in his own little group.

We glance at one another a couple of times. We both hold back from one another, as educated people will. Finally, one of us makes a *namaskār* and the restraint is broken.

We introduce ourselves. I tell him (like I tell everyone else), "I've just come along to see the *pālkhī*." I tell him about my survey work, and I give him one of my forms to fill out. It all goes according to what has become by now pretty much a standard procedure. Like an insurance agent this pet survey project of mine pushes itself forward without the slightest timidity.

Fortunately, in this instance the form was put aside. He started to speak—his very own mind! Instead of just giving me information, he made an effort to win me over from my lack of faith. He started right off with, "This is a pilgrimage of joy. Here we don't have special forms of worship for special times. You can just close your eyes at any time and make your heart quiet for a moment. You just keep right on walking. And there's real satisfaction. Dnyanobaray says, 'When I behold your feet, my mind stays calm and still.' The saints and holy men have spoken about this Path for hundreds of years. What is the very highest of high goals—but the attainment of God! That is achieved through this Path. You've come along once now—you'll always continue to come along. There's no way out of that. That's the greatness of Pandhari. 'First I built the town of Pandhari, then I built Vaikunthanagari.' And this is what Tukobaray says—'Though he's been on ten million pilgrimages, but never has gone to see Pandhari, let his attainments all go up in flame.'

"There's no other pilgrimage like this one throughout the whole of India. I'm telling you from my very own experience. I've gone on all the pilgrimages around India three times. I went first class on the train to Badrinath and Kedarnath three times. I've seen the Kumbha Melas. It's all just frolic and fun! Processions of horses and elephants, the glitter of gold and silver. Go to Kashi, go to Rameshwaram, they all ask for nothing but money. You can't sit down quietly for two minutes in any one of those temples. But how free you feel here! The *Wārkarīs* go walking along singing their *bhajans*. Every footstep is taken in the name of Vitthal! Nobody asks anything from anyone. There's nothing that compares with it in all of India. I speak from experience."

I asked him, "Which *diṇḍī* are you with?"

His face grew troubled. He said, "I have just one complaint about them. They are very strict about the purity-pollution restrictions in our *diṇḍī*! They have separate rows at meals and distinguish between the pure and the impure. Have the saints ever advocated this kind of distinction-making? On the Pathway of God there shouldn't be any discrimination."

I asked him, "Then why do you go with that *diṇḍī*?"

"Other than the purity-pollution business everyone's behavior is faultless. These people are really very good. There's always a *bhajan* or a reading or something going on. You learn a lot about the saints. If you don't know something, you just ask them and they explain it. Folks like us need the company of the learned ones."

❀

Smelling the fragrance of the flat bread baking all around me made me grow very hungry. I had come back to the far side of the stream from the temple looking for our *diṇḍī*. I went up to each one of the trucks and asked the location of our *diṇḍī*. After I had inquired in ten different places, I began to feel that I was lost.

As it turned out, our *diṇḍī* had gone on a whole mile farther before it stopped—near a wide, open-mouth irrigation well. Some of the other *diṇḍīs* had also stopped there. It was mealtime, and everything was in commotion. I quickly ate my food, and then I turned and headed over to where a *diṇḍī* of people from the *Koḷī* community had stopped.[1]

1. The name *Koḷī* includes a variety of tribes which are settled predominantly in the Konkan or coastal districts of Maharashtra. The major tribe is the *Mahādev Koḷīs*, who are settled largely in Thana District.

As I was ambling along there, I felt as if I was back wandering about in my home region. It felt really good to see that style of clothes I had known before from the Konkan and to hear the Konkan dialect. Compared with the *diṇḍīs* from up on the Desh, this *diṇḍī* had greater enthusiasm, and it was noisier and more lively.

There were some very tall trees standing around the well. Clusters of people were sitting under each tree. Right at the well itself, others were busy scouring the huge cooking pots. A barber was engrossed in giving a man a shave under one of the trees. Two or three other men were lined up there waiting their turns.

It suddenly occurs to me that there would be a certain special felicity in having yourself shaved out here in the middle of the Dindiravan.[1] Compared with sitting in a soft chair in a barbershop, where you count your white hairs, the gaps in your teeth, and the wrinkles on your face in the mirrors both before you and behind you, how much more fun it is to have your whiskers dispatched where you can watch the grass, the trees, and the earth. It can't have a good effect on you always to see the constantly growing signs of your age in the mirror. Out here an occasional leaf will come fall on your head, or a butterfly might even playfully perch on your ear. Once a month regularly for the past twenty years I have sat in the barber's chair, dripping with sweat underneath the tightly bound apron, suffering from the prickling of the fresh-cut hair down my neck, seeing the hurry in the eyes of

1. Traditionally, "Dindiravan" is the name of the forest that once grew along the bank of the Bhima River. One of the temple sites in Pandharpur still retains this name.

the other customers sitting in a line behind me, and hearing the restless rustling of newspapers. Right now I am tempted to go just as I am and sit down in front of this barber here. Having your hair cut here seems just about as natural as an antelope casting his horns.

I start to talk with the barber sahib in an easy, familiar way. He too is chatting with me while he does his work. This is his tenth time going along with the *pālkhī*. He just covers the expenses of the pilgrimage by plying his trade. On rare occasions he has five or ten rupees left over. But his main purpose is not simply to ply his trade. After all, all those who go along with the *pālkhī* are saints. There is a true joy in serving them.

His face shows complete satisfaction. The most contented people you meet up with are always the carpenters, the blacksmiths, the cobblers, and the other small-time craftsmen like them. Is that because their ambitions are so limited? Or do they get their contentment from having an art they can call all their own? Whatever may be the case, I think that of all people, they really know best what is required for contentment.

❀

We have left the Sadhubuva temple. A loudspeaker, which has been mounted on top of a car, is following after us screaming *bhajans*. The car belongs to a *biḍī* factory owner, and it isn't about to leave the *Wārkarīs* in peace. The noise the speaker makes is so loud it drowns out the *Wārkarīs*' own *bhajans*. Is this stupid aggravation going to continue with us like this all the way to Pandharpur? To me it feels as if everything that is interesting, everything that is serious and important about the *pālkhī* is being spoiled.

The thought occurs to me that that factory owner ought to be brought out here himself and told to listen. He might feel ashamed of himself and shut off the speaker.

The sun is striking down at us from above. Thirst has once again begun to trouble us. The government water tanker comes along, and everyone runs toward it. Just within these five miles I have grown very tired. I look at the *Wārkarīs* ahead of me and at those still behind me—am I the only one who is tired, or are all of them also? That *Wārkarī* man over there, that elderly woman, that fat man—like machines, they all keep right on moving their feet. Nobody is prepared to stop. So of course I don't stop either.

The fatigue you feel here is very different from the usual kind. It is a crowd phenomenon. No one is allowed to get tired on his own account. When the person in front takes a step, the person behind him takes a step. When the whole *diṇḍī* starts to lag from fatigue, they all start singing a new *abhaṅga* very loudly. They strike the heavy brass cymbals together with renewed force. People's attention is distracted from their feet.

It isn't that the people who are really tired don't stop. They sit down to rest by the side of the road, but they won't let the last *diṇḍī* in the procession pass by them. Before that can happen, they summon up their strength and get up and mix back into the procession.

I saw one of the women from our *diṇḍī* sitting on the ground with her back up against a mile stone—as if she were trying to hide the distance. Whenever somebody else gets tired and stops, you feel a little better. It gives you the excuse to stop, too. I said to her, "You sure look tired!"

"I just couldn't take another step."

"But what are you going to do just sitting there?"

"What do you mean, just sit? I'll come along, slowly, slowly. I'll just arrive a little bit late."

"Go and get a ride in the *diṇḍī*'s truck."

She told me vehemently, "Oh no! I won't ride in the truck even if my feet break."

❀

Our stopover in Natepute is in tents.

After the *pālkhī* has been properly settled in its place for the night, everyone heads off to his own spot. People's faces are all drawn with fatigue.

We have arrived at our tents. There in the middle is a heap of bedding rolls they have unloaded from the truck. We each find our own and sit down on it right there. We don't have the strength left to pick them up and carry them into the tents. When I have sat down I am truly amazed at how my legs could have stayed upright for so long!

The tea is all ready. But we don't even have the wish to get up and get some in our tumblers. Just as soon as we have actually drunk the tea, however, we start to brighten up. One after another we pick up our bedding rolls and go to our tents.

❀

After the evening meal is over, all the people get busy in their tents tending their feet—just as we are. We share our vaseline or coconut oil with each other. These are the days when people really pamper their feet! Would they otherwise have spread their toes apart and carefully examined the cracks between them? Would they ever have turned up the soles of their feet and gingerly run their fingers over the blisters?

One of the gentlemen in our *diṇḍī* has just come into our tent. I suddenly realize how incredibly dark he has become. I remember how his face looked when I saw him at Saswad. I tell him, "How dark you've become!"

He laughs and then tells me, "You've gotten dark too."

I look around at the others, and I realize how dark the sun has tanned us all. And our skin has gotten all dried out.

❀

I had established the rule, before going to bed each night, of wandering about here and there to see things. The people in my tent were starting to get sleepy. I got up and went outside.

I bought some tea at one of the pushcarts. At another one I got some *pān*. Then I set off in the direction of the *pālkhī*'s tent.

Except for the glare of the pressure lamps the shopkeepers had hung up high here and there, it was completely dark all around us. I could hear a *bhajan* coming from somewhere beside the *pālkhī*. In between there was a compound fenced in with barbed wire. I bent my head and started to go through the wires because that was the shortest way, when a thorn stuck in my foot. As I was trying to pull it out I raised my head, and the barbs on the wire scored my neck.

Farther along, the tents were crowded together so close they were touching. Several times I tripped as I made my way through the middle of the pegs and ropes. There was total silence amidst all those tents. I had been planning on going as far as the *pālkhī*'s tent. But in the end I didn't get there either, and I continued wandering among the dark tents. I stood and stared out into the darkness with my hands on my hips, and I asked myself once again, "Why did I come here?"

At that very moment the sounds coming from the *bhajan* beside the *pālkhī* stopped. The abrupt stillness made me feel even more unsettled. I began to envy all these *Wārkarīs* who were sleeping so soundly back there in our own tents as well as all those still beyond me. They had all fallen asleep in the perfect contentment of the pilgrim journey. Making their feet tired had become the major accomplishment of their lives! Once they had sung a couple of *bhajans*, they felt completely fulfilled.

I envied them. But not with any sort of great regret. It certainly wasn't a case of their being the fortunate and of my being the unfortunate. I understood that this kind of satisfaction wasn't for me. I needed something more besides.

I came back around toward where the shops were. I hadn't gone more than a dozen steps beyond the bazaar when I heard a shout behind me, "Thief! Thief!"

A young fellow ran rapidly right past me. He was clutching a sheet, which he had wrapped around his shoulders. He had scarcely gone ten steps farther when the people who were chasing after him came up, shouting, "Catch him! Catch him!" In a moment they had caught him, and they started to beat him up with their feet and their fists.

This was the first time I had ever seen anyone so frightened—or anyone who got so badly mauled in such a short time. He had put his head down and held it between his hands. His whole body was jerking with the force of each blow. And he kept shouting just this one sentence, "I'm not a thief! I'm not a thief!"

When he could bear the beating no longer he started to wail. He banged his head on the ground in front of them all and said, "I'm a *Wārkarī* just like you. I'll even tell you the name of my *diṇḍī*. I just came to get some tea. I'm a poor man. Please don't beat me!"

But the men who were beating him were in no state to listen to him. As they continued pounding him, two of them grabbed hold of his shirt and hauled him to his feet. I could hear the sound of the shirt tearing. They held him from both sides and forced him to walk. His feet dragged along like a prisoner going to the gallows whose limbs turn to water. His pants were torn up above the knee, and his shoulder was bared. One corner of the sheet that had been wrapped around him caught on something, and for a few steps it hung stretched-out behind him before it fell to the ground. His head was hanging forward, and he was weeping loudly as he told them, "I'm not a thief! Don't take me to the police. I have little kids. I'll lose my good reputation back home. If you want to, beat me up some more."

The men who were dragging him along took him away. In no time at all a crowd of thirty or forty people had gathered around. Somebody swore violently, and they all disappeared into the darkness beyond the lamps.

I went back to our tent. But not without bringing something with me that kept gnawing at my mind—was he really a thief?

*July 18, 1961*

303. *When the wind of concern with the body ceases to blow, O warrior, the individual soul attains to union with Brahma as the waves merge in the ocean.*
304. *Such a man immediately becomes one with Me; as the clouds merge with the sky at the end of the rainy season,*
305. *he has indeed been united with Me, then although he remains in the body he is no longer at the mercy of those qualities of which the body is born.*

Jnāneshvari *Fourteen*

CHAPTER NINE

# Malshiras

The stream of the Mandavi River is flowing by, after artfully dodging around a great sheet of protruding bedrock. We have come walking four miles from Natepute in the fresh morning air.

I stand on the sheet of rock by the river and cast a glance in all directions. The expansiveness of the scene greatly delights me. There is this same kind of sheetrock around the river back in our hometown in the Konkan; but there the river is all pent up within it.

I contrast the two parts of the country in my mind. There are rocky knolls standing all around our river back home that seem to smother it. Even if you were to stand right at the level of the river, you wouldn't be able to see another person standing just a little beyond you. Here you can stand anywhere and feel that everyone's eyes are on you. When I go traveling out on the Desh I feel startled—caught by surprise. There is no place to take cover and hide.

I can still remember how I felt when I first came up to the Desh, as if I had come onto something quite grand. Such expansive fields! And people wore clothes that covered up their entire bodies. Even the simple farmers here could recite the sayings of the saints. Where we come from the clothing consists of a loincloth and a blanket to wrap up in. Our holy "sayings" are curses and quarrels. The Desh has produced one saint after another. In our part of the country, who has the time to become a saint? Anyone who sat around writing *abhaṅgas* simply couldn't survive. And if he did survive, it could only be in a mental hospital.

I am watching the *Wārkarīs* as they bathe in the stream. Both in front of me and behind me saris and dhotis have been spread out in the sun to dry. The clothes are held out upright in the current of the stream and then wrung out. Some are pounding and squeezing their clothes on the rock. The hair on many people's heads has turned white from the soapsuds. Some of them are scrubbing each other's backs. Others are scraping the mud off their feet with jagged stones.

I feel as if I am seeing it all for the first time! I fill my eyes with it as if I were looking at a beautiful picture. I look at it for a long time before I start to descend toward the stream myself, jumping over the clothes that are spread out in my way.

I have found a nice big boulder and wrapped the towel around me. I take off my shirt and then my undershirt. But I do all this very hesitantly. There are also women bathing nearby, and I feel terribly self-conscious. The moment I actually stand right in the middle of the scene, which I had been watching all this time as being so beautiful, I somehow lose all trace of its beauty.

The next small rest stop was at Chitalewadi. Here a *riṅgaṇ* took place.[1] Everyone tells me that from here onward there will be *riṅgaṇs* all the time: both circular ones and standing ones. During all the preceding trek there had been two *riṅgaṇs*, one at Lonand and the other one beyond Phaltan—at Vedhani. I had missed both of them.

Even though I was present there, I as good as missed the *riṅgaṇ* at Chitalewadi too. The *riṅgaṇ* was taking place among the thick trees of a hamlet. A wall of people was standing in between watching it. Even the trees were loaded full of spectators. When the *riṅgaṇ* actually started, I was thrown back by the vast thronging of the crowd.

So it was from some distance away that I tried to trace the pattern of the *riṅgaṇ* from the movement of the people. One man, in the very effort of trying to stay standing aloft on a tree branch, came tumbling down. A couple of the branches broke, and the children who were sitting up there came falling down one after the other like large beads off a broken string. The *riṅgaṇ* must be in full swing—I told myself.

I got up and came back to the road and sat down in the garden plot across the way. To escape the shafts of the sun I kept my head in the shade of a papaya tree and spread my arms and legs out into a little irrigation channel. Just beyond me two young *Wārkarīs* were lying sprawled on the ground. I asked them about the *riṅgaṇ*: "Didn't you go to see the *riṅgaṇ*?"

They both just barely smiled. I looked at them more carefully. They had the *tulsī* necklace around their necks. But they didn't seem to be like the other *Wārkarīs*. They

---

1. A *riṅgaṇ* (or *raṅgaṇ*) is a mass ritual performance during which the two horses that accompany the *pālkhī* are made to run before the assembled devotees. For a description see pp. 241–42.

both had books with them. When he saw that my eyes had strayed to the books, one of them told me, "We're students at the *Wārkarī* school in Alandi. So we have to go along with the *pālkhī*."

I asked him out of surprise, "A *Wārkarī* school?"

"It's a four-year course. We're in our last year."

"What are you going to do when you graduate?"

"*Kīrtans* and *pravacanas*."[1]

"You must have had some other education."

"No."

"So then what are you going to do to make a living?"

"Just this."

I asked him, "Do you get any money from this?"

"Not really. We are supplied with clothes and whatnot from people here and there. Villagers invite us to live in their villages—even for as long as a month."

"How are you going to support a family on that?"

"This isn't just some kind of business."

"Are you married?"

"Yes."

"Then how are you going to support your wife and children?"

"We have a farm."

"But you must surely have some brothers too."

"I have four brothers."

"So you're going to go wandering about giving *kīrtans*—and they're going to be doing all the farming. Misunderstandings are bound to arise sometime."

"My brothers have agreed to it."

I was asking him all these questions with a great show of being myself a practical man of affairs. But inside me I could feel the laughter bubbling up.

1. A *pravacana* is a recitation or discourse of a religious nature.

The *pālkhī* has started out again from Chitalewadi, onward to Malshiras. Once again the sun beating down. Once again the thirst. Once again a straggling pace!

Then the sun starts to decline and the wind begins to blow. The *pālkhī*'s spirit is reviving. The cymbals and the drums have begun to sound loudly again.

I also feel fresh vigor as I walk alongside the *diṇḍī*. Sometimes I go briskly on ahead. Sometimes I stop and let the whole procession pass by me, and then I walk along with the old and lame *Wārkarīs* who are lagging behind.

I've counted the *pālkhī* again. It has gone above eight thousand. Now it keeps growing continuously. You see *Wārkarī* men and women standing in groups at the side of the road. When the *pālkhī* comes by, they apply the dust of the road to their foreheads and join in. But before they do so, the others who have come to bid them farewell prostrate themselves at their feet. If the person who is doing the prostration is someone older than himself, the *Wārkarī* raises him up while he is still bending down, and he in turn falls at the feet of the other. Those the same age embrace each other. The women also meet in the same way and prostrate themselves at one another's feet. One of them wipes the tears from her eyes with the loose end of her sari. A pampered child among them thrashes about with his arms and legs and starts to cry.

The *pālkhī*'s pace has picked up. Feet, feet, feet! All you see in every direction is moving feet. Occasionally an echoing sound of "Om—Om" draws near and passes on ahead. Everyone stares. A huge dark-skinned *Wārkarī*, clad in a jacket and striking the nine-inch brass cymbals in his hands, goes rushing past us like a locomotive. Every fifteen or twenty minutes he comes and he goes, making a circumambulation of the *pālkhī* procession.

❀

Somebody right at my side asked me, "How do you like it here?"

I said, "Fine!"

The man who had spoken glanced at my notebook and said, "I make a note in my diary, too, every day. Then I can tell all about the *pālkhī* to the school children when I get back home."

He begins to tell me stories then about the village where he is a teacher. It is in the mountains, very remote and poor. The children there don't know anything about the outside world. They themselves really ought to have been brought along with the *pālkhī*. While he was talking he pointed to the green touring car ahead on the road and said, "That car belongs to our Madam."

There must have been at least a mile left to Malshiras. I suddenly sensed that the teacher, who had been speaking to me so equably all this time, was starting to become uneasy. I suggested to him, "Let's go on together now. I'll give you the information I've collected, and you can show me yours."

The teacher quickly replied, "I've got to go on ahead. Our bullock carts must have arrived already at the stopover."

I asked him, "What are you going to do when you get there?"

"The tents where we'll be staying have to be put up. I have to help out with the cooking. And if everyone doesn't do the work that's assigned to him, the Madam gets angry. I have to go. We'll meet tonight."

I said, "How about near the *pālkhī*'s tent?"

He gestured yes with his hand as he was turning away and went on ahead.

There was still a good mile left to Malshiras. I started talking with anyone I met. Whenever a *Wārkarī* came near me I would just talk to him about being tired or about the growing numbers of people joining the *pālkhī*. Some of them looked at me suspiciously. Others just answered the particular question I asked them and went on ahead. Except for me everyone was walking too fast and was feeling too tired to want to talk. But then there was this troubled *Wārkarī* man who told me a few things. He told me all about how his store in a certain village had failed and how he had gone then to another village. And about how he had just settled down there nicely when he lost seven or eight thousand rupees in a robbery. And about how he suffered because he had no offspring.

Or there was this other very ambitious *Wārkarī* whose restless toil and trouble hadn't grown quiet even here. He was telling me about his efforts to start a new *diṇḍī*. He had gathered together all the *Wārkarīs* in his village and put up seventy-five rupees for a tent. Now they wanted to gain entry into one of the established *diṇḍīs*. He had been working on it for the last two years. When the *pālkhī* returned to Alandi after the pilgrimage they were going to make a decision about it at the meeting of the *diṇḍī*-leaders.

Here at last is Malshiras. The *Wārkarīs* have unfurled their ochre banners, and they have started to flutter in the breeze. There is no time now for talking. We begin to see the people from the town who have come out to meet us. School girls have come, laughing and playing, in their groups. Some boys have arrived on their bicycles. One family has been sitting waiting for the *pālkhī*, and now they leap to their feet. The father picks up one of the little boys. The mother is filling a bag with what they had brought along to eat. The town leaders must be standing now waiting at the entrance of the town. There will be a *pūjā* for the *pālkhī*, and with new vigor the *bhajan* groups in the town will dance and sing the *pālkhī* to its place of rest.

❀

Our tents at this stopover ended up near the town's *kacerī.*[1]

When we have finished looking after our feet, a few people decide to write letters. Some of them sent letters home at every overnight stop it seemed. As he was writing a letter, one man told me, "Except for this pilgrimage with the *pālkhī* I can't be away from my wife even for a few hours. When the children have all grown up I'm going to bring her along too."

There are three married couples in our *diṇḍī.* The habit they had from home of caring for each other didn't forsake them here either. At every stop the husband and wife would be coming and going between their respective tents. The wife would come over and ask her husband, "Did you have any trouble on the walk today? Do you want anything to

1. The courthouse, jail, and administrative offices of a town.

eat? Do you need a new handkerchief? Have you changed your clothes?" The husband in turn would go over to her tent and ask, "I'm writing a letter home. You want to write something to the kids?" Or, "If you're tired, go ride in the truck tomorrow. You've taken care of your bundle of saris, haven't you?"

Hearing all these questions right there in front of everyone, the wife would become very proper and demure. Sometimes the two of them would even be teased. But neither of them would pay any attention to it. They couldn't bear to be without this constant caring for each other, that much was true.

It struck me that this kind of love is the magic charm people apply as a remedy against God's evil trick of making each and every one of us be born all alone into this life. Let it be forty, fifty, or even sixty years, the charm still does its work.

I also wrote two letters while everyone was at it. One to my wife and the other to my older brother. I had sent letters previously from Lonand. I came to understand that we could even receive mail while we were walking with the *pālkhī*. For an address it is enough just to write "The Dnyaneshwar Palkhi Pilgrimage" and the name of your *diṇḍī*. The letters are delivered to whichever town the *pālkhī* happens to be in at the time and are given to the people who are in charge of the *pālkhī*. When the *pālkhī* starts moving again, one of the *pālkhī*'s assistants takes the letters and distributes them among the *diṇḍīs*. The head of each *diṇḍī* takes the letters that are addressed to his *diṇḍī*, and as he walks along he shouts out people's names and hands them their letters.

"It must be hard to be living in Poona now. Please come and stay here," said a letter from my brother. It had gone to Poona first and then come on to me. The only thing is, I didn't get the letter until after I had arrived in Pandharpur.

But you *do* get letters.

I have finished writing my letters and given them to one of the assistants to mail. I have just been lying around here in the tent. I don't feel like going out. I don't feel very much like seeing the town either.

As a matter of fact I haven't really gone out and taken a look at any of the towns where the *pālkhī* has made its stopovers. Whenever the *pālkhī* enters a town, it adds its own color to the town. The normal appearance of the town gets hidden—by the crowds that come for the inevitable fair that accompanies the *pālkhī*, by the thousands of people waiting in lines for *darśan*, and by the great heaps of things specially put out for sale at the time of the *pālkhī*! The things that are prepared as food are usually made just as badly as they possibly can be. There is no tea in the tea. There is no milk in the milk. The vegetables are dealt out in meager bunches. The scales are rigged to weigh light.

I can't remember that a single one of the *Wārkarīs* in our *diṇḍī* ever ate outside the *diṇḍī*. Nobody even talked about going to see a movie. Along the way I met a man with a pushcart who told me, "Our customers usually aren't the *Wārkarīs*. They are usually the people who come out for the fairs." I could see for myself how little the *Wārkarīs* care about buying anything to eat or drink. A town is just another place to make a stopover. Today that is how I have started to feel about it too.

As I am lying around in the tent I take out a book of *abhaṅgas* to read. I bought it at the last overnight stop because I couldn't make out the words in all the *abhaṅgas* they were singing. As I read the *abhaṅgas* in the book one by one, I find myself becoming more and more engrossed in them. There are places where the saints become so utterly anguished, where they plead with Vitthal, or where they even revile themselves. Even if I don't have the kind of anguish the saints experienced, I do understand it: the state of mind—that pang—that exists there before the words emerge. The joy I feel comes out of the understanding I have for this anguish of theirs.

I have also been seeing the *Wārkarīs*' anguish up to this point on the pilgrimage. It is something quite different. Its manner seems reversed. It starts out from where the saints' words leave off. It almost never reaches that state that precedes the creation of the words.

I wonder—is it this that has been bothering me about the *pālkhī* till now? As I have listened to all the many little things that people from every side have been telling me, what I have heard is the words and the sayings of the saints. Nobody seems able to speak without furnishing some proof from the saints for what they say.

*July 19, 1961*

*218. O Arjuna, devotion to Me is so mysterious that I will now describe some other ways in which it is practised.*

*219. As there is but one thread running through a woven garment from one end to the other, so they recognize no one except Me in the whole universe.*

*222. Unaware of their own greatness, they do not distinguish between the worthy and the unworthy, classing all together, they like to bow down before all.*

*223. As water pouring from a height flows downwards without effort, so is it their nature to pay respect to every creature that they see.*

*224. As the branches of fruit-laden trees bend towards the earth, so they humble themselves before all creatures.*

*225. They are always free from conceit; humility is their wealth which they offer to Me with words of homage.*

*226. Being thus always humble, honour and dishonour do not exist for them, and they easily become united with Me; always absorbed in Me, they worship Me.*

Jnāneshvari *Nine*

CHAPTER TEN

# Velapur

We left Malshiras behind. It began to seem then that the name "Malshiras" (high plain) was very apt: a flat plain, clasped right to the sky! You feel the curvature so distinctly you can actually sense that the earth is round. You get the feeling that the earth is falling away deeper and deeper. If you were to let some object go rolling away, it would just go right on rolling.

Our meal stop was to be at the stream at Khadus. But before this the *pālkhī* stopped to take a fifteen-minute rest stop. I went to find a place for myself to sit down by the side of the road. A *Wārkarī* man was sitting nearby examining the yellow pole of his banner over and over and patting it affectionately with his hand. He had a broad, full moustache and a strong, heavily built body. And what enormous *rudrākṣa* beads he had around his neck!

I asked him, "You got a new pole there?"

He said, "The pole I had first split. I somehow managed with it this far. Those bastards took six annas for this new one back at Malshiras! At home we pass out these poles for free. Thieving bastards!"

Back home he didn't just distribute banner poles for free. On the occasion of every pilgrimage he had been spending a thousand rupees. Year after year he had paid for the arrangements to feed all the *Wārkarīs* who went from his town. When the *pālkhī* returned to Alandi, he always provided a meal for 250 *Wārkarīs*! And here these bastards had taken six annas from him for the pole!

Then he told me a little about his own family. He had married his daughter off in Poona. Her home there had been washed away in the flood; but since his son-in-law had a good job, they weren't overly worried about it.

❀

The fifteen-minute rest was over. The *pālkhī* started moving on. The flat plain, the flowing breeze, the morning's fresh vigor—it was fun to be out walking.

Four men on bicycles were finding their way through the crowds. The *Wārkarī* man nearby said, "These boys are doing the pilgrimage on their bicycles. At their age we used to go in groups of twenty."

I asked him, "How many days does it take to go to Pandharpur by bicycle?"

"From our town it required just one overnight stop. We would spend one whole day in Pandharpur for *darśan*. Then we would turn around at night and cycle back."

I looked at him with particular attention. He was tall and fair-skinned and he had a large yellow turban on his head and a clean shirt and dhoti. He must have easily been six feet tall. I asked him, "How many years have you been going on foot?"

"It's been at least fifteen years. I go along with the Jaitunbai *diṇḍī*."

I had been hearing Jaitunbai's name ever since Phaltan. I had seen the crowd that had gathered at her *kīrtan*, and I had stood there a couple of minutes. I hadn't much liked the shrill style of her *kīrtan*, which she did in Muslim-style clothes.

I had been hearing her name, though, at every stop along the way. Everyone was attracted by the fact that she had become a *Wārkarī* even though she was a Muslim. Another attraction about her was that in her *kīrtans* she mingled Urdu *ghazals* with the *abhaṅgas* of the *Wārkarī* saints.[1] Her manner of singing was very bold.

I asked, "Just who is this woman?"

He replied, "She is one who has the bountiful hand of Panduranga himself upon her. She has Saraswati in her speech. There is a *gandharva* in her voice—"[2]

And so he started on his praise of her. When I realized that he wasn't going to stop, I just listened silently to him.

"When Jaitunbai became a *Wārkarī* it raised a serious threat from the Muslim community. But she faced up to them boldly. She stays apart from her own family, and she is unmarried. Her father and mother are always accompanying her in her *diṇḍī*. And what is so special about her *diṇḍī*? All the men and women in it are like brothers and sisters under one guru to each other. There is never any kind of confusion. They get along on just whatever people give them. Now she has bought a place in Pandharpur and has started work on a religious center."

I asked him, "Just where is Jaitunbai's *diṇḍī*?"

He said, "It always comes along a mile behind the rest of the *pālkhī*."

---

1. *Ghazals* are a form of Persian lyric poetry, based chiefly on themes of love, which is also very prevalent in Urdu.

2. Saraswati is the goddess of learning, music, and the arts. *Gandharvas* are a class of demigods who are known as the musicians of heaven.

And then he started to tell me about his children. He had five daughters whom he had married off. He had spent five thousand rupees for each one of them. He was sending one of his sons to college. The other two were still in high school.

He started to talk with somebody else, and I took leave of him. I stood by the side of the road and let the whole *pālkhī* procession go past me. Then I turned my face about and set off in the direction of Jaitunbai.

❀

Jaitunbai's *diṇḍī* comes half a mile behind the rest of the procession. After I had been walking along for a while, I started to see the *diṇḍī*. Right in the middle of it there was this very broad-beamed gentleman in a khaki coat. Behind him were two women dressed in Muslim-style clothes. It looked as if the *diṇḍī* had two or three hundred *Wārkarīs* in it.

I came up to the *diṇḍī* and made my way straight into it. I made a *namaskār* to Jaitunbai and asked her if I could ask her a few questions. She pointed to the man in the khaki coat ahead of her and said, "Ask him. He's my guru."

This gentleman looked as if he might be in his sixties. I asked him, "Why does your *diṇḍī* come along behind the procession?"

"They don't allow us in with the *pālkhī*'s other *diṇḍīs*."

"What town do you come from?"

"Baramati."

"Why did Jaitunbai feel that she should become a *Wārkarī*?"

"She has been drawn that way ever since she was a child. She would sing the most beautiful *abhaṅgas*. We've been watching her all this time. Her father and I are in the same trade. We're both masons, and we've worked together. It was Jaitunbai herself who made me her guru. I look after all the arrangements for the *diṇḍī*. Those people who go along with the *diṇḍī* have their expenses paid by the *diṇḍī*."

The guru ended his interview, and I turned back toward Jaitunbai. I asked her, "Have you taken the *tulsī* necklace?"

She showed me the necklace around her neck.

"How old are you?"

"Twenty-eight."

"You wear the necklace, but do you honor any other god besides Vitthal?"

She said, "Yes! Paigambar."[1]

I asked her, "Haven't you given up your Muslim faith then?"

She said, "No."

I said, "You honor Paigambar. Do you also keep all the rules of your religion?"

"Yes."

"You give performances as a *Wārkarī*. Do you then propagate the Muslim religion in them?"

She said, "No. But I do say a lot of things about it."

"Have you decided to do only this work for the rest of your life?"

"Yes! We have a center coming up in Pandharpur. Slowly, slowly people will start believing in me."

I had already heard about Jaitunbai's center. I remembered the sadhu I had met at Lonand. The technique for building up a center stood before me clearly—as if I had put it all to memory. Enticing *abhaṅgas*, a beautiful voice, perfect recitation, and boldness—if you had that much capital, that was quite sufficient. The people gather around you in big crowds. You start some kind of scheme like the feeding of a thousand or a pilgrimage to the four

1. The Prophet Mohammed.

holiest places. Once you start a *kīrtan* you don't end it until a specified sum has been collected. One person gives. Somebody else hears his name and feels as if he must also give. One entire town gives, and when the other town hears about it, they open wide their pockets.

I left Jaitunbai's *diṇḍī*, and by walking fast I came back up and joined the *pālkhī* procession. I entered our *diṇḍī* and told them the news about my "interview."

I started walking again outside the *diṇḍī*. The stop at the stream at Khadus is still a mile-and-a-half away. The procession had grown sluggish. I was also walking along very sluggishly. Somebody came up to me just then and asked, "You came to the *pālkhī*'s tent once, didn't you?"

I said, "Yes."

"I'm in the *pālkhī*'s own *diṇḍī*. I'm responsible for doing some of the *pālkhī*'s work. So you're collecting information, are you?"

I told him the nature of my work.

He said, "In my family we've been going on this pilgrimage for more than three hundred years."

I asked him, "Are you from Alandi?"

He said, "No. From near Nasik. One of my ancestors built a temple for Vitthal in our town. He saw the image of Vitthal in a dream. It told him, 'Take me out of the river. I'm in such and such a place.' In the morning my ancestor went down to the river to bathe and to say his prayers. He dived in at the place he had been told. He took hold of the image with both his hands and came back up. He set it up and built a temple for it. Ever since then the oldest person in the family has gone on this pilgrimage."

We went on talking for almost a whole mile as we walked along. He was in his forties, rather dark, a brahman by caste. From the way he acted, it appeared that he was none too happy with things. Being so very close to the *pālkhī* as he was, there was nothing new for him in it. The remarks he made were clear and bold. He told me sharply once that the *Wārkarīs* were stupid—like rhinoceroses. He gave an analysis of the classes of people that go along on the pilgrimage. There were just two classes that go. The one is extremely rich, the other extremely poor. The middle class very nearly didn't go at all. His statement was very true. I had counted the number of middle-class people of all castes among the *diṇḍīs* with the *pālkhī*. It had remained the same from Saswad on. Ninety-two men, thirty-three women.

Later on he also made this statement: "The middle class is scarcely represented in the *pālkhī*. And as long as the middle class doesn't come along, there is not going to be any change for the better in the *pālkhī*."

I remembered what one of the women in our *diṇḍī* had told me. At her in-laws' house they went every year on the *pālkhī* pilgrimage. So she also started going along. Her family back at home and her friends started laughing at her. At first she used to feel embarrassed. But later on it just became a part of her. She simply had to follow the customs of her in-laws.

If the middle class were to come along, would the *pālkhī* really and truly "change for the better?" I think it would simply stop. I asked the man what he meant by "change for the better." He couldn't tell me. It seems to me that the *pālkhī* operates just as much on people's lack of education as it does on faith. If one of these two wheels falls off, what use is the other going to be?

It looks as if today is the day for discussing as well as for witnessing just these sorts of things. As I was walking along in one *diṇḍī*, one of the men in it moved forward and started to walk ahead of the man who was carrying the *vīṇā*.[1] The man with the *vīṇā* immediately got back at him for violating his authority: he grabbed him hard under his arm and shoved him right back!

I met one college graduate who was accompanying the *pālkhī* procession when we were approaching the stream at Khadus. He told me, "I always go in a *diṇḍī* now. One year I went walking alongside the procession just like you are today. The *pālkhī* seemed completely different."

He couldn't tell me what he meant by "different." Perhaps he saw it just like I am seeing it now—and yet he had come back again and again!

❀

The stop for the afternoon meal is at the stream at Khadus. The moment we arrive, three of us from the *diṇḍī* set off to find a place to take a bath.

We avoid bathing in the stream itself. The water there has become all muddy. There is too much of a crowd there too. But there is a well over in the orchard across the way.

We zigzag across a couple of open fields, and there suddenly stands the well right before us. Trees and vines hem it in on all sides. On the far side, the handsome plumes of sugarcane. On this side, the heavy bobbing ears of sorghum. A bullock cart stands unyoked under one of the trees. The two white bullocks are resting nearby chewing their cuds.

To me it feels as if this well might have been left behind just the way it was by some strange oversight after *gandharvas* from the time of the *Mahābhārata* had created it for

1. The *vīṇā* is a traditional fretted string instrument, which the leader of a *diṇḍī* carries as a symbol of his authority.

their own pleasure. Birds are hidden in the tall trees, and they sing from time to time. A flock of sparrows is flying about in the bushes. This really and truly is a well of the *gandharvas*! It doesn't even surprise me that the night crickets here continue with their shrill melody unafraid in the middle of the day.

There are three other men like us who had learned beforehand about the location of this well. One *Wārkarī* man in his seventies, wearing just a loincloth, is getting ready to take a bath. Two young boys out swimming in the water are shooting up and catching hold of the long dangling roots of a banyan that hang out over the water.

Two more *Wārkarī* men arrive. As they are taking off their clothes they all start to make their enquiries about their respective villages. It turns out that one of them comes from Khandesh, one from Marathwada, and a third man from Satara. The three of them start to talk about their crops. One of them asks the old man, "Grandpa, where are you from?"

"Satara."

"How are the crops doing there?"

The old man says, "I've left the farm to my nephew to take care of. I've been away from it now for ten years. I just keep moving arom Alandi to Pandharpur and from Pandharpur to Alandi."

I have started to feel, as I listen to their talk, as if we are standing on the riverbank at some sacred pilgrimage site. The well has lost its small form and become instead the vast channel of the Ganges. The trees standing all around us begin to seem like the Dandaka Aranya itself.[1] From time to time silence overlaps our talk. And those are the moments

---

1. The forest in which Ram, Sita, and Lakshmaṇ went for their twelve-year exile.

when I feel the utter worthlessness of all my roles: the roles of interviewer, of survey-taker, of writer. Even the *pālkhī* doesn't seem real.

❀

All our surroundings have changed now, like a change of scene in a movie. We have left the stream at Khadus behind us, and now all the roads seem to go running straight off to the horizon. Whenever there is a bend in the road, how broad and spreading it is! I can see the entire two-mile procession of the *pālkhī*. It is so long anymore that it can't all fit at once within the compass of my eyes. The colorful line of men and women against the rain-darkened earth looks like a festive *rāṅgoḷī* pattern on the floor.

All the *Wārkarīs* can't fit now onto this road. When we left Saswad there were four *Wārkarīs* in a rank. Now it has gone up to twelve. Like an overflowing measure of grain the *pālkhī* has poured these *Wārkarīs* prodigally onto the earth. It is getting hard to stay on your feet. Many *Wārkarīs* are walking rapidly along in the fields by the side of the road. The *pālkhī* is coming alive and beginning to resound.

Watching all this has turned me altogether softhearted. I stop thinking anymore about how many of them are true *Wārkarīs*, how many are mere hypocrites, how many come along with the name of God on their lips while all their lives they have preyed on others. Nor does it occur to me to wonder how it is, when they are sending up sputniks and preparing for wars elsewhere, that we go on with whatever this is here.

I take myself way back into former times. Such a short, short while ago human beings were tearing each other to pieces as food to eat in order to live, and here today right before my eyes these thousands of people are walking together, joyfully and voluntarily, singing *bhajans*. What a grand scene it is! What progress this is!

❀

There were two miles left to Malshiras when the *diṇḍīs* suddenly left the main road and turned off into the fields. Had we come to a rest stop? I started to ask around, but instead of slowing down, the *diṇḍīs* actually started moving faster. I could see the leveled road going straight on up an incline ahead of us. *Diṇḍī* after *diṇḍī* was turning off it and with ever greater speed descending into the wet fields. Nobody was stopping. Our feet were getting caked with mud. Behind me somebody shouted to somebody else, "It's time for the 'run'—It's time for the 'run'!"

So I started to ask people what they meant by the "run." Nobody had the time to listen to my question. Before I could get my question out of my mouth, they would rush on ahead. Finally I grabbed hold of somebody and didn't let go of him until he gave me an answer. He told me that it was from this road that Tukaram Maharaj saw the pinnacle of the temple at Pandharpur. Unable to restrain himself, he had set off running toward it. So everybody has to run here.

A cart trail had cut a way across the fields. They had taken the *pālkhī* down off its "chariot," and the bearers, who were carring it on their shoulders, were struggling to keep their footing in the wheelruts of the trail. The *pālkhī* itself kept jerking and swaying wildly. Billowing waves of people were rushing up behind, threatening to break over the *pālkhī*. Everyone was pressing and driving forward and even running on ahead of the *pālkhī*.

Again there was a loud shout, "It's time for the 'run'—it's time for the 'run'!"

I also ran forward, ahead of the *pālkhī*. Only twenty-five feet farther along, the road suddenly made a sharp descent. The slope was so steep you would have had to pull back hard on a bullock's reins. As the *Wārkarīs* came up to the edge they had no choice but to run down it—because of the steepness of the slope and because of the press of people behind them.

I made my own way down—to one side of the crowd—and stood at the bottom of the slope. The *Wārkarīs* were pouring over it like a waterfall. Feet were tripping over feet, dhotis were getting tangled and caught, sandals went flying. Anyone who bent to pick them up was hurled forward. Caps went flying away and turbans were coming unravelled. The *Wārkarīs* themselves were shouting and screaming as they tried to guard themselves and their things. They were also laughing.

A row of *Wārkarīs* would come to the top of the slope like soldiers. When they saw the descent, they would try to hold themselves back as best they could, but before they knew it they would come crashing down. It was a parachute jump that was taking place. And now came the *Wārkarīs* bearing the banners. For an instant their banners and poles could be seen against the sky, and then they started down, clashing and crashing together.

Those of us who were looking on from below at this melee were shouting and laughing and clapping our hands. Finally the *pālkhī* itself arrived. The bearers hesitated for a moment at the very edge. Then, jolting and crashing, they started down. The *pālkhī* jostled about like water in a pot. At any moment it might have slipped away!

The "run" was over. I lagged behind the others a little bit. The road on which the "run" had just taken place was empty. All that remained behind was great piles of sandals and one-sandled *Wārkarīs* standing around looking for the sandals they had lost!

The *pālkhī* is taking a rest a little ways farther out on the high open plain. How completely out of the blue this whole business of the "run" had come and gone! I am sitting silent and still on the grass.

The *Wārkarīs* in the *pālkhī* procession very rarely laugh and have fun in this way. The *riṅgaṇ* is one other such occasion when they perform various kinds of dances and games. The fact is I ought to feel good about this. But somehow it just doesn't seem to fit the image of the *Wārkarī* I have in my mind. I somehow feel that something is wrong. This is a very different type of *Wārkarī* here. This whole *Wārkarī* sect is something very different. This isn't Tukaram's *Wārkarī*, nor is he Dnyaneshwar's—this *Wārkarī* who watches *riṅgaṇs*, who performs dances and games, who takes part in the "run."

I can understand that an urgent upsurge of feeling would have overcome Tukaram Maharaj when he saw the pinnacle of Vitthal's temple. And that he would have run down that slope—to shorten the distance. Or that *abhaṅgas* could emerge spontaneously from his lips. But when these others descended by this same sloping road clapping their hands, laughing, shouting, and throwing their caps in the air, it could only be something artificial. The thought occurs to me that these can't really be Tukaram's *Wārkarīs*, can they?

A man out of the mountains in the Maval area came and sat down near me, and I felt as if I were sitting in a scene from the novel *The Stronghold Conquered But the Lion*

*Lost.*[1] He had a red turban, a full bushy white moustache, a massive chest and neck. Suryaji himself—or at least the Suryaji I have in my mind.[2] We became fast friends. We had some tea and chatted about inflation. He tossed a piece of betel nut in his mouth, and as he was vigorously kneading his chewing tobacco in the palm of his hand he told me, "I've been after someone the whole way from Poona. When I find him I'm really going to tell him off. The first thing I'll do is give his face a couple of good hard slaps."

Naturally I asked him, "What's he done?"

"What has he done? He's made a wreck of my daughter's life. He sent her back home to us and then got his son married again to somebody else. And he hasn't said a word about alimony for my girl either. I've been on the lookout for him all the way from Poona. I'm certain the old guy came along on the pilgrimage. I'm not the kind of man who lets people get away with this kind of mischief."

I asked him, "Are you going to send your daughter back to live with them?"

"Oh no! I'll get her a divorce. And then I'll get her married again. But before I do that I'll take a few people along and soften his bones a bit."

The old man simply couldn't contain his anger. The hand he was using to knead this tobacco was trembling.

But in keeping with my own character I asked him, "Have you gone and talked to him about it?"

"No! First I'm going to demand that alimony from him. We can only talk about it in court."

---

1. Published in 1903, this historical novel by Hari Narayan Apte, the first major Marathi novelist, is based on the heroic exploit of Shivaji's military commander, Tanaji Malusre, in conquering the fort at Sinhagad. He himself was killed in the battle: hence the title.

2. Suryaji Malusre was Tanaji's brother. They came from the Maval area, the rugged country along the eastern flank of the Western Ghats.

I said, "At least try to ask him if he'll give you the alimony. You'll see—he'll agree to it. It'll look better that way."

The old man plunged into thought for a while. Then he said, "Here's what I'll do. When we get back to Poona I'll call together some of the experienced leaders in our caste, and I'll do what they tell me to do."

I had to laugh at myself. One of Tolstoy's stories suddenly came to mind. There is this man who has adopted a son. He only forbids him to do one thing—to sit on the throne that is kept locked up in a room. But the boy steals a chance and sits on the throne. He begins to see the future. A robber has broken into their home and is threatening his father with an ax. The boy can't bear to see it and he shouts, "Father! Father!"

At that very instant the throne disappears. The room itself disappears. And the boy wakes up in the middle of the wilds somewhere. His father takes him to task then for his disobedience and for having meddled with the future. It was the father who was meant to die, but instead of that it is the thief who dies.

I remembered this story, and it occurred to me that this was exactly what I myself was doing. The girl's father-in-law would have been properly humiliated. The whole affair would have been dragged through the courts. There would have been grief and remorse. And I had come in the way of that future.

But then again it occurred to me that this was probably how it had to be—that I would meet him and give him my advice without his even asking me for it.

Deep in his own thoughts the old man got up and without saying a word to me started to walk away. Staring straight before him. It occurred to me that he must have made this entire one-hundred-fifty-mile trek simply working himself up to a boil—deciding just how he would catch hold of his daughter's father-in-law, what curses he would use, and how he would humiliate him.

❀

I have also gotten up and started to walk. The *pālkhī* has started out again. The main road bends to the right, and it seems to hang right over our heads because of the long climb up to it. The bullock carts from the various *diṇḍīs* are moving up the road in a long line. Their roofs look very handsome and trim outlined against the black sky. The occasional ochre banner tied to one of the carts looks, against that sky, an even brighter orange. The movement of the carts and the steps of the bullocks are steady, slow, and solemn. They have also become serious here in the company of the *Wārkarīs*.

Slowly, slowly the entire *pālkhī* procession climbs back up onto the road, and it resumes its full, immense form. We reach the road, and suddenly the flat countryside spreads out before us like a vast arena. Things are quiet again. The "run" is finished. The feeling that we are nearing Pandharpur is spreading. In spite of the ground being so flat, nobody is in any hurry. The cymbals and drums are beaten slowly. The sound of the *bhajans* is subdued.

We have started to see Velapur some distance away.

❀

Tonight we are at Velapur, tomorrow night at Shegav. There are just two more stops left now. Pandharpur is almost here. The trek is nearly over.

I have begun to feel that I have accomplished very, very little. I ought to have seen more and talked more.

Here at Velapur I first got some tea, and now I am out wandering about. Unconsciously my feet have brought me toward the god's tent. During this entire trek I had omitted the god! I try to recall. This whole time I haven't taken *darśan* of the *pālkhī* even once. I had only made *namaskārs* from a distance. Whenever I entered the procession I had touched the road with my hand and made a *namaskār* along with all the others.

When you consider it, how simple a thing *darśan* is! At every town the people had stood waiting in long lines. And in every lane and road of each new town they had positively clung to the *pālkhī*. The *prasād* couldn't even be given properly into people's hands. The people who were with the *pālkhī* would simply fling it broadcast from inside, and the people would start pushing and shoving each other to pick it up. But except for the guards and the assistants, during the many intervening miles there was nobody near the *pālkhī*. I could have gone up at my own leisure, and walking quietly along beside the *pālkhī* I could have gazed upon Dnyaneshwar's silver *pādukās* to my heart's content.

In fact I can remember two occasions when I did walk beside the *pālkhī*. Once it was so that I could talk to the government guard. (The other time it was with the *pālkhī*'s assistants.) Our talk was very superficial. I mentioned something to the effect that he—the guard—automatically got a chance to go on the pilgrimage as a part of his job. He replied, "Yes. But I'm not going with it all the way to the end. When we get to the border of this District I'll leave. Then the Sholapur District police will take over."

The District had to end somewhere! It was rather like when I was a kid and used to sit staring at the railway signal so that I would see it when it fell—I kept my eyes peeled now to see when we crossed the District's border. But just as the signal always used to fall the very moment my eyes looked away, I never did know when the border came and when the police were changed.

I have reached the *pālkhī*'s tent. At this stopover it has been concealed by a large bamboo canopy, which they have erected in front of it. There are sugar factories in the vicinity—and money consequently. So here they pamper the god rather more than usual. There is a *jāgar* taking place before the god.[1] Today I can see the people who are doing the *jāgar* very clearly inside the colorful, cloth-festooned canopy. I had seen a *jāgar* at Saswad from some distance away. It had been going on right out in the middle of the rain.

There is also a line for *darśan* of course. At least once at one of the stopovers along the way the individual *Wārkarīs* from the *diṇḍīs* will choose a time when the crowd is somewhat less and go have *darśan*.

I would even like just to sit down here with my back up against one of the supporting poles of the canopy. Just as I would do at any temple. In fact there are a few people sitting here in this way, their eyes withdrawn into themselves. In our society these are the only places where you can just sit down and nobody is going to ask you why, or what your caste or your position in society is.

I have maintained the feeling that it is best for the *pālkhī* to make its nightly stopovers outside the towns along its route. I remember the big dispute that flared up in Phaltan. I had heard it myself. The Rani of Phaltan had insisted that the *pālkhī* should stay in the new Dnyaneshwar temple she had built, and the *pālkhī* was stuck there.[2] This

1. A *jāgar* is a ritual performance in which the participants maintain a night-long vigil before the *pālkhī*.

2. A princely state during British rule, Phaltan has since been absorbed into Satara District. The former Raja and Rani continued however to enjoy special prestige and privileges.

sudden change from the former place didn't at all please some of the people in the *diṇḍīs* accompanying the *pālkhī*. The police were called on the scene, and the *pālkhī* leaders also came. I even heard that the Rani had brought pressure to bear from the Honorable Yashwantrao Chavan to carry out her demand.[1] And the *pālkhī* ended up in the Dnyaneshwar temple. Some of the *diṇḍīs* got angry, and they went by the usual route to the former stopover.

In previous times also, when the *pālkhī* was growing in prestige, the wealthy people in the towns along the way must have offered to donate buildings, bungalows, and land. But the *pālkhī should* make its stopovers out on the open plain and maintain an atmosphere in which all can come without any inhibition and have *darśan*.

I didn't take *darśan* this time either. There was a long line there waiting. I went off and walked on beyond the main tent. All those tents in a row, large and small—how nice they looked! The gentleman I had just met on the road between Malshiras and Velapur stepped out of one of the tents when he spotted me. He told me, "Come on! I'll help you get the information you want."

He brought me up to one of the tents a little ways ahead, and he told someone there to spread out a rug for us to sit down on. Then he sent someone else off to call the people in some of the other tents. After fifteen minutes of earnest entreaty, two or three of these people came. I told them what information I needed and started to hand them the questionaire. One of them jumped to his feet when he got his, and as he tore it to shreds he shouted, "We don't have to give you any information! Why do you outsiders come here anyway? All these outsiders who squeeze into the *pālkhī*.

1. Yashwantrao Chavan was for years the foremost political leader of Maharashtra. At the time he was Chief Minister of the state government.

Make themselves important. Wasn't our experience with the Rani of Phaltan enough?"

I tried to make him understand. But I hadn't said more than a couple of words when he raised his fists and ran at me—and threatened to punch me. Two of the others there held him back. I got up on my feet too. I asked him, "Why do you get so mad? Listen to what I have to say. I don't want to join the *pālkhī*. I just want some information. If various kinds of information about the *pālkhī* are gathered, that will be useful even to you. You call yourself a *Wārkarī*. Getting mad like this doesn't befit you at all."

My words were all for nothing. He was glowering at me, and glowering he went away. When he had gone, his companion said, "The boy's a little off his rocker. Yesterday he brought us to the point of almost breaking heads over where to put up the tent."

To myself I thought, "Maybe I should have spent some more time before this around the *pālkhī*'s tent." I would have learned a lot. It is by living at court after all that you learn all the politics. But I really wasn't interested in politics—whether belonging to the court or here.

Our meeting broke up, and I set off back to our tent. The man who was helping me accompanied me a short way. He said, "The *pālkhī* is also cursed—like everything else—by this brahman-non-brahman dispute.[1] It keeps growing from day to day. It's come to the point where all these groups of people don't like the position of leadership the brahmans have in the Dnyaneshwar *pālkhī*."

He left me then and went back to his tent. But I couldn't see myself agreeing with what he had just told me. That man who just quarreled with me had also spoken angrily

1. This "dispute" has been a serious aspect of Maharashtrian social and political life for nearly a hundred years, especially since Independence, when the non-brahmans (i.e., Marathas) have attained political ascendancy.

about the Rani of Phaltan, who is not a brahman. In my opinion there are really just two classes in the *pālkhī*. The educated and the uneducated. It isn't that some element of the brahman-non-brahman dispute isn't involved in it. That is everywhere. But in the same way that an uneducated and orthodox *Wārkarī* wouldn't like the Rani of Phaltan, he wouldn't like Sonopant Dandekar either.[1]

❀

Our chatting this evening is very lively and full of spirit—just like a house where they are going to have a wedding. As if we actually had come together for a wedding in which the silver *pādukās* of Dnyaneshwar were the bride and Vitthal was the groom.

Even those who normally don't talk are talking today. The fact that we shall very soon be going our separate ways has touched all of us somewhere deep in our hearts. Even though we still have a good ways to walk tomorrow morning, nobody is in any hurry to stop talking.

The night is getting deeper. And now at last the chatting is starting to drag. One by one they become silent and start to nod. I get up and go out.

As usual there is a sermon going on over at the big tent in our *diṇḍī*. Our *buvā* won't leave off without giving us a sermon to hear at every stopover. The same thing today.

Should I sit in on this sermon?—I stand there and think about it. This *buvā* has ruined my firm intention to look upon everything when I went with the *pālkhī* with an open

1. Sonopant Dandekar, a brahman, was one of the foremost spiritual leaders of the *Wārkarīs* in recent years and the acknowledged head of the Dnyaneshwar *pālkhī*. He was a professor of philosophy and the Principal of Sir Parshurambhau College in Poona.

mind. The unfavorable prejudice I had developed from my first sight of him beating up on that "robber" at Phaltan still stands between us. Then too there is his immaculate grooming, his way of living separate and apart, his women disciples, and that first boring sermon of his that I heard at Lonand!

I turn toward the big tent anyway and sit down among the listeners. Within the first five minutes I start to yawn. I look around me: the other listeners are yawning too. I can see right through every one of the preacher's tricks of speech. He apparently thinks that what he is saying is funny because he himself is laughing. But those who are listening all look very solemn. The *buvā* doesn't even *know* that he is not being amusing. I feel like shouting at him. The idea even occurs to me how funny it might be if right in the middle of it all I were to make some strange noise.

I promptly banish the idea. I feel somehow that the fault is mine. Why do I harbor such suspicion in my mind about this man? I must free myself from it before the pilgrimage ends. I must not let it turn into something morbid.

I consider why these doubts about the *buvā* might have arisen in my mind. Was it because he lives apart from all the rest of us? Because he demands recognition of his own importance? Because he has his men and women disciples with him? Because he takes a special tent all for himself? Because he acts with special familiarity with his women disciples?

*July 20, 1961*

185. *He who, for the sake of the bliss of the Self, feels aversion for all objects of sense, in whom there is no thought for the senses,*

186. *to whose mind desires make no appeal, who has no interest in the material world and who takes pleasure in the enjoyment of faith,*

187. *is surely sought out by wisdom, in which perfect peace is found.*

188. *When that wisdom is established in the heart and the tender shoots of peace break through, then at once the light of the Self shines forth.*

189. *Then wherever he looks, he will see only peace of which no limit is conceivable.*

190. *In short it would be impossible to describe how the seeds of wisdom are spread far and wide.*

Jnāneshvari *Four*

CHAPTER ELEVEN

# Shegav

The night came to an end, and we left Velapur. I spent a whole hour then counting the *pālkhī.* It had filled out to about eleven thousand.

The afternoon stop was to be at Tondlabondla. A *riṅgaṇ* took place before that.

I still had not seen a *riṅgaṇ* properly. I went ahead with all the others and pressed into the crowd. This *riṅgaṇ* was to be a circular one. A large number of *Wārkarīs* had sat down very crowdedly in a huge circle on the open ground. All around this circle a ten foot space had been left open, and *Wārkarīs* were standing along the outside perimeter of this open space. Occasionally the shape of the *riṅgaṇ* would be broken because of the huge press of the crowd. The space that had been left open as a pathway would start to fill up. All this time, even in the *riṅgaṇ*, the *bhajans* were still going on.

The *pālkhī*'s two horses came toward the place of the *riṅgaṇ*. The people made a way for them to get through to the open pathway in the middle. One of the horses had no rider.[1] On the other one was seated one of the *pālkhī*'s attendants. He let his horse go around the pathway of the *riṅgaṇ*. The other riderless horse started to run along behind. They made one circumambulation of the *riṅgaṇ*. At the end of the second circumambulation the second horse crowded ahead, and during the third circumambulation it went running on ahead, left the *riṅgaṇ* when it had finished the circle, and went and stood beside the *pālkhī*.

Then, here, there, and everywhere, in every manner and style, the *bhajans* began. The people stood in lines facing each other. They were springing rhythmically backward and forward and squatting and whirling about. The *Wārkarīs* who were not attached to *diṇḍīs* started playing *phugaḍī*.[2] Mixed *phugaḍī*. Anyone could put out his hand and begin it. Men and women were doing the *phugaḍī* together. They had no inhibitions at all. The women were shouting, "Phu-phu," as they did a squatting *phugaḍī*. They weren't embarrassed even though there were men all around them. And there was our *buvā* enjoying himself among them—once again the *buvā*!

I have never liked the *riṅgaṇ* or the *phugaḍī* and all the other things that go along with them. About a dozen years ago I had gone walking along with the *pālkhī* procession for the last few miles of the pilgrimage. On that occasion, at the Wakhari stopover, I had squeezed myself into the crushing

1. *Wārkarīs* believe that the spiritual presence of Dnyaneshwar rides on this horse.

2. The *phugaḍī* is a kind of gambol or dance, generally done by girls, in which two or more, clutching hands, whirl themselves around, keeping time to their movements by puffing *phugaḍī phu* with their mouths.

crowd and seen an entire *ringaṇ*. After it was over I had heard all the many different kinds of *bhajans* that were being performed by various groups out there on that same open plain, and I had also seen the *phugaḍīs* and other such things then.

But what had given me the biggest shock on that occasion was the affair I saw at Gopalpur.

The Gopalpur temple is roughly a mile's distance from Pandharpur. The temple is up on a hill. There is a wall all around it. The chief deity is Gopalkrishna.[1] But there is even one temple, in the cluster of other small temples there, that is dedicated to the parents of Rukmini.[2] In a certain grotto they have Janabai's woolen wrap and her grind stone on display.[3] You can go to this place from Pandharpur either by road or on the river. I went that time by a boat on the river. I could see the crowds trudging there along the riverbank. At various places on the hill where the temple was located *Wārkarī kīrtans* were going on.

I climbed up the hill and went into the temple. The moment I set foot inside, I stopped short and just stood there. What I was seeing before me was so unexpected. It came as a complete shock to the idea of the *Wārkarī* sect I knew and for which I harbored a feeling of warmth deep in my heart. As I was climbing up the hill outside, I had kept seeing puffed rice strewn all over the road, and there were little shops selling the puffed rice at various places. Here in the courtyard of the temple there had been a veritable shower of the puffed rice, and *Wārkarī* men and women were doing the *phugaḍī* together. Those people who weren't doing the *phugaḍī* were pulling the puffed rice out of their pockets or

---

1. Krishna as a cowherd.

2. Rukmini is Krishna's principal wife. Her father was Bhishmaka, king of Kundina in the Vidarbha area of what is now Maharashtra.

3. Janabai is one of the revered saint-poets of the *Wārkarīs*. She lived in the fourteenth century.

from the knotted ends of their saris, and they were stuffing it into the mouths of anyone who came before them. The rule was, I saw, that no matter who held out a handful of puffed rice to someone else, that person was obligated to open his mouth and accept it. In the same way, if someone just crossed his hands in front and held them out to someone else, they would twine their hands together and start a *phugaḍī*. When one *phugaḍī* was over another would start up in its place. Throughout the entire courtyard these *phugaḍīs* were going on.

If one particular *phugaḍī* became especially lively, the people all around would draw back or stop the other *phugaḍīs* nearby and would all look on admiringly.

I was watching this for a long time. There was a young widow there who was doing the *phugaḍī* with one and all. When one partner stopped she would hold out her crossed hands to someone else. Her liveliness and her quickness were more than a match for anyone else. At the end of one *phugaḍī* one of her partners lost his balance, dizzy from all the whirling. Someone else's turban came undone as he was doing the *phugaḍī* with her. One man tried to pull away to one side after only two or three turns because he was so outmatched by her, and he started to drag behind. The onlookers thought it was all very funny,and they were laughing. She had taken down the end of the sari that covered her head and had tucked it in tightly around her waist. The wind from all the whirling had disheveled her hair, and it had come down over her forehead and was sticking to her sweaty face. From being out of breath and still laughing at the same time, her face had flushed all red. Occasionally she would take the knot of her hair, which had come lose, and pull it tight.

One old man came forward excitedly to take his turn. After only three turns around he fell panting to the side. All the people burst out laughing. A wrestler came forward.

But he was so ponderous that the *phugaḍī* kept stumbling and stopping. Finally, a girl even younger than the widow, who was very skinny, joined in. And then of course both of them really started outdoing themselves.

As I was watching this whole business of people stuffing puffed rice into other people's mouths and doing the *phugaḍī* together, I was quite dumbfounded. I just couldn't grasp the fact that these really were *Wārkarīs* and in Pandharpur itself—whom I was seeing with my own eyes. Compared to the *Wārkarīs* in my imagination, these seemed totally different and alien.

While I was still looking on, I heard a voice at my side, "Shameless bastards! Don't the sons-of-bitches have their own wives?"

I turned with a start and looked to my side.

I had been standing all that time right beside the police officer who had been assigned to the temple to supervise security. He had spoken to me only because he had seen from my clothes that I was educated. When I looked at him, he went on to say, "And see how utterly shameless these women are! They hold hands with anyone just exactly as they please. Shameless hussies!"

I didn't say a word in reply. He also remained unspeaking for some time. But he was still sputtering angrily to himself. I began to realize that the things going on in front of him were becoming more and more unbearable to him by the minute.

The wall around the temple was nice and wide, and there was a way to go up the wall to the top. Part of the crowd was moving up there. The people who had climbed up all made *namaskārs* when they saw the pinnacle of the temple of Vitthal in Pandharpur. The police officer just then happened to look up and see the crowd of people that was climbing up the wall. He jumped up and yanked down one of the *Wārkarīs* who had climbed up onto the stairs. The man came crashing down from four or five steps up. "Stupid bastards!" the police officer shouted as he was beating the man with the stick in his hand, "You want to go up there and get killed? What if you fall down? Don't you think we have anything better to do than write accident reports? They came on a pilgrimage, the bastards!"

Then he shouted at the policeman who was standing over on one side, "Useless runt! You blind or something? Drag them all down!"

The crowd up there on top all started coming down at once. And the policemen were helping, pulling at them as they were descending. The crowd they made down at the bottom mixed in with all the people who were doing the *phugaḍī* in the courtyard, and the confusion got worse and worse. One man lost his balance in the press and fell heavily against the police officer.

His face just went red with rage. There are some occupations, it seems, in which you have to keep your anger at a boil all the time. Otherwise it wouldn't have been possible for a person to become so angry so frequently. The police officer picked himself up, brandished his stick in a paroxysm of rage, and he shouted as he struck at some of the people who were doing the *phugaḍī*, "Throw them all out! Playing *phugaḍī*, are they?"

I saw the people squeezing out toward the doorway, so I just stood right where I was for some time. The *Wārkarīs* who had been doing the *phugaḍī* left, and others arrived in their place. But these had not come to do the *phugaḍī*. They were only taking *darśan*. And they were stepping warily over the puffed rice that had fallen all over the ground.

❀

The *riṅgaṇ* is over and the *pālkhī* has started to move again. It is past ten o'clock in the morning. Beside me an old man, who is carrying a banner, is telling me his story. He has been making the pilgrimage on foot for the last ten years. As he tells the story: "I've left home for good. I go there only once a month. But I don't go into the house farther than the porch—and I don't stay overnight. I never say anything about any of the domestic affairs at home. I don't even give my opinion. I keep on walking the whole year round from Alandi to Pandharpur and back. I've told the folks at home that I've died."

To tell the truth, even though I want very much to hear what is being told me, it is scarcely possible. The crowd has grown too big. But as I keep trying to listen, I seem to catch something quite new and different, and my ears perk up. This *Wārkarī* here is from a village near Saswad. He has given over his fruit business in Bombay to his nephew and come back up to his home village to live. Now he isn't going to go back. He can't tolerate the Bombay weather. The doctor has warned him that his health would fail if he continued to live in Bombay. When he came back up here to the Desh he had started doing the pilgrimage. Before that he used to go by the train.

He had come back to spend his last days in his home village. He had thought on the way there that after all the rush and noise of Bombay he would find peace and quiet in his village.

As he tells it: "To tell the truth, my experience was exactly the opposite. You may not agree with me. But life in the village has gotten to be the worst of all. Constant bickering, vices, immorality—the times are ripe for them all. In our village no one is really friendly with anyone else. I was Sarpanch of the village for four years.[1] So I'm telling you this out of my own experience. All the villages in the vicinity have the same sad complaint as our village. No one thinks of anyone else in the village. In Bombay, on the contrary, I was happy. Just call for help and a hundred helping hands are there to aid you. Such was the harmony. Nobody's problems are left unattended. There's fellow feeling in the city. My son got sick late one night. I went to the Parsi man next door to phone the doctor. He let me make the call, surely, but when he understood the situation he got out his own car and took my son to the hospital. There he took it upon himself to pay the doctor's fifty-rupee fee. The next day when I went to return the money, he wouldn't take it. He told me, 'He's just like my own son.'

"Everyone leaves some village behind when he comes to Bombay. So the people there understand the pain of broken ties. Here people aren't even welcome, so it seems. Everything has turned into sheer rowdyism in the villages. There is a Kulkarni in our village.[2] A really godly man. He labored selflessly for the village year after year. If called upon he would get up at any hour of the night to help. We put him up as a candidate for the election to the *pañcāyat.*[3] In order to get him elected I had to expend every bit of my own merit. He ought to have been elected without anyone saying so much as a word. But the opposing party paid people bribes, played rough, and campaigned on the slogan 'Beat the Brahman.' That's how things go in the village. Now I'm going to withdraw myself from all of that."

When he has finished speaking I tell him, "You're a

1. The Sarpanch is the elected head of the *pañcāyat*—the local village assembly—and the village representative at the district level.

2. The Kulkarni, brahman by caste, was the traditional village record-keeper.

3. The *pañcāyat* is the local elected village assembly, which is responsible for village welfare and development.

*Wārkarī*—a man who wears the *tulsī* necklace. They must give you a lot of respect."

At first he replies, "Oh, yes." But then he says, "It really doesn't count for anything in everyday life."

Before lunch I went down to the stream at Tondlabondla to bathe. There were a great many hollows in the stream bed at this spot. Hundreds of *Wārkarīs* were bathing in them. The water had taken on the color of tea.

As we were wandering about looking for an open hollow, we heard the *buvā* calling to us from the water, "Come on in! Today is the ninth day of the bright half of Ashadh. That is the day for Krishna-*līlās*—the day on which he subdued the serpent Kaliya.[1] It ought to be celebrated in this way with *līlās*."

One of his women disciples was massaging his one arm, while another was rubbing his back. With his free hand the *buvā* started to splash both of them with water. Then all the disciples began playfully splashing the water around.

It was clear that those who saw this whole scene thought it was very peculiar. This manner of behavior, in the company of the *pālkhī* no less, came as a real shock to a lot of people. But neither the *buvā* nor his disciples thought anything of it. They were really and truly enjoying themselves in their Krishna-*līlā*. Through the splashes of water you could see the joy on their faces.

When we had bathed and were returning to the *diṇḍī*, we started discussing the *buvā*, of course. One of the men told us something funny that had happened to him earlier. One

1. *Līlās* are the divine deeds of Krishna, which his devotees enact as a ritual of worship.

day the *buvā* had called him and asked what they were whispering about him in the *diṇḍī*. "Oh, no, no!" the man had replied, "They have complete faith in you." Then the *buvā* asked him, "Why do they always remain so distant?" He replied, "They're a little bit afraid." Then the *buvā* had told him to come and stay in his tent. "If you stay here with us, you will receive a special joy."

The man didn't say a thing. Then the *buvā* said, "You seem to enjoy singing. You come with us. I'll arrange it so you have a program on the radio." But when he kept silent even after that the *buvā* said, "I've recognized that your character is a spiritual one. If you stay among us to receive spiritual guidance, just think how far you'll go. Go close up your business and sell it off. Just bring all your money with you. I'll make everything flourish for you."

They were all laughing as they listened to him. I didn't get angry this time either when I heard him joke about the *buvā*. I laughed heartily right along with them.

The *buvā* was the sole topic of conversation that day in the *diṇḍī*. Everyone was saying that the *buvā* was giving the *diṇḍī* a bad name. One of them even told the leader of our *diṇḍī*, "Don't let the *buvā* into our *diṇḍī*. Everyone's laughing at us."

The leader replied, "Just let it be. Each person is responsible for his own sins. Why do you bother to look at him?"

I asked him, "What does it all mean—these oil massages, the women disciples, the sanctimoniousness? It doesn't fit in with the *Wārkarīs*."

I got the following answer: "It's a part of the Dada Maharaj sect, which is a part of the whole *Wārkarī* movement. His entire method is based on the *rājas* quality."[1]

1. *Rājas*, the quality of passion and activeness, is one of the three fundamental properties of all existent things in traditional Hindu philosophy, the other two being *sattva* (purity, virtue) and *tamas* (ignorance, darkness).

❀

As I was wandering around after lunch, a *Wārkarī* man made a *namaskār* to me and said, "Sir, turn your attention toward us once in a while."

I realized that here was another man who mistook me for a government official. I told him, "What could I possibly do for you?"

"How can that be? Write down my name. Every year I do the meritorious service of bringing along a group of twenty people on the pilgrimage. I gather up the money wherever I can and pay for all their expenses. I've spent twenty years in this way all for the sake of the *Wārkarī* religion. But still I have to worry about feeding myself. The government must give some thought to that. Self-sacrificing *Wārkarīs* like myself ought to be given a yearly stipend. That's the only way these religious deeds can be kept going. Write down my name! Ask anybody about me. I've never taken a bribe from anyone. Recommend my name to somebody right at the top. Nowadays the thieves are devouring everything."

What could I say to him?

I counted the multitude when we left Tondlabondla. It had grown to more than eleven thousand.

❀

We have left Tondlabondla behind us. The *pālkhī* is taking its short rest stop just now. There is a hill over on the right. I can see pits of all sizes on it where they have been excavating gravel. In places there are piles of broken-up rocks. In a dell to the left *bhāruḍs* are being performed.[1] One of the people in the troupe has draped a rough blanket over himself. Another one has the end of a sari pulled over his head. The man in the blanket is calling out to the others at the top of his voice and dancing.

Very suddenly it starts to pour! So hard it reminds me of Saswad. Everyone goes scurrying about helterskelter. Like an old woman chasing after a rat with her broom. I don't know of any place to go for shelter. My raincoat has gone on ahead with the truck. The very first gust of rain soaks me through.

The entire *pālkhī* is standing frozen in place. Their heads bent low, the *bhāruḍ* performers are just standing there dripping in the rain. All the people have stopped in clusters here and there. There must be twenty *Wārkarīs* under each umbrella. For them it is quite enough just to have the feeling that at least there is an umbrella somewhere in the vicinity. It becomes virtually a game of hide and seek as they try to find cover one from the other. Some people are hiding in the trenches on the hillside, as if they were hiding from a bombing attack.

For ten minutes I just walk around here and there and look. The entire time my state is no better than that of an exposed wooden post left out in the pouring rain. Occasionally I wipe my streaming face with my handkerchief. But the handkerchief itself is no longer really a handkerchief. It has become nothing but a soaking rag.

There is no way to know now whether the *pālkhī* is staying put or is moving on. It's not that old joke again, is it, where the whole army goes merrily on its way, and we are the platoon that gets left behind? The air has started to get colder. It really would be better to start walking than to stand here getting wet!

---

1. *Bhāruḍs* are a form of dramatic dialog on religious themes, which are performed as a kind of folk theater.

❀

I had just decided to set out when I heard a voice calling from behind me, "Hey, look at this! You've gotten completely soaked!"

I turned to look. It was the gentleman I had accompanied to Saswad! I told him, "Well, I certainly have gotten wet. Chalk one up to experience!"

He said, "It's Saswad all over again. Don't keep on getting wet! We can go on together under this one rain coat of mine!"

He started unbuttoning the coat. I told him, "I'm completely soaked through. You'll just get wet too. At least you should stay dry."

We started off walking. Once again, a bath of mud and those sharp, protruding stones in the road. Only this time it wasn't dark. We put our sandals on our heads, and jauntily pretending that it wasn't raining, we went walking on. We didn't even bother to wipe the dripping water from our faces. Nor did we pause to wring out the ends of our clothes.

❀

Farther along I begin to see how the rain has put the entire *pālkhī* to rout. Everyone is struggling along, head bent low, just as fast as he can. The *pālkhī* has long since gone on its way. I meet up with two of the women from our *diṇḍī*. Apparently, even in our *diṇḍī* the people have all been scattered here and there. I ask one of them about it. She doesn't know either who has gone on ahead and who has been left behind. She has had quite enough as it is to manage on her own. The other woman has brought an umbrella with her, and she is some distance farther along. I start to walk with her. She sees that I am getting wet and asks me to share the umbrella with her. But nobody could get decent shelter under such a tiny umbrella as that, and I tell her so. But I can see what a time she is having of it, holding the umbrella up against the wind while at the same time she is trying to manage the long, hanging folds of her sari. So I reach out and take hold of the umbrella.

As we are walking along we start to talk. She tells me about how at Baradgav her saris had been stolen. She is in the group that manages the *diṇḍī*. We start talking about that. She tells me, "The preparations for the *diṇḍī* begin four months ahead of time. We start sorting the wheat and rice and storing them up. Then it's a matter of getting the wheat ground, making all the pickles, grinding the spices, collecting enough pans to cook for a hundred or a hundred and fifty people. We have to decide on a cook and a maid servant and keep account of the salt, the pepper, the sugar, and the leaf plates and cups. There's also the tea and coffee, of course. And peanuts and sago for the days of fasting. Then the boxes for all these items. And labels on the boxes. The work goes on right up to the day the *diṇḍī* leaves. Meanwhile, the men's work outside is going on also: getting the tents back in shape, hiring a truck, getting the fuel. They have to make arrangements to bring the charcoal and firewood with us. It's too expensive to get it along the way. That's the sort of trouble we go to getting the *diṇḍī* ready. And on top of that, there are always more and more people coming and going. You have to give them all tea. And some of them you have to have for dinner. Every year we prepare as much as we would for four weddings. The only reason for this whole fuss and bother is to bring a handful of people together to share the joy of the *pālkhī*. If a lot of folks join the *diṇḍī*, we break even. But often enough we're left with a deficit."

There is still time before it gets dark. I have arrived in Shegav, and I have found the place where we are staying. I feel just as if I have come home. I am standing in the "courtyard" in the middle of our tents drinking some nice hot tea. I am remembering how my legs were just ready to give way under me only a furlong away from Shegav. But once I was sure about where we were staying, the aching of my feet seemed like just so much fun.

This is where we are staying tonight! We have begun all our by now normal evening occupations. I enter the tent and untie my bedding roll, change my clothes, and rub my feet with a medicated balm. I spread out my bedding roll neatly, and I lie down for a bit. When anyone else comes in we chat. I get up soon and go ambling about the other tents. Everything feels just like "home." All the movements I make inside the tent have become as natural as if I were an Arab. When I enter the tent my head automatically lowers. My feet now cross over the tent ropes without my giving it a thought. At first the sloping roof of the tent had felt very confining, but now it has begun to seem like a palace. The first night the tent had felt too crowded for me to sleep, but now it seems nice and roomy. Whenever there is a sudden downpour, my hands move unerringly to lower the flaps. As if I had been living in nothing but a tent all my life.

This is the last stop on this trek, the last meal together, the last time sleeping in the group, the last chance to chat together, and perhaps the last real fatigue.

While we were eating today, one of the women went around and served us each salt—as a service to the "saints" gathered there. I also feel myself becoming warm inside with feeling. I remember my first day back at Saswad. It was in this very same group that I had felt myself so alone.

Now after fifteen days on the march, these same people have started to feel like part of my own family. These are the faces that were strangers to me then—homely, decorous, washed, or unwashed—but now all these distinctions have disappeared. Only the joy of being together has remained.

I don't know the past history of a single person in the entire group: neither their jobs or businesses nor their families. I haven't felt the need for any of that. Neither do I now.

Later in the evening I purposely went to hear the *buvā*'s *kīrtan*. In order to expunge that blot from my mind. He was making his commentary on the scripture with the use of various illustrations. I listened to it all. I couldn't stop myself from feeling that he himself knew that he was doing the *kīrtan* without the proper training or study for it. But I began to understand what urge might impel him to give his talks even when he didn't have the imagination it requires.

I really pitied the *buvā*. It seemed to me I could see the tension on his face that came from always having vigilantly to guard his own importance. Finding new disciples, looking after the old, always running about collecting money to keep his "church" going—are these such small matters? Whatever he receives for all these troubles is quite alright. Nothing troubles me now either about those who have accepted discipleship from him. There are all different levels of people in society. Some gain realization of Krishna from his *Gītā*, others from his *līlās*. And some have a taste for none other than the Way of the passions.

When the scripture reading and commentary are over and we are going to bed, we really start to feel that the pilgrimage is coming to an end. It will be Wakhari tomorrow. But nobody stops there. People usually want to go on and reach Pandharpur.

Everyone is talking now about the return home. Someone is asking about how he can get a return reservation. Someone else is already worrying about how he is going to have *darśan* in Pandharpur in the huge crowds.

*July 21, 1961*

When the afternoon meal is over today the *pālkhī* is going to move onward to Wakhari. Today the trek is coming to an end. At Wakhari only the *pālkhī* will make a stopover. We people in the *diṇḍī* are not going to stay there overnight. We will leave the *pālkhī* settled in at its stopover in the evening and then go on to Pandharpur.

This morning I got up bright and early. It had suddenly occurred to me that I ought to go and have a look at the *pālkhī*'s *pūjā*. So I presented myself at the tent of the god.

The *pūjā* that was taking place there was just like one at any major temple. The man who was doing the *pūjā* was dressed in his pure ritual clothes. While he was saying the sacred *mantras* of the *pūjā*, he was successively wiping the *pādukās* and making offerings of flowers and scent. The people who were moving about in the vicinity carefully kept their distance in order to preserve the ritual purity.

The *āratīs* and the chanting of *mantras* took place exactly in the usual way. There was only one difference. At the end they sang *abhaṅgas*.

The final *āratī* ended, and I turned toward the tent of the *pālkhī*. The one in which the *pālkhī* leaders sit. I bent low and went in. Sonopant Dandekar and some of the others were sitting there. I had met Sonopant before this about the work I had undertaken, and I had also gotten a letter from him saying that I should be given full cooperation in my work.

I made a *namaskār* and sat down on the floor. The other people were touching their heads to Sonopant's feet. I couldn't see myself doing that. I didn't have that kind of faith. Sonopant asked me, "How's your work coming along?"

I told him, "There are a lot of obstacles. The *Wārkarīs* outside there speak freely enough. But the closer you come to the *pālkhī*, the greater their obstinacy becomes."

I told him about the occasion when I almost got beaten up. He laughed a little and said, "It's hard to make these people understand! Here you have to deal with real illiterates. But even so I'll do for you what it is in my power to do."

Just then the *prasād* from the *pūjā* was brought in: sweets made from milk and fruit. We had pretty much finished our talk. But I stayed on and sat there for a while. I took some of the *prasād*.

I started to think about Dandekar. On the one hand this gentleman was the principal of a college, while on the other hand he was the leading advocate of that sect for which our educated people have no respect.

It appeared that in the role of *Wārkarī* also he had to perform two duties. The *Wārkarīs* who constantly kept coming and going through the tent would always touch their heads to his feet. The ultimate leadership of the *pālkhī* was his of course. And the responsibility with it for all the *pālkhī*'s arrangements and for the policy decisions that from time to time had to be enforced. Then, on the other hand, he was a scholar of the *Wārkarī* philosophy and its chief propounder. How could he carry out both these roles successfully without a conflict? People said of him, "Even such a highly educated man as he has accepted the *Wārkarī* faith." This point has become a veritable weapon for the *Wārkarīs*. I had heard it any number of times. But how had he managed to link in his mind the scientific knowledge of college education with the *Wārkarī* principles? Or perhaps he hadn't linked them but had kept them as two separate things? But if he has managed to form some compromise, then it is important that we should hear about it.

During the time I was there, fifty to seventy-five people had entered, touched his feet with their heads, sat there a while, and gone out again. Every time he drew his feet back. He himself would make a *namaskār* in return, and he would hand out some of the *pālkhī*'s *prasād*. In the midst of this, he would turn his head and talk to us.

When I looked at his face he seemed to me to be very tired. Was this tiredness only something temporary, or was it because he has worked his whole life for the faith and has not had as much success as he had wished? I give my imagination some rein: was it the very position of esteem he has attained that made him tired? Every single day he had to let people come and touch their heads to his feet, and he had to say a few words each time. Then, too, there was the fatigue of having to put up with those who came in without any apparent reason and just sat for a long time without saying anything.

Whatever the case, *I* got tired from the lines of people who had come to have *darśan* of him. People just cannot leave you alone for a minute. I would have said, "Why can't each person simply live his own life?"

I have always felt that a carpenter is a happier man than a king. That is how I felt on this occasion too. Not in that primary school sense in which the simple life is always so fulsomely praised. But because it strikes me as really being true. Dreams of being famous, of becoming a government minister or a major artist are fine until you actually attain them! Then what of the burdens that descend on you? Everyone just assumes that you have found something; and when you really haven't, then what do you do?

But then it occurred to me—shouldn't anyone become a Dandekar or a prime minister then? How would that work? Who would there be to lead society?

But I provided an answer to my own question. Society's unprogressiveness lies exactly in the fact that anyone has to become a Dandekar or a prime minister. Everyone should be mindful and alert, everyone should understand the needful.

*July 22, 1961*

98. *As, also, owing to the rising and setting of the sun, it seems to move, though in reality it is stationary, so realize that freedom from action lies in action.*

99. *Such a man seems to be as other men, but he is not affected by human nature, like the sun which can never be drowned in water.*

100. *He has seen the universe without seeing it, he does all without doing it and he enjoys all pleasures without involvement in them.*

101. *Though seated in one place, he travels everywhere, for even while in the body he has become the universe.*

Jnāneshvari *Four*

CHAPTER TWELVE

# Pandharpur

The afternoon meal at Shegav is over, and the *pālkhī* has set off once again. Its impetus is now unrestrainable like water running down a slope, the force of which cannot be controlled. When I was small I particularly liked the sentence, "The thronging tide of the people surged in"—without even clearly understanding what it meant. Now it keeps coming to mind again and again. Without realizing it I find myself muttering, "The thronging tide of the people surged in."

The *pālkhī*'s procession seems like storm clouds now—storm clouds that go swirling over and under each other and billow and whirl! The fields on all sides are overflowing with *Wārkarīs*. When the leaves of the roadside trees shake in the breeze, it seems instead that the very force of our movement makes them shake.

The tops of the trees are tossing and swaying even more forcefully now. Like children who beckon above their heads with both their arms and shout, "Come on! Come on!" The branches of the trees have started bobbing up and down. Like children when their favorite uncle comes to visit, the trees are making merry at the sight of the approaching *Wārkarīs*. As I look down the road, the trees way on ahead of us also start to sway. The "Joyous Message" has reached them too.

❀

The *riṅgaṇ* that took place after Shegav was an extremely energetic one. The open plain was spread out on all sides. The *Wārkarīs* were all running toward the place of the *riṅgaṇ*, planting their feet in the black, dusty earth. Scarcely had I looked before the crowd had assembled.

The height of the afternoon was past, but the hot sun still made its presence known. I sat down a little distance from the *riṅgaṇ*. I threw my raincoat down and sat on the black, rain-swelled ground. Then I lay back and stretched out. The pungent odor of the ground tickled my nose. The sky above me became suddenly immense.

An old *Wārkarī* man had sat down a few feet away. Right beside him a young woman was drawing lines on the ground. The people were passing right by us on the way to the *riṅgaṇ*. There was this one woman who went running past with her child dangling about her waist. The child suddenly slid off and fell down. When he tried to run after his mother he tripped and fell. His mother grabbed him under his arms then and dragged him off behind her.

From a distance I saw her take the child with her and squeeze into the crowd. The kid was being crushed as he went in, and he screamed loudly.

The old man nearby said, "The people go running as if a carnival had come to town! What's there to see at a *riṅgaṇ*? They certainly don't see what they ought to see. People just want some fun. The *riṅgaṇ* isn't one of the *pālkhī*'s festive rites at all. It's just a game! I just cannot accept it."

I replied, "I can't fathom it myself. It's just not befitting of the *pālkhī*."

The old man said, "How right you are! In the month of Ashadh the true devotee doesn't go running off to the temple. He absorbs himself in *bhajans* or in doing some kind of good work. You know what? Since the true devotee is never to be found in Pandharpur during Ashadh, God doesn't stay in the temple there either."

"Then why are all these people going there?" I asked him.

"Because they're fools. Do they really go there just for the sake of God? I'll tell you a story so you'll see what I mean. Come and sit a little closer."

I picked up my raincoat, came over and sat down in front of thc old man, and started to listen to the story. The old man began, "Once again it was the eleventh day of Ashadh, and the *Wārkarīs* started gathering in Pandharpur. As the crowd of *Wārkarīs* kept growing, Panduranga kept getting more and more uneasy. His wife, Rakhamai, could see this. She said to him, 'Oh Lord! The *Wārkarīs* are all crowding here to have *darśan* of you. How can it be that you don't feel pleased about it?'

"Now you know the character of women of course. They like all these festivals an awful lot. When the *Wārkarīs* started to arrive in huge crowds making their *diṇḍīs* resound with the noise they made, Rakhamai's self-importance would swell up. But with Panduranga it was just the opposite. As the eleventh of Ashadh drew near he would start to fidget! And on the eleventh itself, well, he would escape out through the pinnacle of the temple. Rakhamai would shout after him, 'Stop! Stop!' But *he* wasn't going to stop! Rakhamai didn't at all like the way he did this every year. So this year she decided for better or for worse to bring it all to a head. She said to him, 'Tell me why you leave Pandharpur on the eleventh.'

"Panduranga replied, 'Rakhamai! Lots of *Wārkarīs* come here, but I don't find my real devotees here. On the eleventh I do feel like meeting with my devotees. So it falls on me to go myself to have *darśan* of them.'

"Rakhamai asked him, 'So many hundreds of thousands come here, and there's never even one true devotee among them?'

"Panduranga said, 'No. Not even one.'

"Rakhamai got a little angry and said, 'Well at least one of these times please show me one of your real devotees."

"Panduranga said, 'Is that all you want? Come on, I'll show you. Follow me.'

"Both Panduranga and Rakhamai went out through the pinnacle of the temple. The roads were all jammed with *Wārkarīs*. All you could hear was "Vitthal-Rakhamai, Vitthal-Rakhamai!' Rakhamai really didn't feel like leaving. But as for Panduranga, he just turned away and didn't even look at the *Wārkarīs*. He looked straight before him as he walked along. Rakhamai set off behind him.

"When they had gotten outside of Pandharpur, Panduranga said, 'Ah! How much better I feel now!'

"Rakhamai tossed her head and said, 'Show me your devotee!'

"Panduranga said, 'Let's go on a little ways farther. We'll surely find him.'

"They both went on a few more miles. Then Panduranga stopped and said, 'Rakhamai! Look there! One of my devotees is coming along—Tukoba! You'll want to see a test of my devotee, won't you? I'll show you what my real devotee is like.'

"Rakhamai said, 'Show me. Just show me.'

"Panduranga said, 'We'll have to change our forms first. I'm going to become a cow. You become a milkmaid. See that pit full of mud over there? I'm going to go and get myself stuck in it. You go and stand on the edge and cry. The *Wārkarīs* who are going to Pandharpur are passing by there. Stop them one by one, and as you cry, say to them, "Please, somebody come and pull out my cow." '

"Panduranga immediately turned himself into a cow. He went and rooted himself deep in the mud. Rakhamai turned herself into a milkmaid and stood on the edge of the pit. As she cried and wept, she said to one of the passing *Wārkarīs*, 'Brother! My cow's gotten stuck. Please help me to pull her out!'

"The *Wārkarī* paused for a moment. He looked at the cow. He said, 'Lady, today is the eleventh of Ashadh. Whatever happens I have to get to Pandharpur. If I don't have *darśan* of Panduranga today, all my twenty-five years of pilgrimage will be wasted.'

"He turned his face and went on his way. Another *Wārkarī* came along. Rakhamai cried a little harder and said, 'Please save this cow of mine!"

"Without even stopping the *Wārkarī* went on his way saying, 'Who has the time, lady? If I busy myself with your cow, I'll squander all my merit!'

"Just then an entire *diṇḍī* came by with great eclat. Rakhamai thought, 'At least one of these people is sure to stop.' This time she cried even louder and fell down at their feet. 'Somebody please pull out my cow!' she said as she ran after them. But the people in the *diṇḍī* were absorbed in the rhythm of their cymbals and drums. They went on without a pause.

"Rakhamai came back to the pit. Panduranga laughed and said, 'Seen the fun? Now just wait. Look there—my Tukoba is coming.'

"Rakhamai said, 'Now don't you go and give him some kind of a sign. I'm watching you. Otherwise you'll wag your tail or something.'

"Panduranga laughed and said, 'All right! I'll get down in even deeper.'

"Tukoba was coming toward them singing a *bhajan* and swaying and nodding to the rhythm. His eyes were closed. He was in *samādhi*.[1] He drew near. Rakhami was weeping and she went running up to him, 'Good sir! My cow has gotten stuck in the mud. Please give me some help!'

Tukoba took just one look at the cow. Rakhamai was getting ready to break into sobs. But Tukoba immediately took the *vīṇā* off his neck and put it down. He set down the cymbals that also hung from his neck. Then tucking up his dhoti he said, 'Come on, lady! Let's see if we can get the cow out.'

"Rakhamai said, 'But, good sir, it's the eleventh today! Don't you have to reach Pandharpur? You might waste the whole day here.'

"Tukoba said, 'Lady! When a cow is stuck in the mud, how can I just go on? Whatever must happen will happen. If I can't have *darśan* of Panduranga on the eleventh, I'll have to have it on the twelfth. All the days are alike to Panduranga. I can't bear to see the cow in such a plight. Poor thing, it's stuck in there up to its neck.'

"Tukoba got down in the mud. Like the cow, he himself was slowly getting stuck. When he reached the cow the mud came up to his chest. He ran his hand over the cow's body and said, 'Just you wait, lady! I'll get you out. Don't be frightened.'

"The cow understood this. It was none other than Panduranga himself. He turned his head and looked at his devotee. The tears started to trickle from his eyes. Tukoba said, "Mother! Don't cry like that. I'm not going to go away and leave you in the mud.'

"Tukoba dived down into the mud. He bent his neck and placed it under the belly of the cow. Straining, he lifted her

1. In this context *samādhi* means a meditative trance, a state of contemplative bliss.

a little. Then he came up for a breath of air. Rakhamai said, 'That's enough, good sir! You're getting late.'

"Tukoba didn't even hear what she was saying. He said, 'Panduranga,' and he dived under again. He lifted the cow up on his neck some more. He did this three times. The fourth time Tukoba lifted her out. His face was coated with mud. He was all out of breath. The tears came to Rakhamai's eyes. Tukoba had the cow on his neck and slowly, slowly began to come out of the pit. When he got out, he put the cow down. Rakhamai ran over and hugged the cow. She said to Tukoba, 'Baba! You've been so kind to me. If it weren't for you, the cow would have died. Then what would my little children have done? You can go now. You'll be late for *darśan*.'

"But Tukoba didn't leave. He said, 'I can't bear to see her in this state. I'll wash her up a bit before I go. It's too much for a woman like you to do.'

"Tukoba took the cow to the neighboring brook and cleaned her up. He washed himself and his clothes. Then he brought the cow back, put the *vīṇā* around his neck, picked up the cymbals, and went off singing a *bhajan*.

"After Tukoba left, the cow and the milkmaid both vanished."

❀

When the story was over there was complete silence, and I found myself starting to look for that cow that had gotten stuck.

The crowd at the *riṅgaṇ* was swelling and surging again. And now the old man was telling me his own story. One of his sons was in college in Poona. He had gotten together a few of his friends to rent a room and was managing there that way. The boy's uncle looked after the farm back home. The boy was all for getting an education. There wasn't any money for it at home. He went to Poona and got a job, and he started to study at his own expense. He had passed the high school exam, and now he was in college. The old man had withdrawn his attention completely from the family's life.

He wasn't the first person to tell me he had withdrawn himself completely from his family. I remembered ten or twenty other *Wārkarīs* like him. Men who had passed sixty and who were maybe nearer seventy. They were all just barely literate. It must require a very special mental preparation to achieve this kind of poise about life.

My conversation with the old man was being interrupted by the crowd. The *riṅgaṇ* had finally dispersed. The woman who was with the old man asked me, "You're from Poona?"

I said, "Yes."

"There was a big flood in Poona, wasn't there? They say there was a lot of damage done."

I said, "A *lot* of damage."

She asked me, "Did the water reach as far as the . . . . . . . section of town?"

I told her, "No. If it did, it was very little."

Out of the blue she asked me, "Will you do something for me?"

I asked her, "What?"

"I want to send a message to Poona."

"To whom?"

"To a certain man, a family friend, who's just like a brother to me."

I said, "Of course I'll take your message."

"Tell him, 'Laxmi is suffering terribly. Please send her a note.' And tell him that she has nowhere to go and that he should come sometime and see Laxmi's plight for himself."

Even while she was speaking, she burst into tears. The old

man told me, "She's fallen on hard times, the poor girl. Her husband left her. She lives all alone somewhere."

I asked him, "How is she related to you?"

The old man replied, "She isn't related to me. I met her along the road. She has my companionship—and I have hers. I give her a portion of whatever I get."

Laxmi had stopped her crying now. She dried her eyes with the end of her sari and blew her nose and looked up at me with reddened eyes. She said to me, "You must go. He's my distant relation. He is especially fond of me. Tell him that Laxmi does nothing but cry, that she doesn't have a husband anymore, that she doesn't have either a father or a mother, and he'll come running and take me away."

I said, "I'll be sure to see him. Give me his address."

She got up and sat down again in front of me. She undid the knot in one corner of her bundle and pulled out a slip of paper from it to show me. When I saw it I told her, "This isn't a Poona address."

From another knot she pulled out a second slip of paper. It was a Poona address. As she handed me the paper she said, "Write it down—and give me back the paper."

I wrote the address down in my diary. As I was writing she kept saying, "Tell him that Laxmi is all alone. She gets work where she can. She's half starved. She doesn't get a thing from her husband. Please send her a note."

When I had written the address down, I put the diary in my pocket and started to get up. Laxmi had her head down and was furtively picking at the grass. When she saw me getting up she suddenly asked me, "Have you come all alone here?"

I said, "Yes."

"Where do you eat?"

"In the *diṇḍī*."

She said, "Why don't you do this? Let's all three go on together. I'll cook for you. Give me enough money for the flour and the vegetables. I'll go gather sticks for the fire. I have a pan with me. The old man has a couple of pans too. We can manage to make rice and bread in them."

For a split second I was tempted to undergo this experience too. But there were no more stopovers ahead. I also must have felt a little bit apprehensive about the experience. But at that moment the memory of Sharad Babu's wanderlust came to me.[1] It amused me to think how the very same kind of thing he described in his novels was happening to me personally. It may be that I wasn't attracted to this experience simply because it would have been a repetition of the kind of experience he had already noted down.

I had gotten up, and I did not sit down again. I told the woman, "I'm afraid I can't stay." At Shegav the leader of our *diṇḍī* had given me a packed lunch to eat at Wakhari. I gave it, just as it was, to the woman. She took it and immediately entrusted it to the old man. She told me, "We don't have any money for tea. Will you give us four annas?"

I searched my pocket. I gave four annas to the old man and four annas to her.

I gathered up my coat, which was spread out on the ground, and saying, "O.K., good-bye—don't get up," I started walking.

❀

I finally came—dragging along—to Wakhari. The *pālkhī* had long since been put in its resting place there. Everyone had set off down the road to Pandharpur. I ran into a

1. Saratchandra Chatterjee (1876–1938), one of the formative Bengali novelists whose translated novels had a profound impact on Maathi fiction, wrote feelingly about the widows, waifs, and runaways in turn-of-the-century Bengal.

gentleman from our *diṇḍī*. He asked me, "Coming along, aren't you?"

I said, "I'm not sure yet. I might just stay."

"O.K. then! We're heading off."

I asked him, "What's become of all the others?"

"Anyone who could, went on."

That is the way it is at Wakhari it seems. Everyone who can, goes on. There are bullock carts standing right there—"Eight annas to Pandharpur," the drivers shout. As soon as the fellowship of the *pālkhī* is over, everyone shifts for himself.[1]

I, too, was all alone with myself. In my loneliness, I started to wander about over the grounds at Wakhari. At various places they had set up water taps. The water was gushing out of them. I went and filled up my water bag. Out of nothing but my usual habit. At one place I had some tea. Again I started to wander around.

They had marked off big squares on the grounds with boundary lines, and it appeared that each separate *pālkhī* had been assigned to one of the spaces. At the corners where the boundaries met there were signs with the names of the *pālkhīs*. There were *pālkhīs* I had never heard of. They had come from all over Maharashtra. Or were going to come. A few of the spaces were still empty.

I got out my diary, and I went around and wrote down each name:

Shri Eknath Maharaj—Paithan
Shri Sopan Kaka—Saswad
Shri Muktabai—Jalgav
Shri Damajipant—Mangalvedhe
Shri Jayram Swami—Wadgav
Shri Rakhamabai—Kondhanapur—Amaravati

1. The following day, however, hundreds of thousands return to Wakhari to join the *pālkhī*'s final procession into Pandharpur.

Shri Lakshminarayan—Saswad
Shri Ramdas Swami—Sajjangad
Shri Shankar—Mahuli

It seemed that a veritable conference of *pālkhīs* was taking place. The thought occurred to me how interesting it would be to go along once with each one of the *pālkhīs*.

There were *pālkhīs* still coming in. Tomorrow morning they are all going to set out together for Pandharpur. With the greatest of festivities. Shri Tukaram Maharaj's *pālkhī* arrived at its assigned resting place right in front of my eyes. The faces of the *Wārkarīs* in its *diṇḍīs* seemed very drawn and tired.

The *pālkhī* of Shri Tukaram Maharaj was put in its place. And I suddenly realized that I had no more work to do. I felt suddenly empty. My legs turned weak under me, and I sat down right there on the grass. I put my diary away in my pocket.

❀

My body was tired, but my mind would not allow me to rest. I felt it suffocating in this sudden emptiness. It was trying to get out of it. I closed my eyes and then opened them again. I lay down on my back.

Just then a white man went hurrying past me. He held some rolls of paper under his arm. I had heard before that someone like this had come along with the *pālkhī*. I scrambled to my feet and started to follow after him.

To my tired legs his pace seemed very brisk. Before I knew it he had turned off somewhere into the crowd.

"Did the sahib go by here?" I kept asking as I made my way toward the main road. A stationwagon was standing there on the road. And there the sahib was standing too. I went running up to meet him, and I asked him his name.

He gave me a look of real surprise. Then he said, "No, no, no! I'm a missionary."

One of his companions put a little booklet in my hands. I read the title: *A Message from the Father in Heaven.*

A white woman got out of the car, and she started to sell books to the *Wārkarīs* who were passing by. I handed back the book in my hand and said, "Why do you go to all this trouble? The *Wārkarīs* don't yield their faith to anyone."

The man who had taken back the book from me was going to say something when his sahib said, "Don't waste time on this man. Let him go."

I stood and watched this effort at proselytizing for a while. The same thing was happening here as had happened at Jejuri where the *Wārkarīs* had gone walking by and just looked at the man with the stone on his chest. Each *Wārkarī* would take the book that was offered to him and then immediately hand it back.

❀

Now the crowd has really thinned out. The only ones left are the shopkeepers! They are sitting with their goods piled up around them: *peḍhās*, puffed rice, sugared gram, batter-dipped deep-fried vegetables, *kuṁkum*, *bukkā*, parched rice.[1] The only other people left here are the ones who are still accompanying their respective *pālkhīs*. It has started to get dark.

---

1. *Peḍhās* are a sweetmeat made of thick evaporated milk and sugar. *Kuṁkum* is a red powder, colored with lemon juice, alum, etc., which is used by women to put the round marking on their foreheads as a symbol of not being a widow. *Bukkā* is a powder made of fragrant substances like sandalwood, which is used to make ritual markings on the forehead.

I realize it has now come time for me to be on my way. I set off down the road. The men in the bullock carts are still shouting away. But their fare has come down. It is no more than four annas now.

For a moment I wonder if maybe I should go by a bullock cart. But that doesn't feel right somehow. This trek has to be finished out on foot. I still haven't reached Pandharpur. The walk isn't over yet.

I have started walking. Pandharpur is coming closer step by step. But how tiresome it has become. The walk out from Phaltan was just like this; but then I had a companion and we could see the *pālkhī* ahead of us.

The road is dark. There is no light in my thoughts either. My body has become utterly weary. I occasionally meet *Wārkarīs*: a *sannyāsī*, a family from Warhad. But I don't have any desire to talk. Nothing even from out of all the uproar of the past fifteen days occupies my thoughts.

❀

I have entered Pandharpur. But I can't figure out from what direction I entered it. The *Wārkarīs* are walking along all jammed together. It almost feels as if they are not the ones who are walking but the streets are. I step along the road and flow along with the rest of them.

I know where I want to go. I'm going to my father-in-law's house. Just up the alleyway to the huge front door, climb up the four stone steps, strike the knocker, and it would be over. But I don't even have the presence of mind left to get there. I'm being driven on with the crowd. I turn when the street turns. Pandharpur looks so different. In the crush of all the *Wārkarīs* and in the light from hundreds of lamps I have lost all my sense of the streets. Like a shirt that has been turned inside out, and I can't recognize it as my own.

❀

It is one o'clock at night when I finally knock at the door of my father-in-law's house.

The moment she sees me, my mother-in-law asks me, "How come you're so late? The *pālkhī* arrived long ago."

I throw down my bag, and just in order to say something I say, "I came here walking."

*July 22, 1961*

# *GLOSSARY*

*abhaṅga*: The most common of the traditional forms of Marathi devotional song, which all the major *Wārkarī* saints used.

*Aṇṇā*: A term of respectful address for an older brother.

*āratī*: The ceremony of waving a burning lamp on a platter around, in front of an image or person, and the verse chanted on the occasion.

*bhajan*: A traditional devotional song—commonly an *abhaṅga*—which devotees sing together as a group to the accompaniment of drums and cymbals.

*bhakta*: a worshiper, devotee, or follower of a particular deity; one who follows the path of religious devotion (*bhaktimārga*).

*bhakti*: Devotion, adoration; the heart's attitude of devotion and love toward God.

*bhaktimārga*: Literally, the path of religious devotion; the way of obtaining salvation through devotion and obedience.

*bhāruḍ*: A dramatic dialog on a religious theme, which is performed as a form of folk theater.

*biḍī*: Tobacco rolled up in a leaf, which is smoked like a cigarette.

*bukkā*: A powder composed of fragrant substances such as sandalwood, which is used to make ritual markings on the forehead.

*buvā*: A term of respectful address or mention for an older person, especially someone of religious attainments.

*darśan*: Literally, "vision" or "sight"; but in the context of a visit to a shrine it carries the implication of a direct and intimate encounter of the deity and devotee.

*diṇḍī*: A neighborhood or local group of *Wārkarīs* (usually formed along caste lines), in which the members worship, sing, and go on the pilgrimage together.

*ekādaśī*: The eleventh day of both the waxing and the waning halves of the lunar months, a special day of fasting and devotions among the *Wārkarīs*.

*gandharva*: One of a class of demigods who are the musicians of heaven.

*ghazal*: A form of Persian lyric poetry, based chiefly on themes of love, which is also very prevalent in Urdu.

*jāgar*: A ritual performance in which the participants maintain a night-long vigil before the *pālkhī*.

*jilebī*: A sweet made of fermented dough, extruded into pretzel-like shapes, fried, and soaked in sugar syrup.

*kacerī*: The courthouse, jail, and administrative offices of a town.

*karmayogī*: One who seeks spiritual liberation not through renunciation but through the performance of his duty without any expectation of reward.

*kicaḍī*: A cooked mixture of rice and pulses or, on days of fasting, of sago and peanuts.

*kīrtan*: A religious performance combining song, dance, and narrative for the exposition of a devotional theme.

*kṣetra*: A pure or sacred spot; a place of pilgrimage; a spot viewed as the field or dwelling place of the gods.

*kuṁkum*: A powder prepared from turmeric which is used by unwidowed women to put the round red marking on their foreheads.

*līlā*: A divine deed of Krishna, which his devotees enact as a ritual of worship.

*liṅga*: The phallic representation of Shiva.

*mantra*: A mystical formula sacred to a deity, which is given at initiation into a religious order.

*Mārwaḍī*: A caste of merchants and traders originating in Rajasthan.

*muni*: A holy sage; an ascetic.

*namaskār*: A salutation performed by joining the palms, inclining the head, and pronouncing the word *namaskār*.

*pādukā*: A type of wooden clog worn by ascetics, which is worshiped as a relic of a god or a guru.

*pālkhī*: a palanquin, which in the present context bears the silver-plated clogs that represent Saint Dnyaneshwar in the yearly pilgrimage in Ashadh to Pandharpur; it also often signifies, as a convenient synecdoche, the entire pilgrim procession that accompanies it.

*pān*: The piper betel leaf folded up with betelnut, spices, lime, etc., which is chewed, especially after meals.

*pañcāyat*: The local elected village assembly, which is responsible for village welfare and development.

*Pāṇḍuranga*: One of the popular names of Vitthal.

*phugaḍī*: A kind of gambol or dance, generally done by girls, in which two or more, clutching hands, whirl themselves around, keeping time to their movements by puffing *phugaḍī phū* with their mouths.

*prasād*: Food offerings made to deities or gurus, the remnants of which are distributed among worshipers as a token of grace.

*pravacana*: A recitation or discourse of a religious nature.

*pūjā*: The entire ritual of worship done before the iconic representation of gods, which involves prostration or bowing before the image, bathing the image, the offering of flowers or coconuts, etc.

*purāṇas*: A class of sacred texts in Sanskrit, which give the stories of creation, and of the gods, heroes, sacred places, etc.

*rājas*: The quality of passion and activeness, one of the three fundamental properties of all existent things in traditional Hindu philosophy, the others being *sattva* (purity, virtue) and *tamas* (ignorance, darkness).

*rāṅgoḷī*: A powder made from a soft white stone, which is used to draw decorative figures by hand before an icon or on a floor where entertainment is to be given.

*riṅgaṇ*: A mass ritual performance during the course of the pilgrimage in which the two horses that accompany the *pālkhī* are made to run before the assembled devotees.

*rudrākṣa*: A tree sacred to Shiva and the berry of it from which are made the necklaces that Shiva devotees wear.

*sādhu*: A respectful term for holy men, saints, and sages.

*śāligrām*: A smooth river pebble, generally out of the Gandaki River, which is worshiped as one of the forms of Vishnu.

*samādhi*: (1) a state of contemplative bliss, a meditative trance; (2) the rite of burying a *sannyāsī* in the earth and the commemorative ediface erected over the site.

*sannyāsī*: One who has renounced worldly life to become a religious mendicant.

*Sarpañca*: The elected head of the village *pañcāyat* and the village representative at the District level.

*śev*: A noodle-like string of deep-fried gram flour, eaten as a snack.

*tīrtha*: A holy or sacred place; a place of pilgrimage.

*tīrthopādhyāya*: The Brahman guide engaged by pilgrims at a *tīrtha* to direct the ceremonies they are required to observe.

*tulsī*: The holy basil plant, which is held in veneration by Hindus as sacred to Vishnu and from the wood of which necklaces are made that are one of the obligatory tokens of a *Wārkarī*.

*vīṇā*: A traditional fretted string instrument, which the leader of a *diṇḍī* carries as a symbol of his authority.

*Wārkarī*: An initiated devotee of Vitthal who performs a regular monthly, semiannual, or annual pilgrimage to Vitthal's temple in Pandharpur.

*yātrā*: (1) traveling to a sacred spot for the purpose of pilgrimage; (2) the periodical festival in honor of a god or saint, to which pilgrims resort.

# *INDEX*

Abbott, Justin: translations by, of saint-poets, 48
*Abhangas*: author reads book of, 214–15; in *pālkhī pūjā*, 258; singing of, in Saswad, 82; use of, in *kīrtan*, 127
Alandi: beginning of *pālkhī* pilgrimage in, 8, 16; return of *pālkhī* to, 22; yearly *yātrā* at Dnyaneshwar *samādhi* in, 15; *sannyāsī* from, 142
Ala-ud-din Khalji: and conquest of Devgiri, 42
Andhra Pradesh: non-*Wārkarī* pilgrims from, 11
*Āratī*: for Dnyaneshwar, 109–10; in *pālkhī pūjā*, 258
Arphalkar, Haibatravbaba: creation of *pālkhī* by, 18
Ashadh: climactic *Wārkarī* pilgrimage during, 16; largest yearly Maharashtrian pilgrimage in, 2

Badrinath: difference of, from *wārī*, 28, 195
*Badvās*: monopolization of ritual worship by, 9
Bahinabai: as disciple of Tukaram, 45
Banaras: pilgrimage to, by uncle and nephew, 167–68. *See also* Kashi
Baradgav: first stopover in tents at, 178; *pālkhī* encampment at, 178; reputation of, for thieves, 96, 178
Baramati: Jaitunbai *diṇḍī* from, 220
Barber: service of, to saints, 198
Bedekar, D.K.: questionnaire prepared by, 62
Berar. *See* Warhad
Bhagwat, Durga: on Maharashtrian "inner link" to Pandharpur, 4; regional meaning of Vithoba assessed by, 31, 36
*Bhajan*: accessibility of, 25; as *Wārkarīs'* principal act of worship, 25; contrast of, with *pūjā*, 183; definition of, 25; importance to *Wārkarīs* of, as *sādhana*, 10; performance of, in group, 183–84
*Bhajans*: after *riṅgaṇ*, 242; at entrance to Jejuri, 108–9; *diṇḍīs* provide support for, 20; ordering of, by Haibatravbaba Arphalkar, 18; palling of, on author, 183; performance of, in Saswad, 96–98
*Bhaktas*: *Wārkarīs* as, 8
*Bhaktas*, community of: as common factor to *kīrtan, bhajan,* and *wārī*, 25; basis of all *bhaktimārga* in, 26
*Bhakti*: as primary goal of *Wārkarī Panth*, 10
*Bhaktimārga*: advocacy of, by saints, 22; as *sādhana* for Kali Yuga, 23; as better for understanding *wārī* than *tīrthayātrā*, 28–29

277
15

40

777
55

2'3'2'